A Common Word

A Common Word

Muslims and Christians
on Loving God and Neighbor

Edited by

Miroslav Volf,
Ghazi bin Muhammad, *and*
Melissa Yarrington

William B. Eerdmans Publishing Company
Grand Rapids, Michigan / Cambridge, U.K.

Published 2010 by
Wm. B. Eerdmans Publishing Co.
2140 Oak Industrial Drive N.E., Grand Rapids, Michigan 49505 /
P.O. Box 163, Cambridge CB3 9PU U.K.

Printed in the United States of America

16 15 14 13 12 11 10   7 6 5 4 3 2 1

ISBN 978-0-8028-6380-5

www.eerdmans.com

Contents

Part II. Muslim Perspectives

Part III. Christian Perspectives

Part IV. Frequently Asked Questions

Part V. Political Significance of "A Common Word"

Foreword

"All of us share this world for but a brief moment in time. The question is whether we spend that time focused on what pushes us apart, or whether we commit ourselves to an effort — a sustained effort — to find common ground, to focus on the future we seek for our children, and to respect the dignity of all human beings.

"There's one rule that lies at the heart of every religion — that we do unto others as we would have them do unto us. This truth transcends nations and peoples — a belief that isn't new; that isn't black or white or brown; that isn't Christian or Muslim or Jew. It's a belief that pulsed in the cradle of civilization, and that still beats in the hearts of billions around the world. It's a faith in other people, and it's what brought me here today."

President Barack Obama, Cairo, Egypt

President Obama's words serve as a fitting opening to this, the first major introduction of "A Common Word" to the public. In his momentous speech, President Obama touched upon many of the most pressing issues that confront the world today. Importantly, and unsurprisingly, many of these issues relate directly to religion.

The significance of religion in this world and in the lives of billions of people is something we simply cannot ignore or write off as a vestige of antiquity. Faith in God guides and gives meaning to the lives of billions of people around the world, myself included. Yet none of us can at the same time ignore the potential for conflict between religious populations — not limited to but including Christians and Muslims.

That is why "A Common Word" is so crucial. With the momentum of globalization, countries and cultures are being drawn closer and closer together with astonishing speed, creating a world that is becoming ever more interdependent. As such, not only peaceful coexistence but active cooperation between Christians and Muslims — who together comprise about 55% of the earth's population — is a necessary component in making the 21st century work more humanely and the earth a better place for all its inhabitants.

Thankfully, as "A Common Word" reminds us, active cooperation with one's neighbours, grounded in mutual love and respect, is part and parcel of being a Muslim or a Christian. Contrary to many people's belief, Christians and Muslims are called to compassionate cooperation with others, regardless of their particular religious affiliation, not *in spite of* their different faiths, but *because of* their respective faiths. The shared commandments to love God and to love one's neighbour are at the core of both religions.

Of course, we must avoid being reductive: we must acknowledge that whilst these commandments are at the heart of Islam and Christianity, they do not constitute the whole of either religion. And "A Common Word" in no way diminishes or disregards the important theological differences between Christianity and Islam. Indeed, part of its power is that it explicitly acknowledges and respects such differences. Yet we still can and must note these two commandments' essential *internal* importance to both faiths, as well as their *external* importance regarding peaceful coexistence and active cooperation between the two faiths — and between them and others as well. The commandments to love God and love one's neighbour serve, as HRH Prince Ghazi notes in his introduction, as "preexisting *essential* common ground between Islam and Christianity, rooted in our sacred texts and in their common Abrahamic origin."

This raises another important point about "A Common Word" that is often misunderstood — its relationship to Judaism. For although it is focused primarily on the relationship between Christianity and Islam, this in turn includes the importance of Judaism in the world today and the possibility of increased involvement of Judaism in the future of "A Common Word." In fact, Jewish observers have already been invited to and attended both conferences at Yale and Cambridge. It is my hope that Jewish participation increases in the future.

Finally, I would like to highlight the practical consequences of "A Common Word." Although a theological endeavour in and of itself, "A Common Word" has very real and important implications within our increasingly globalized world. If religious leaders of both faiths appreciate the shared emphasis on love of God and love of neighbour within Christianity and Islam, they can help instil a similar appreciation of this fact amongst their congregations and communities. This is no small step. Indeed, although many would argue that the language or concept of love itself is incapable of addressing the truly thorny and important issues that challenge Muslim-Christian coexistence and cooperation, such an argument misses the point. As Professor Volf makes clear in his introduction, "love is not a soft and a nebulous emotion but a tough, practical virtue of benevolence and beneficence, a virtue of which justice is an absolutely integral part." I take this to be what President Obama means when he describes "faith in other people" — that love demands an acknowledgment of the inherent value of each and every person, and a corresponding commitment to help those in need, regardless of their religious affiliation.

In spite of the enormous problems that face the world today, I am hopeful and confident that we are on a path towards finding solutions, thanks in large part to efforts like "A Common Word," which itself is increasing in importance and prominence daily. The work of "A Common Word" is far from complete. There is still much to be done. Again, one of my strongest hopes is for the increased participation and inclusion of Judaism. Yet there is no doubt that "A Common Word" has the potential to effect radical and positive change in relations between Muslims and Christians. For all these reasons and more, I am delighted that my Faith Foundation and I are involved in this process initiated by "A Common Word" which holds so much promise for the future of the world.

TONY BLAIR
Tony Blair Faith Foundation

Preface

The Muslim signatories of the October 2007 letter, "A Common Word Between Us and You," proposed that the two greatest commandments according to Jesus Christ, namely to love God and to love our neighbors, were later affirmed by the Prophet Muhammad and therefore describe the most basic attitudes, values, and practices that Muslims and Christians hold in common. Shortly after the letter was released, many key Christian leaders from a wide spectrum of Christian traditions welcomed the Muslim initiative by signing "Loving God and Neighbor Together," a Christian response to "A Common Word." Each of these two documents affirmed irresolvable differences as well as this central commonality between the two religions. They also left much room to explore fundamental questions undergirding the claim that Muslims and Christians share the command to love God and neighbor: Do Muslims and Christians understand the same thing when they envision and endeavor to live out their love for God and their love for neighbor?

The authors in this book seek to explore these important questions in order to uncover foundations for peaceful coexistence between Christians and Muslims. In doing so, they specifically address and engage the religious commitments of adherents of these two great religions who strive to take their faith seriously. Religion is too often branded as merely a contributor to violence, and faith questions are therefore frequently avoided at the peacemaking table. But while recognizing that religious and non-religious peacemaking efforts best work in tandem to promote nonviolence, the contributors of this book believe that an essential foundation to effective peacemaking consists precisely in Christians and Muslims intentionally drawing on the resources of their respective faiths and approaches to devotion to God.

This book contains articles by some of the most prominent theologians and leaders in Islam and Christianity today. They were presented, discussed, and debated in July of 2008 at Yale University. The first two chapters are written by the co-hosts of the Yale conference and editors of this book, and they outline the current crisis in Muslim-Christian relations, along with the reasons why any solutions to that crisis must draw on the resources of our respective faiths. After the opening chapters readers will find the original letter, "A Common Word Between Us and You," and then "Loving God and Neighbor Together: A Christian Response to 'A Common Word Between Us and You,'" which has come to be known as the Yale Response. In addition to the original text of the Yale Response as published in the *New York Times* on November 18, 2007, the reader will also find an extensive commentary that gives insight into discussions surrounding the wording of the original Yale Response.

The second section addresses the questions of what it means to love God and love one's neighbor from the Muslim perspective. The authors represent four different continents and both the Sunni and Shi'i branches of Islam. Their perspectives also range from those of academicians, as in the cases of Seyyed Hossein Nasr and Reza Shah-Kazemi, to the popular Yemeni spiritual teacher, Shaykh Habib Ali al-Jifri, and a judge and member of the Nigerian Owu Royal family, Prince Judge Bola Abdul Jabbar Ajibola.

The third section addresses the important questions of what it means to love God and to love neighbor from the Christian perspective, with contributors from around the globe representing a wide range of backgrounds. The Christian scholars hail from three different continents and represent individuals who not only have thought deeply about these issues but have sought to put them into practice over the course of many years, as academics, institutional leaders, and community developers (Martin Accad, David Burrell, Harvey Cox, Joseph Cumming, and Miroslav Volf).

The fourth section includes two chapters on frequently asked questions. The first was written by Muslims to answer questions about "A Common Word," and the second was written by Christians to answer the questions that other Christians ask about the Yale Response. The volume concludes with the speech given by Senator John Kerry at the Yale conference describing the role of this dialogue in global peacemaking efforts.

What are our hopes as we send this book into the world? That it will inform people about a central aspect of the two largest faiths in the world today — love of God and love of the neighbor — and stimulate critical discussion of the possibilities of Christians and Muslims living in peace with one another without compromising their own authentic identity or disrespecting the other.

THE EDITORS

PART I

Invitation and Response

In the Name of God, the Compassionate, the Merciful
May Peace and Blessings be upon the Prophet Muhammad

On "A Common Word Between Us and You"

H.R.H. Prince Ghazi bin Muhammad of Jordan

"A Common Word Between Us and You" was launched on October 13th 2007 initially as an open letter signed by 138 leading Muslim scholars and intellectuals (including such figures as the Grand Muftis of Egypt, Syria, Jordan, Oman, Bosnia, Russia, and Istanbul) to the leaders of the Christian churches and denominations of the entire world, including His Holiness Pope Benedict XVI. In essence it proposed, based on verses from the Holy Qur'an and the Holy Bible, that Islam and Christianity share, at their core, the twin "golden" commandments of the paramount importance of loving God and loving one's neighbor. Based on this joint common ground, it called for peace and harmony between Christians and Muslims worldwide.

Introduction: The Birth of "A Common Word"

In the middle of the eastern Jordanian desert, in a place called Safawi, miles away from anything, from any landmark or any human traces, there stands a unique, solitary tree. This tree is around 1500 years old and there are no other trees to be seen for dozens of miles in any direction. Despite its age and breadth, it is only about 6-8 meters tall. It is a *butum* tree, a kind of pistachio tree found in Jordan and surrounding countries, and it was under this particular *butum* tree that "A Common Word" was born. For in September 2007, one month before the launch of "A Common Word," I had the privilege of visiting this tree twice — once in the company of a

3

number of the scholars behind the "Common Word" initiative — and it was under this tree that we prayed to God (or at least I did) to grant "A Common Word" success.

In what follows, we will endeavor to outline the reasons why the Common Word initiative was so necessary at this time in history by describing the current state of Muslim-Christian relations, the causes for tension between these two religious communities, and the subsequent concerns for the future. After this background, we will describe the goals and motives for launching "A Common Word"; explain what we did *not* intend by this initiative; discuss the reasons for primarily engaging religious leadership; and, finally, summarize the initial results.

Background: The Current State of Muslim-Christian Relations

In the early 1990s, after the collapse of the Soviet Union, there surfaced various influential political theories regarding the future of the world, including Samuel Huntington's 1993 thesis of a *Clash of Civilizations*, Francis Fukayama's *The End of History and the Last Man*, written in 1992, and Robert Kaplan's seminal article *The Coming Anarchy* of February 1994. In this article, Kaplan uses the image of a luxury car driving one way on a highway and a stream of destitute refugees walking the other way to suggest that while one part of the world is moving comfortably and prosperously forward, much of the rest of the world is suffering horribly and disintegrating due to poverty, disease, crime, conflict, tribalism, overpopulation, and pollution. Assessing each of these theories can help us better understand the historical context of where we are today.

Huntington gets a B. He was right about tension and conflict between Muslims and the West (e.g., Bosnia 1992-95; Kosovo 1996-99; Chechnya 1994-96, 1999-2001; 9-11-2001 and Afghanistan; Iraq 2003-07, etc.) but dead wrong about either side unifying, never mind Muslim countries uniting with China. Moreover, every single Muslim country in the world has denounced terrorism, and the vast majority of governments of Muslim countries have sided with the West in one way or another. Inside Syria and Iran, the two notable exceptions to siding with the West, Christian-Muslim relations are excellent (witness Orthodox Patriarch Ignatius of Antioch's open letter rebuffing the Pope after his September 2006 Regensburg address).

4

Fukayama, who declared the triumph of Western-style democracy, gets a C. President George W. Bush's plan for a new more "democratic" Middle East as outlined on November 6, 2003, to the National Endowment for Democracy still languishes. The most "democratic" (in the Western sense) Muslim countries in the Middle East (Iraq, Afghanistan, Palestine, and Lebanon) are either in civil war or close to it. And as we should know from Hitler's 1933 election — or from the actions of the majority of Hutus in Rwanda in 1994, or of the majority of Serbs in Bosnia from 1992-95 — western-style democracy simply does not work where: (a) there are no pre-existing democratic institutions that can overrule demagoguery; (b) there is no democratic culture that can control and channel fear and hatred; and (c) the majority seeks to gain power in order to slaughter the minority, for reasons that go back hundreds of years. Plato warns us of this in the eighth book of *The Republic,* and Herodotus hints at it in the third book of his *Histories.*

Kaplan gets an A-. He was right about increased anarchy and wealth in the world, but he failed to see the unique tensions existing between Muslims and the West. Since Muslims and Christians together constitute over 55% of the world's population, his omission is significant.

So where are we now? Sectarian wars, and political and religious distrust dominate the peoples of the Middle East and its relationship to the West. Chaos, conflict, and disease ravage the horn of Africa and Darfur. Terrorism threatens everywhere in the world. We pray conflict does not break out in the Persian Gulf.

It is true that polite and educated company all over the world make positive and optimistic comments about the other side, but there is not enough trickle-down to the masses and to popular culture. Moreover, as the current Pew Global survey shows, religious attitudes between Muslims, Christians, and Jews are generally hardening and getting worse, not better. A cursory review of the world's biggest bookseller, Amazon.com, shows that Americans are buying more books about Islam written by vitriolic former Muslims now touted as experts and sponsored by Christian fundamentalist groups than written by serious Muslim or non-Muslim scholars. In the West there are whispers of a "Long War" — an idea which in the Islamic world is taken to be directed against all Muslims.

Roots: Causes for Tension in Muslim-Christian Relations

We will only briefly sketch some of the major causes of tension, as they are well known. On the Western side are the fear of terrorism; a loathing of religious coercion; suspicion of the unfamiliar; and deep historical misunderstandings. On the Islamic side is first and foremost the situation in Palestine: despite the denial of certain parties, Palestine is a grievance rooted in faith (since Muslim holy sites lie occupied). Added are discontentment with Western foreign policy (especially the Iraq War and Occupation 2003-09); fear and resentment of the massive missionary movements launched from the West into the Islamic World; wounded pride arising from the colonial experience, poverty and unemployment, illiteracy, ignorance of true Islam and of the Arabic language, social and political oppression, and a technology gap. On both sides are vast centrifugal forces unleashed by fundamentalist and extremist movements, and by missionary activity. These far outweigh the centripetal forces set in motion by hundreds of interfaith and intercultural centers all over the world and by world governments (e.g., the Spanish-Turkish "Alliance of Civilizations"; the Russian "Dialogue of Civilizations"; the Kazakh "Dialogue of Confessions"; the *Amman Message;* the French *Atelier-Culturel;* the British Radical Middle Way; the Malaysian *Islam Hadari;* the new *Saudi Interfaith Initiative of 2008;* etc. — and the umpteen "declarations" of this or that city). The fundamentalists are better organized, more experienced, better coordinated, and more motivated. They have more stratagems, more institutes, more people, more money, more power, more influence.

We are reminded of the words of W. B. Yeats:

Turning and turning in the widening gyre
The falcon cannot hear the falconer;
Things fall apart; the centre cannot hold;
Mere anarchy is loosed upon the world,
The blood-dimmed tide is loosed, and everywhere
The ceremony of innocence is drowned.
The best lack all conviction, while the worst
Are full of passionate intensity.

In short, Muslim-Christian relations are characterized by deeply rooted, historical, cultural, and racial misunderstanding, suspicion, and even loathing. Thus now, according to the results of the largest international religious surveys in history (as outlined in a recently-published seminal book by Professor John Esposito and Dalia Mogahed and discussed at the Yale conference), 60 percent of Christians harbor prejudice against Muslims and 30 percent of Muslims reciprocate. Quite clearly, the grounds for fear of war and religious genocides are starkly real.

Fears: The Future of Muslim-Christian Relations

With such an explosive mix, popular religious conflicts — even unto genocides — are lurking around the corner. Indeed, one such conflict took place a few hundred miles away from where the Pope sits only fifteen years or so ago (that is, from 1993-95) in the heart of Europe, when 300,000 innocent Muslim civilians were slaughtered and 100,000 Bosnian women were raped as a method of war. And our feeling is still that, God forbid, a few more terrorist attacks, a few more national security emergencies, a few more demagogues, and a few more national protection laws, and then internment camps (like those set up for Americans of Japanese origin during World War II) — if not concentration camps — are not inconceivable eventualities in some places, and that their fruition would inevitably spawn global counter-reactions.

The Holocaust of six million Jews — then the largest religious minority in Europe — occurred sixty-five years ago, still within living memory. This is something that Muslims in the West, now the largest minority, should contemplate as seriously as Jews do. For unfortunately we are not now inherently immune to committing the crimes of the past — our nature and worst potential has not fundamentally changed. Moreover, as the Gallup survey showed, we are now actually at the stage where we (as Christians and Muslims) routinely mistrust, disrespect, and dislike each other, if not popularly and actively trash, dehumanize, demonize, despise, and attack each other. This is the stage at which Hutus and Tutsis (both Christian tribes, by their own confession at least) were in Rwanda before the popular genocide-by-machete of nearly one million people in 1994. How much easier would it be for Muslims and Christians — who have been fighting for over a millennium and have viewed each other with the deepest suspicion since St. John of Damascus — to slaughter each other? And how much more likely is this possibility to become reality when we are all finally struck with the apparently looming catastrophes of global climate change, and when competition for food and natural resources becomes fiercer?

Goals and Motives behind Launching "A Common Word"

Our goal was very clear. We wanted — and want — to avoid a greater worldwide conflict between Muslims and the West. We wanted to — and must — resolve all our current crises. To do both, we had — and have — to find a *modus vivendi* to live and let live, to "love thy neighbor"; this idea must be expressed from within our religious scriptures, and must then be applied everywhere.

The intention in sending out the *Common Word* missive was simply to try to make peace and spread harmony between Muslims and Christians globally — it was and is an extended global handshake of religious goodwill, friendship and fellowship and consequently of interreligious peace. Of course, peace is primarily a matter for governments, but Huntington's 1993 vision of global conflict between Muslims and Christians was wrong in one important sense: post September 11, 2001, the only government as such to have opposed the West in its various demands is that of Iran (but even Iran has sided with the West against terrorism); more than fifty other Islamic nations have sided with the West. This is to say, then, that the governments of Islamic majority countries have not banded together against the governments of Christian-majority countries (much less in alliance to China), or vice versa. Nevertheless, Huntington was very correct in his prediction of heightened tensions between Christian and Muslim populations as such *globally* after the collapse of atheistic communism, albeit with *religiously affiliated, non-government actors taking the lead.*

Thus, exactly one month after His Holiness Pope Benedict XVI's controversial and potentially incendiary Regensburg lecture on September 13, 2006, an international group of thirty-eight Muslim scholars and intellectuals (many of whom would later form the nucleus of those behind the Common Word initiative) issued an *Open Letter to His Holiness* (in retrospect, a letter that would prove to be a "trial run" for "A Common Word") in what we thought was a very gentle and polite way of pointing out some factual mistakes in His Holiness's lecture. We did not get a satisfactory answer from the Vatican beyond a perfunctory courtesy visit to me, a month later, from some Vatican officials. So exactly one year after issuing our first letter (and thus one year and one month after the Regensburg lecture), we increased our number by exactly 100 (to 138, symbolically saying that we are many and that we are not going away) and issued, based on the Holy Qur'an, "A Common Word between Us and You."

We repeat that we had honestly — as is evident from the genesis of this story, and as is evident, we believe, in the very text of "A Common Word" itself — only one motive: peace. We were aiming to try to spread peace and harmony between Christians and Muslims all over the world, not through governments and treaties but on the all-important popular and mass level, through precisely the world's most influential popular leaders — that is to say, through the leaders of the two religions. We wanted to stop the drumbeat of what we feared was a growing popular consensus (on both sides) for worldwide (and thus cataclysmic and perhaps apocalyptic) Muslim-Christian *jihad*/crusade. We were keenly aware, however, that peace efforts also required another element: knowledge. We thus aimed to spread proper basic knowledge of our religion in order to correct and abate the constant and unjust vilification of Islam, in the West especially.

What Was *NOT* Intended by Launching "A Common Word"

Having said what our motive was, we want to emphasize what our motives were *not,* in view of some of the strange suspicions and speculations we have read about on the internet.

(1) "A Common Word" was *not* intended — as some have misconstrued — to trick Christians or to foist Muslim theology on them, or even to convert them to Islam. There is deliberately no mention of the "Christian Trinity" in "A Common Word" because Jesus (peace be upon him) never mentions it in the Gospels — and certainly not when discussing the Two Greatest Commandments. Indeed, we believe the word "Trinity" (or "triune," for that matter) itself does not occur once in the whole Bible, but comes from the Christian creeds some time later. Of course, Muslims and Christians differ irreconcilably on this point, but the Christian part of "A Common Word" is based on Jesus' (peace be upon him) own words — which Christians can obviously interpret for themselves. Besides, as we understand it, Christians also insist on the Unity of God, and so we sought, through Jesus' (peace be upon him) own words, to find what we do have in

common in so far as it goes, not denying what we know we disagree upon beyond that.

(2) "A Common Word" was *not* intended to reduce both our religions to an artificial union based on the Two Commandments. Indeed in Matthew 22:40 Jesus Christ the Messiah (peace be upon him) was quite specific: "On these two commandments *hang* all the Law and the Prophets" (Matthew 22:40) — "hang," not "are (reduced to)." Ours was simply an attempt to find a theologically correct, preexisting *essential* common ground (albeit interpreted perhaps differently) between Islam and Christianity, rooted in our sacred texts and in their common Abrahamic origin, in order to stop our deep-rooted religiously mutual suspicions from being an impediment to behaving properly toward each other. It was, and is, an effort to ensure that religions behave as part of the solution and are not misused to become part of the problem. Indeed, the Two Commandments give us guidelines and a concrete, shared standard of behavior not only for what to expect from the other but also for how we must ourselves *behave* and *be.* We believe we can and must hold ourselves and each other to this shared standard.

(3) "A Common Word" was *not* intended to deny that God loved us first, as some Christians have opined. The knowledge that God loved man before man loved God is so obvious in Islam that we did not think we had to make it explicit. It is obvious because God obviously existed before His creation of the world and man. It is also evident in the very sacred formula that starts every chapter in the Holy Qur'an but one, and that begins every single legitimate act of a Muslim's entire life — *Bism Illah Al-Rahman Al-Rahim,* "In the Name of God, the Compassionate, the Merciful." Indeed, there is a *Hadith Qudsi* (a "holy saying")[1] wherein God says that His Name is *Al-Rahman* (the "Lovingly Compassionate") and that the word for "womb" *(al-rahm)* comes from His Name, thus implying that God created the world out of an internal overflowing of love. Indeed, creation out of *Rahmah* ("Loving Compassion") is also seen in the Holy Qur'an in the beginning of the *Sura* of *Al-Rahman,* which says:

Al-Rahman / Has Taught the Quran / He has created Man / He has taught him speech. (*Al-Rahman,* 55:1-4)

---

1. *Sunan Al-Tirmithi,* no. 1907.

In other words, the very Divine Name *Al-Rahman* should be understood as containing the meaning "The Creator-through-Love," and the Divine Name *Al-Rahim* should be understood as containing the meaning "The Savior through Mercy."

(4) "A Common Word" was *not* intended to exclude Judaism as such or diminish its importance. We started with Christianity bilaterally simply because Islam and Christianity are the two largest religions in the world and in history, and so in that sense, Islamic-Christian dialogue is the most critical; for there are about 2 billion Christians in the world and 1.5 billion Muslims, compared to 20 million Jews. But this demographic does not preclude Muslims from dialoguing with those of faiths other than Christianity, bilaterally or multilaterally, or even with those of no faith at all. Moreover, Muslims do not object to the idea of a Judeo-Christian tradition (even though Islam shares with Judaism and Christianity the same Abrahamic origins and traditions), nor to not being invited to all Jewish-Christian dialogues; so there is no need for Jews to feel excluded by a Muslim-Christian conversation. For that matter, there is no need for Christians to feel excluded by a Judeo-Islamic dialogue. We can all, however, understand the reason for Jewish fears about Christian-Muslim dialogue, and we note that Jewish observers have been invited attendees of the conferences in Yale and Cambridge.

(5) On the other hand, "A Common Word" does *not* signal that Muslims are prepared to deviate from, or concede one iota of, any of their convictions in order to reach out to Christians — and we expect the reverse is also true. Let us be crystal clear: "A Common Word" is about equal peace, not about capitulation.

(6) Neither does "A Common Word" mean Muslims are going to facilitate foreign "evangelism opportunities" in the Islamic world in the name of "freedom of religion." This topic is an extremely sensitive one with much bitter history, and it has the potential to create much tension between Christians and Muslims, just as it has between Protestant, Catholic, Orthodox, and Eastern Orthodox Christians. Our intention with "A Common Word" is to focus on popular rapprochement and mutual understanding between Christians and Muslims.

(7) Some have suggested that framing our extended hand in the language of "love" *is* such a concession, but assuredly this suggestion is not at all accurate, nor is it a "concession": rather, it has been a particular pleasure to be able to focus our initiative on this frequently underestimated as-

pect of our religion: the Grand Principle of Love. Indeed, the Holy Qur'an uses over fifty near-synonyms for love; English does not have the same linguistic riches and connotations, as was discussed in particular during the Yale workshop and conference in July 2008. If Muslims do not usually use the same language of love as English-speaking Christians, it is perhaps because the word "love" for Muslims frequently implies something different for Muslims than it does for Christians.

Our use of the language of love in "A Common Word" is simply, then, a recognition that human beings have the same souls everywhere, however pure or corrupted, and thus that the experience of love must have something in common everywhere, even if the objects of love are different, and even if the ultimate love of God is stronger than all other loves. God says in the Holy Qur'an:

> Yet of mankind are some who take unto themselves (objects of worship which they set as) rivals to God, loving them with a love like (that which is the due) of God (only) — [but] those who believe are stauncher in their love for God. . . . (*Al-Baqarah*, 2:165)

The Recipients of "A Common Word"

"A Common Word" was addressed from religious leaders to religious leaders of the largest two religions in the world in recognition that while religious leaders do not generally make public policy, they are nevertheless still the ultimate touchstones for morality and thus the final safety net for public opinion and non-government actors. Religious leaders have a great public following; their opinions matter — many of them at least — and have enormous influence with the general public.

It is important to note on the other hand that getting secular, Westernized Muslim academics together with Westerners to influence Muslims in general *cannot* work, because "man does not live by bread alone, but from every word that issueth from the Mouth of God" (Matthew 4:4). Moreover, secular modernists command no following in the Islamic street; to the contrary, their promotion in the West creates popular outrage in the Islamic world, which drives the moderate, traditional majority of Muslims into the embrace of fundamentalists. The 9-11 Commission report, the current Rand report, and all who subscribe to this approach (or relying on secularized Muslims to speak for and influence the Islamic world) are simply wrong. "Love thy neighbor" is in all Islamic scriptures in different ways: let the authentic, traditional Muslim authorities bring it out. If we do not let the orthodox voices of our religions speak for peace, they risk being misused and manipulated to move us toward conflict.

The Results of "A Common Word" Initiative During Its First Year

Since the launching of the Common Word initiative in October 2007 (see www.acommonword.com), it has in many ways become the world's leading interfaith dialogue initiative between Christians and Muslims specifically, and "A Common Word" has achieved historically unprecedented global acceptance and traction as an interfaith theological document. Over 60 leading Christian figures have responded to it in one form or another, including H.H. Pope Benedict XVI, H.B. Orthodox Patriarch Alexi II of Russia, the Archbishop of Canterbury Dr. Rowan Williams, and the Presiding Bishop of the Lutheran World Federation, Bishop Mark Hanson (see "Christian Responses" at www.acommonword.com). In November 2007, over 300 leading Protestant church leaders and academics, including many of the most prominent evangelicals, also responded in an open letter in the *New York Times*. In the meantime, the Muslim scholars signing the initiative increased to around 300, with over 460 Islamic organizations and associations endorsing it. "A Common Word" has led to a number of spontaneous, local, grass-roots and community-level initiatives all over the world in places as far apart as India, Pakistan, Bangladesh, Canada, South Africa, the United States, and Great Britain (see "New Fruits" at www.acommonword.com).

Over 600 articles — carried by thousands of press outlets — have been written about "A Common Word" in English alone. Over 200,000 people have visited the official website of "A Common Word" for further details, with over 6,000 people having fully endorsed "A Common Word" online alone. "A Common Word" has already been the subject of a number M.A. and M.Phil. dissertations in Western universities in various countries (including at Harvard University; the Theological Seminary at the University of Tübingen, Germany; and the Center for Studies of Islam in the U.K.). It has been the subject of major international conferences at Yale

University, United States, and Britain's Cambridge University and Lambeth Palace, and studied at the World Economic Forum in the spring of 2008 and the Mediterranean Dialogue of Cultures in November 2008. "A Common Word" was also the basis for the First Annual Catholic-Muslim forum held at the Vatican in November 2008.

"A Common Word" was the central impetus behind the Wamp-Ellison Resolution in the U.S. House of Representatives, which passed in 2008, and it was commended in that Resolution. It received the U.K.'s Association of Muslim Social Scientists 2008 *Building Bridges Award,* and Germany's *Eugen Biser Award* of 2008.

Finally, "A Common Word" was even cited at the traditional Post-Inauguration Service at the National Cathedral for President Obama on January 21, 2009, during the main sermon by Reverend Dr. Sharon E. Watkins, General Minister and President of the Christian Church (Disciples of Christ) in the United States and Canada, as follows:

> Recently Muslim scholars from around the world released a document, known as "A Common Word Between Us [and You]." It proposes a common basis for building a world at peace. That common basis? Love of God and love of neighbor! What we just read in the Gospel of Matthew!

*   *   *

The year 2009 witnessed an equal barrage of activity. "A Common Word" has truly become a world movement. All over the globe symposiums, lectures, workshops, conferences, and other interfaith activities have spontaneously arisen without any formal coordination by those who spearheaded the original initiatives. Indeed, for this reason we cannot give an account of all that has happened, but we have come to hear of the following during 2009: lectures or workshops were given on "A Common Word" in Cambridge University, Oman, Philippines, Virginia, Egypt, and Sudan. Larger symposiums were held relating to "A Common Word" by the Brookings Institute in Qatar (January), Fuller Theological Seminary (May), ISNA (2009), Yale Center for Faith & Culture (September), and the Evangelical Theological Society (November). Full-blown conferences were held on "A Common Word" in Portland, Oregon (March); in the UAE and South Carolina (March), in Pakistan (April), and in Australia (May). And the fourth conference of the Common Word initiative brought together many of the original signatories of the open letter and its responses at Georgetown University in October. In short, in just two years, "A Common Word" has gained, by the Grace of God/*Al-HamduLillah,* historically unprecedented "global traction," and we hope in the coming year, with the Will of God/*in sha Allah,* that it will achieve historically unprecedented "global trickle down." God is Bounteous!

Despite our prayers for success (in truth I remember praying that God grant the initiative success beyond "what can possibly be imagined"), we had no expectations whatsoever — only some hope in God's generosity — and we were all resolved to accept a complete failure. This prayer itself was a gift from God, for it is not within a human's power to achieve sincerity and detachment if God does not grant them, and with God all things are possible. *Praise God/Al-HamduLillah* that we are continually astonished by the spectacular way God has answered the prayer that was His gift in the first place. One of the great wonders of God's love for humanity is that He rewards human beings for gifts He has given them in the first place. He keeps giving and giving, and all that He requires from us is to accept! *Subhan Allah!* Glory be to God!

Conclusion

Let us now return to the tree mentioned at the start of this chapter, the tree under which prayers were offered for "A Common Word" — a tree which today stands in a completely desolate place. But until the last century there lay not far from this tree the clear remains of an ancient Roman Road and of a later but also ancient Byzantine Monastery. And according to the earliest Islamic historical sources, some fourteen hundred years ago, on one of the caravan roads from Arabia to Syria, a nine-year-old Meccan boy named Muhammad bin Abdullah, from the clan of Hashem (may peace and blessing be upon him), traveled with his uncle Abu Talib to Syria from his home in Eastern Arabia. A cloud hung over him wherever he went, and when he sat under a tree in the desert, the tree, too, lowered its branches to shield him from the desert heat. A local Christian monk named Bahira noticed these two miracles from a little distance and summoned the caravan and the boy, and after courteously examining and speaking to him, Bahira witnessed the boy as a future Prophet to his people. The monk had a book with him that led him to expect a Prophet among the Arabs, who were descended from Ishmael, the eldest son of the Prophet Abraham (peace be upon him). Perhaps that book was the Torah, for Genesis 49:10 and Deuteronomy 18:15 seem to predict a prophet who is not the Messiah and not Judah but who is from the "brethren" of the Jews. We do not know for certain the identity of the book; but what is most important here is that the selfsame blessed tree underneath which "A Common Word" was born also itself gave rise, fourteen hundred years ago, to the first harmonious contact between Christianity and the founder of Islam! Indeed, it is immensely significant that God draws a direct analogy between a good word and a good tree (and both their fruits) in the Holy Qur'an as follows:

> Seest thou not how God coineth a similitude: A good word is as a good tree, its root set firm, its branches in heaven, / Giving its fruit at every season by permission of its Lord? God coineth the similitudes for mankind in order that they may reflect. / And the similitude of a bad word is as a bad tree, uprooted from upon the ground, possessing no stability. / God confirmeth those who believe by a firm saying in the life of the world and in the Hereafter, and God sendeth wrong-doers astray. And God doeth what He will. (*Ibrahim*, 14:24-27)

Nor, I believe, is it a coincidence that in the Holy Qur'an the blessed virgin Mary — for both Muslims and Christians, the greatest woman who ever lived (and after whom the nineteenth chapter of the Holy Qur'an is named) — is described as having birth pangs under a tree:

> And mention in the Book Mary when she withdrew from her family to an easterly place. / Thus she veiled herself from them, whereupon We sent to her Our Spirit, and he assumed before her the likeness of a well-proportioned human. / She said, "Lo! I seek refuge in the Compassionate One from you! If you fear God." / He said, "I am only a messenger of your Lord, that I may give you a boy [who shall be] pure." / She said, "How shall I have a boy when no human being has [ever] touched me, neither have I been unchaste?" / He said, "It shall be so! Your Lord has said: 'It is easy for Me, and so that We may make him a sign for mankind, and a mercy from Us. And it is a thing [already] decreed.'" / Thus she conceived him and then withdrew with him to a distant place. / And the birth pangs brought her to the trunk

of the palm-tree. She said, "O would that I had died before this and become a forgotten thing, beyond recall!" / Then he called her from below her, "Do not grieve. Your Lord has made below you a rivulet. / And shake the trunk of the palm-tree towards you — there will drop on you dates fresh and ripe. / So eat and drink, and [let] your eye be comforted; and if you [happen to] see any human being, then say, 'I have vowed to the Compassionate One a fast, so I will not speak to any human today.'" (*Maryam*, 19:16-26)

Finally, a word about the Christians who answered the invitation of "A Common Word," wrote responses, and attended the various resulting dialogues. These men and women have welcomed strange people whom they did not know from far parts of the world which they have never visited, and from a religion that has always been considered by their own to be heretical at best. They have given much effort, time, and money to do so, and since "where your treasure is, there will your heart be also" (Matthew 6:21), we Muslims know they gave from the heart, for indeed they were not obliged to do so. They met us with open hands and with even more open hearts, for they all knew that many other Christians might criticize them, yet they did so anyway, out of conviction. Thus I say that they have loved their neighbors as themselves, as called for in the Gospel[2] by Jesus Christ (may peace and blessings be upon him), and have even loved the stranger as themselves, as called for in Leviticus (19:34). They have fulfilled the law spoken of by St. Paul in Romans (13:8), and have, in their own way, accepted "A Common Word Between Us and You" in the way called for by the Holy Qur'an. So may God bless them as peacemakers and reward their beautiful intentions. *Wal-Salaamu Alaykum, Pax Vobiscum.*

---

2. In Matthew 22:34-40; Mark 12:29-31; and John 13:35; 15:12 and 17.

A Common Word for a Common Future

MIROSLAV VOLF

Gloomy Clouds — Sun's Rays

Most people today see a heavy and dangerous storm of tensions between Christians and Muslims that is menacing the world. Since the Crusades, relations between our two faith communities — currently comprised of just slightly under half the human race — have rarely been at a lower point than they are today. Tensions, deep conflicts, and often murderous violence between us are leaving a trail of blood and tears as well as a mounting deposit of deeply painful and potently dangerous memories. These clashes undermine the hopes and efforts of many to live in peace, to flourish as individuals and communities. Worse still, this stunted living enveloped in hopelessness often sucks people even deeper down into a whirlpool of violence.

But many of us sense a new wind of hope beginning to blow — we feel the warm sun's rays penetrating the stormy gloom around us. "A Common Word Between Us and You" — likely one of the most important interfaith

---

This article represents a revision and amalgamation of two presentations: (1) opening remarks at the Yale conference, "Loving God and Neighbor in Word and Deed: Implications for Muslims and Christians" (July 28-31, 2008), which was jointly hosted by Professor Dr. H.R.H. Prince Ghazi bin Muhammad bin Talal and Professor Miroslav Volf; and (2) an address at the Cambridge conference, "A Common Word and Future Muslim-Christian Engagement" (October 12-15, 2008). In a slightly different form it was originally published in *Islamica* (2/2009), 63-68.

documents to appear in the past four decades — is one such ray shining through the barely parting clouds. The central message of this Muslim letter, endorsed by some of the most prominent Muslim leaders worldwide and addressed to Christian leaders across the planet, is as simple as it is profound: a belief in the Oneness of God and the commitment to love God and neighbor are resources found in both our respective faiths on which we can build more peaceful relations between Muslims and Christians. This same belief and the same commitment, of course, bind Christians and Muslims to their elder sibling, Judaism, the Abrahamic faith that originally transmitted to the world these two divine commandments.

Signs of Hope

As a reminder, "A Common Word" was issued not just in an atmosphere of stormy relations between Muslims and Christians but as a response to what many Muslims experienced as a Christian provocation. Its occasion was the famous Regensburg address of Pope Benedict XVI delivered in September 2005. In it Pope Benedict said of the Byzantine emperor Manuel II Paleologos that he "addresse[d] his interlocutor with a startling brusqueness, a brusqueness that we find unacceptable, on the central question about the relationship between religion and violence in general, saying, 'Show me just what Mohammed brought that was new, and there you will find things only evil and inhuman, such as his command to spread by the sword the faith he preached.'" Notwithstanding the Pope's disclaimer, many devout Muslims worldwide felt insulted.

Yet despite the perceived provocation, uttered in a context of deteriorating relations between Muslims and Christians — perhaps in part *because* of the provocation — key Muslim leaders, gathered around "A Common Word," did not respond in kind. Despite the present conflicts, they chose to speak of benevolence and beneficence, not to express hatred or dream of revenge. As is plain from the opening chapter by H.R.H. Prince Ghazi bin Muhammad in this volume, it is not that they simply shrugged off multiple ways they experience being violated by Christians and that they have forgotten the history of past violations. Instead, they turned felt provocation as well as experienced violence into an occasion to send into the wider world what seemed to many an utterly novel idea: For Muslims the commitment to love God and neighbor is central, and they share it with Christians as well as Jews. It has been said that God knows how to write straight even on crooked lines. The signatories of "A Common Word" also wrote "straight" on the crooked line of painful memories and deep tensions. The whole Christian community, indeed the whole world, should be grateful to them.

I trust it will not be taken as self-serving if I mention another smaller ray that penetrated the stormy clouds of Christian-Muslim relations. It was the Yale Response to "A Common Word," titled "Loving God and Neighbor Together." We took the conciliatory hand of the authors of "A Common Word" and responded in kind and out of the heart of the Christian faith. What is significant about the Yale Response, of course, is not so much that it was written, but that it was endorsed by over five hundred Christian leaders, many of whom are leaders of large, worldwide constituencies comprised of literally hundreds of millions of believers. Why did they endorse it? Because their Holy Book says, "as far as it depends on you, live at peace with everyone" (Romans 12:18), and because they sensed a danger of global proportions if a just peace between Muslims and Christians does not triumph over tensions and injustice. Neither the drafters nor the endorsers of the Yale Response were blind to the experience of violence and oppression from the hands of Muslims that many Christians report (e.g., persecution of Christian minorities and converts in many majority Muslim countries, as well as communal violence against Christians in places such as southern Sudan). Nor did they forget the long history of violence experienced in the past (e.g., disappearance of Christians from the Arabian peninsula or the oppression of Christians during Turkish conquests of the Balkans). Yet they felt that their faith called them to love their Muslim neighbors even in situations of enmity. Thus, with intentional obedience to the foundational principles of their faith and a deliberate decision to follow the example and teaching of Jesus Christ, these Christian leaders shook the hand extended to them.

The Yale Response, though early and widely endorsed, was not the only response to "A Common Word." Many Christians from all corners of the world have responded favorably as well, notably and with great theological depth and ecumenical sensitivity the Archbishop of Canterbury Rowan Williams.[1] The broad support of "A Common Word" in the Mus-

---

1. See Rowan Williams, "A Common Word for the Common Good," July 14, 2008, http://www.archbishopofcanterbury.org/1892.

lim community and the favorable response to it in the Christian community suggest that we may be poised for a sea change in Muslim-Christian relations. A day of transition from deep conflicts to mutually beneficial coexistence may be dawning.

Commonalities and Differences

Lest someone suppose that this assessment is a too-quick and somewhat cheap triumph of religious convergence over conflict, let me make plain what I am *not* saying about the significance of finding commonality between Christianity and Islam in the dual command of love. First, to have the dual command of love in common does *not* equate with being amalgamated into one and the same religion. Even if there is significant agreement on love of God and neighbor, many differences remain — differences that are not accidental to each faith but that have historically defined them. Some of these differences concern their basic understandings of God, love, and neighbor.

For instance, Christians believe that the One and Unique God, who is utterly exalted above all creation, is the Holy Trinity, and that God has shown unconditional love for humanity in that Jesus Christ as God's Lamb bore the sin of the world. Muslims generally do not share these beliefs. Other differences concern the sources of revelation. Muslims revere the Prophet Muhammad as the "seal of the prophets" and the Holy Qur'an as sacred Scripture. Christians do not. Significant agreement on love of God and neighbor does not erase these undeniable, deep, and consequential differences. What agreement on love of God and neighbor does is this: It enables those of deep faith to respect and protect others despite these differences, it leads them to get to know each other in their differences, and it helps them live together harmoniously notwithstanding their differences.

Second, to agree on the dual command of love is *not* to say that all the practical problems causing tensions between these two communities have now been resolved. Many thorny issues remain — large and small wars in which Christians and Muslims are involved, persecution and lack of full religious freedom, problems concerning evangelism and *da'wa* (the Islamic practice of inviting another to embrace Islam), and many others. The common commitment to love of God and neighbor does not eliminate all conflicts. What common commitment does is this: It provides a basis on which Muslims and Christians can productively discuss and overcome these conflicts.

Third, and equally significant, agreement on the dual command of love encourages each community to hold the other accountable to its best insights and commitments. A Muslim as the target of Christian verbal attacks can now say to a Christian, "How can you claim that you love me when you only speak ill of how I understand and worship God, when you malign my Prophet, and when you despise my way of life?" A Christian convert from Islam can now say to a hostile Muslim, "How can you say that you love me if you want to kill me just because I have followed my conscience and embraced the Christian faith?"

The common commitment to love of neighbor has real consequences on the ground. If practiced, it has the potential to defuse many serious conflicts of a global reach (such as that of the Danish cartoons of the Prophet Muhammad).

Transforming Love and Orienting Faith

But can one bring about a shift from what feels like a clash of civilizations to peaceful coexistence of faith traditions by promoting what some people may deem an esoteric feeling of human devotion to God and a soft and nebulous sentiment of love? Shouldn't we grapple with the harder realities of life instead? Shouldn't we discuss poverty and economic development, freedom of expression, education, stewardship of the environment, pluralism and democracy, the balance of power, resistance to extremists of all stripes, or modes of countering violence with effective force? If religion has anything to do with conflicts between Christians and Muslims, the critics may continue, religious passions stemming from single-minded devotion to God as the champion of one's cause are the source of these conflicts, not a means to overcome them. Less religion is what we need, not more. Take God out of it all, critics conclude. Let people keep religious devotion locked in the privacy of their hearts. Restrict the virtues and delights of love to friendship and family. Let instead individual and national interests, as well as the balance of power tempered by the claims of hardnosed justice, regulate worldly affairs.

So what worldly good can come of promoting love of God and love of neighbor? Why do we see a sign of hope in "A Common Word"? Partly because, properly understood, love is not a soft and a nebulous emotion but a tough, practical virtue of benevolence and beneficence, a virtue of which justice is an absolutely integral part. And religious faith is not impractical at all! For people of faith, Christians and Muslims alike, God is a motivating and sustaining power, the Holy One who gives meaning, weight, and direction to their life. In the current jargon, faith is what "makes them tick."

Faith Matters

It is not just love's toughness and the orienting character of faith, however, that makes these two shared loves of Muslims and Christians — love of God and love of neighbor — socially important. Consider the undiminished vibrancy of faith in the contemporary world. To the surprise of many — notably, those who believed that religion would gradually retreat before the light of reason and the wonders of technological development — the world today is becoming a *more* religious rather than a less religious place. The world is not progressively secularizing; to the contrary, it is *de*secularizing.[2] This trend is likely to continue into the foreseeable future.

Religious faiths, including Christianity and Islam, are reasserting themselves in two important senses. First, the number of their adherents in the world is growing in absolute and relative terms as compared to nonreligious worldviews. Second, religious people increasingly consider their faith not as simply a private affair but as a significant shaper of their public engagements. Religion matters profoundly, and matters in the public as well as the private sphere. I hope this claim will not be heard as a statement of religious triumphalism. I am aware that religion is often employed to wrap appallingly base causes in the aura of the sacred and to legitimize, even promote, violence. My point is not to deny this obvious fact. Neither is it to suggest that disbelief will be pushed out of existence or that nonbelievers' freedoms ought to be restricted. My aim is rather to remind us that religion matters and to point to a significant and unavoidable consequence of this fact.

What is this consequence? Negatively, if religion matters, no peace be-

2. See *Desecularization of the World: Resurgent Religion and World Politics,* ed. Peter Berger et al. (Grand Rapids: Eerdmans, 1999).

tween religious people will be achieved by pretending that it is merely a veil hiding some undeniable economic, political, or other interest. Positively, if religion matters, we have to find resources for the peaceful coexistence of religious people within each faith tradition itself.

Deep Faith and Social Pluralism

It is because faith matters that the "Common Word" initiative is so significant. First, "A Common Word" points both Muslims and Christians to what is undeniably essential in each faith and common to both — love of God and love of neighbor. Second, it shows how that which is essential in each faith and common to both has the power to bind them together because it encourages — indeed, demands — that their adherents seek the good of others, not just their own good. If it is true that the dual command of love binds the faiths together, the consequences are revolutionary in the best sense of the word. We no longer have to say, "The deeper your faith is, the more at odds with others you will be!" (provided, of course, that "deep faith" means not just emotionally strong faith but also intelligent and informed faith). To the contrary, we must say: "The deeper your faith is, the more in harmony with others you will live!" A deep faith no longer leads to clashes — it fosters peaceful coexistence.

What some people deride as an impractical and soft commitment to love God and neighbor — but what is actually the attachment to the Source of all reality and practice of active care — has real-life effects in defusing conflicts and fostering peace. It makes possible what would otherwise remain unattainable in a world of personally vibrant and socially assertive faiths. We can embrace deep faith while at the same time respecting the rights and promoting the well-being of those who do not share it. Deep faith expresses itself in love, and love, understood as active care, leads to respect of and struggle for others' rights. Put differently, and maybe surprisingly to some, *commitment to the properly understood love of God and neighbor makes deeply religious persons, precisely* because *they are deeply religious, into dedicated social pluralists.* When Christians and Muslims commit themselves to practicing the dual command of love, they are not satisfying some private religious fancy; instead, they are actively fostering peaceful coexistence in our ineradicably pluralistic world, which is plagued by deep divisions. They are making possible the constructive col-

24

laboration of people of different faiths in the common public space and for the common good.

Planetary Common Good

The significance of the "Common Word" initiative goes beyond relations between Muslims and Christians. The initiative holds the potential for providing a good platform for Christians and Muslims together to engage great and troubling problems facing humanity today. If, as Muslims say, God's mercy encompasses all, or if, as Christians might say, God's love is universal, then so should the love of Muslims and Christians be — a love for all humanity that is concerned for all aspects of every person's life. We live in a thoroughly interconnected and interdependent world that also knows itself as such (as we have been made painfully aware by the ongoing deep financial crisis, and as the ecological crisis attests). We're all in the same rocking boat, so to speak, and the good of one is the good of all; the ill of one is the ill of all. It is also a world caught in a whirlwind of unprecedented change. It seems that nothing is stable and that everything can — and eventually will — be overturned.

In the context of such highly dynamic societies marked by thorough-going interdependence, a "common word" between Muslims and Christians should not just be about mutual relations between these two faiths. It should also be, and maybe above all be, about the common good for the little boat that is our common world. In addition to sitting face to face and trying to make peace with one another, we need to start walking shoulder to shoulder in trying to heal the deep wounds and inspire the noble hopes of all people in our common world. Human flourishing and even human survival may depend on it.

An Encounter of Seven

What would it take for Muslims and Christians to have an effective common word with one another aimed at a better common future? How can we make fruitful the encounters of those committed to love God and each other as neighbors? An important first step is to attend carefully to the character of their encounters.

Someone has said, somewhat surprisingly, that in an encounter between you and me, *four* are always involved, not just two. Two of those four are, obviously, you and I. But also present are my image of you and your image of me. If this is so, then an encounter is fruitful when my image of you has become more as you truly are, and your image of me has become more as I truly am. As a Christian, I will engage carefully with my Muslim friend long enough for my perception of him to come in line with his perception of himself — and this is so whether I eventually end up agreeing or disagreeing with his perception of himself. That's a helpful way to think about encounters between people of different faiths. It isn't quite complete, however.

In every encounter *seven* are involved — a perfect number for Christians. There are you and I, and my image of you and your image of me — the obvious two and somewhat surprising four. But there is also my image of myself (which may not be true to who I am and may be very much *un*like who *you* think I am). And there is your image of yourself (which may not be true to who you are and may be very much *un*like who *I* think you are). So that makes six in one encounter. The consequence? I have to learn to see *myself* as I truly am, not just demand that *you* see me as I am (which is often a demand that you see me not as I *truly* am but as I *think* I am). Similarly, you have to learn to see *yourself* as you truly are, not just demand that *I* see you as you are (which is, again, often a demand that I see you not as you *truly* are but as you *think* you are). More concretely, as a Christian I will engage my Muslim friend long enough for his expressed perception of me actually to help me more accurately understand myself.

But I spoke of *seven* in every encounter. Where does the seventh come from? In every encounter there is also another one present — the categorically unique and utterly incomparable One, the absolutely truthful and infinitely merciful One. God is present in every encounter. As the truthful One, God sees each of us truthfully rather than distorting our identities. And God's truthful perception of us demands our truthful self-perception as well as the truthful perceiving of others. Further, as the merciful One, God desires us to be merciful in all our dealings with one another and with the world. Indeed, God desires of us to be *as* truthful and *as* merciful with ourselves, with one another, and with the world as he himself is truthful and merciful.

If God is always involved in any fruitful encounter, then it is clear that the seventh one is really the First One — not first among others, but the first one who makes all others and their encounter possible. Fruitful encounter between those who love God and neighbor is possible only because the God of love makes it possible — makes possible the encounter as well as the love of God and of neighbor around which the encounter takes place. Hence both our love of God and our love of neighbor appropriately must start with the recognition that we and our world are loved by the God of infinite love. The dual command of love is rooted in the simple and the most sublime reality of the God who "*is* love," as the Epistle of John states (1 John 4:8).

A Watershed?

It is not too much to say that the "Common Word" initiative, with its emphasis on the dual command of love, has the potential of becoming a historic watershed defining the relations between the two numerically largest faiths in the world today for the good of all humanity. But will it? Will it remain just a document that gathers the dust of history? Or will it become a common platform made out of a web of partly overlapping convictions from which to address effectively many areas of tension between Muslims and Christians, as well as many of the burning issues in our interconnected world?

Which of these possibilities will be realized? If Muslims and Christians embrace the initiative and commit themselves to love of God and neighbor, the "Common Word" initiative will open up a new future for Muslims, Christians, and Jews — a future in which many swords will be turned into plowshares and countless clashes will be replaced by peaceful coexistence.

In the Name of God, the Compassionate, the Merciful

A Common Word Between Us and You

(Summary and Abridgement)

Muslims and Christians together make up well over half of the world's population. Without peace and justice between these two religious communities, there can be no meaningful peace in the world. The future of the world depends on peace between Muslims and Christians.

The basis for this peace and understanding already exists. It is part of the very foundational principles of both faiths: love of the One God, and love of the neighbour. These principles are found over and over again in the sacred texts of Islam and Christianity. The Unity of God, the necessity of love for Him, and the necessity of love of the neighbour is thus the common ground between Islam and Christianity. The following are only a few examples:

Of God's Unity, God says in the Holy Qur'an: *Say: He is God, the One! / God, the Self-Sufficient Besought of all!* (Al-Ikhlas, 112:1-2). Of the necessity of love for God, God says in the Holy Qur'an: *So invoke the Name of thy Lord and devote thyself to Him with a complete devotion* (Al-Muzzammil, 73:8). Of the necessity of love for the neighbour, the Prophet Muhammad ﷺ said: *"None of you has faith until you love for your neighbour what you love for yourself."*

In the New Testament, Jesus Christ عليه السلام said: *"'Hear, O Israel, the Lord our God, the Lord is One. / And you shall love the Lord your God with all your heart, with all your soul, with all your mind, and with all your strength.' This is the first commandment. / And the second, like it, is this: 'You shall love your neighbour as yourself.' There is no other commandment greater than these"* (Mark 12:29-31).

28

*   *   *

In the Holy Qur'an, God Most High enjoins Muslims to issue the following call to Christians (and Jews — the *People of the Scripture*):

> Say: O People of the Scripture! Come to a common word between us and you: that we shall worship none but God, and that we shall ascribe no partner unto Him, and that none of us shall take others for lords beside God. And if they turn away, then say: Bear witness that we are they who have surrendered (unto Him). (*Aal 'Imran* 3:64)

The words: *we shall ascribe no partner unto Him,* relate to the Unity of God, and the words: *worship none but God,* relate to being totally devoted to God. Hence they all relate to the *First and Greatest Commandment.* According to one of the oldest and most authoritative commentaries on the Holy Qur'an the words: *that none of us shall take others for lords beside God,* mean "that none of us should obey the other in disobedience to what God has commanded." This relates to the Second Commandment because justice and freedom of religion are a crucial part of love of the neighbour.

Thus in obedience to the Holy Qur'an, we as Muslims invite Christians to come together with us on the basis of what is common to us, which is also what is most essential to our faith and practice: the *Two Commandments* of love.

In the Name of God, the Compassionate, the Merciful,
And may peace and blessings be upon the Prophet Muhammad

A Common Word Between Us and You

In the Name of God, the Compassionate, the Merciful,
  Call unto the way of thy Lord with wisdom and fair exhorta-
tion, and contend with them in the fairest way. Lo! thy Lord is Best
Aware of him who strayeth from His way, and He is Best Aware of
those who go aright.

The Holy Qur'an, *Al-Nahl,* 16:125

(I) Love of God

Love of God in Islam

The Testimonies of Faith

The central creed of Islam consists of the two testimonies of faith or *Shahadahs*,[1] which state that: *There is no god but God, Muhammad is the messenger of God.* These Two Testimonies are the *sine qua non* of Islam. He or she who testifies to them is a Muslim; he or she who denies them is not a Muslim. Moreover, the Prophet Muhammad ﷺ said: *The best remembrance is: "There is no god but God."* . . .[2]

---

1. In Arabic: *La illaha illa Allah Muhammad rasul Allah.* The two *Shahadah*s actually both occur (albeit separately) as phrases in the Holy Qur'an (in *Muhammad,* 47:19, and *Al-Fath,* 48:29, respectively).

2. *Sunan Al-Tirmidhi, Kitab Al-Da'awat,* 462/5, no. 3383; *Sunan Ibn Majah,* 1249/2.

The Best That All the Prophets Have Said

Expanding on *the best remembrance,* the Prophet Muhammad ﷺ also said: *The best that I have said — myself, and the prophets that came before me — is:* "There is no god but God, He Alone, He hath no associate, His is the sovereignty and His is the praise and He hath power over all things."³ The phrases which follow the First Testimony of faith are all from the Holy Qur'an; each describes a mode of love of God, and devotion to Him.

The words: *He Alone,* remind Muslims that their hearts⁴ must be de-

---

3. *Sunan Al-Tirmidhi, Kitab Al-Da'awat, Bab al-Du'a fi Yawm 'Arafah, Hadith* no. 3934.

It is important to note that the additional phrases, *He Alone, He hath no associate, His is the sovereignty and His is the praise and He hath power over all things,* all come from the Holy Qur'an, in exactly those forms, albeit in different passages. *He Alone* — referring to God ﷻ — is found at least six times in the Holy Qur'an (7:70; 14:40; 39:45; 40:12; 40:84 and 60:4). *He hath no associate* is found in exactly that form at least once (*Al-An'am,* 6:173). *His is the sovereignty and His is the praise and He hath power over all things* is found in exactly this form once in the Holy Qur'an (*Al-Taghabun,* 64:1), and parts of it are found a number of other times (for instance, the words *He hath power over all things* are found at least five times: 5:120; 11:4; 30:50; 42:9 and 57:2).

4. **The Heart**

In Islam the (spiritual, not physical) heart is the organ of perception of spiritual and metaphysical knowledge. Of one of the Prophet Muhammad's ﷺ greatest visions God says in the Holy Qur'an: *The inner heart lied not (in seeing) what it saw (al-Najm,* 53:11). Indeed, elsewhere in the Holy Qur'an, God says: *[F]or indeed it is not the eyes that grow blind, but it is the hearts, which are within the bosoms, that grow blind (Al-Hajj,* 22:46; see whole verse and also: 2:9-10; 2:74; 8:24; 26:88-89; 48:4; 83:14 et al.; there are in fact over a hundred mentions of the heart and its synonyms in the Holy Qur'an).

Now there are different understandings amongst Muslims as regards the direct Vision of God (as opposed to spiritual realities as such), be it in this life or the next — God says in the Holy Qur'an (of the Day of Judgement):

> That day will faces be resplendent, / Looking toward their Lord. (*Al-Qiyamah,* 75:22-23)

Yet God also says in the Holy Qur'an:

> Such is God, your Lord. There is no God save Him, the Creator of all things, so worship Him. And He taketh care of all things. / Vision comprehendeth Him not, but He comprehendeth (all) vision. He is the Subtle, the Aware. / Proofs have come unto you from your Lord, so whoso seeth, it is for his own good, and whoso is blind is blind to his own hurt. And I am not a keeper over you. (*Al-An'am,* 6:102-104)

Howbeit, it is evident that the Muslim conception of the (spiritual) heart is not very

voted to God Alone, since God says in the Holy Qur'an: *God hath not assigned unto any man two hearts within his body* (Al-Ahzab, 33:4). God is Absolute and therefore devotion to Him must be totally sincere.

The words: *He hath no associate,* remind Muslims that they must love God uniquely, without rivals within their souls, since God says in the Holy Qur'an: *Yet there are men who take rivals unto God: they love them as they should love God. But those of faith are more intense in their love for God . . .* (Al-Baqarah, 2:165). Indeed, *[T]heir flesh and their hearts soften unto the remembrance of God. . . . (Al-Zumar,* 39:23).

The words: *His is the sovereignty,* remind Muslims that their minds or their understandings must be totally devoted to God, for *the sovereignty* is precisely everything in creation or existence and everything that the mind can know. And all is in God's Hand, since God says in the Holy Qur'an: *Blessed is He in Whose Hand is the sovereignty, and, He is Able to do all things (Al-Mulk,* 67:1).

The words: *His is the praise* remind Muslims that they must be grateful to God and trust Him with all their sentiments and emotions. God says in the Holy Qur'an:

> And if thou wert to ask them: Who created the heavens and the earth, and constrained the sun and the moon (to their appointed work)? they would say: God. How then are they turned away? / God maketh the provision wide for whom He will of His servants, and straiteneth it for whom (He will). Lo! God is Aware of all things. / And if thou wert to ask them: Who causeth water to come down from the sky, and therewith reviveth the earth after its death? they verily would say: God. Say: Praise be to God! But most of them have no sense. (Al-'Ankabut, 29:61-63)[5]

For all these bounties and more, human beings must always be truly grateful:

> God is He Who created the heavens and the earth, and causeth water to descend from the sky, thereby producing fruits as food for you, and

---

different from the Christian conception of the (spiritual) heart, as seen in Jesus's ﷺ words in the New Testament: *Blessed are the pure in heart, for they shall see God* (Matthew 5:8); and Paul's words: *For now we see in a mirror, dimly, but then face to face. Now I know in part, but then I shall know just as I am known* (1 Corinthians 13:12).

5. See also: *Luqman,* 31:25.

maketh the ships to be of service unto you, that they may run upon the sea at His command, and hath made of service unto you the rivers; / And maketh the sun and the moon, constant in their courses, to be of service unto you, and hath made of service unto you the night and the day. / And He giveth you of all ye ask of Him, and if ye would count the graces of God ye cannot reckon them. Lo! man is verily a wrong-doer, an ingrate. (*Ibrahim,* 14:32-34)[6]

Indeed, the *Fatihah* — which is the *greatest chapter in the Holy Qur'an*[7] — starts with praise to God:

In the Name of God, the Infinitely Good, the All-Merciful. /
Praise be to God, the Lord of the worlds. /
The Infinitely Good, the All-Merciful. /
Owner of the Day of Judgement. /
Thee we worship, and Thee we ask for help. /
Guide us upon the straight path, /
The path of those on whom is Thy Grace, not those who deserve anger nor those who are astray. (*Al-Fatihah,* 1:1-7)

The *Fatihah,* recited at least seventeen times daily by Muslims in the canonical prayers, reminds us of the praise and gratitude due to God for His Attributes of Infinite Goodness and All-Mercifulness, not merely for His Goodness and Mercy to us in this life but, ultimately, on the Day of Judgement[8] when it matters the most and when we hope to be forgiven for our sins. It thus ends with prayers for grace and guidance, so that we might attain — through what begins with praise and gratitude — salvation and

---

6. See also: *Al-Nahl,* 16:3-18.

7. *Sahih Bukhari, Kitab Tafsir Al-Qur'an, Bab ma Ja'a fi Fatihat Al-Kitab* (*Hadith* no. 1); also: *Sahih Bukhari, Kitab Fada'il Al-Qur'an, Bab Fadl Fatihat Al-Kitab* (*Hadith* no. 9), no. 5006.

8. The Prophet Muhammad ﷺ said:

> God has one hundred mercies. He has sent down one of them between genii and human beings and beasts and animals and because of it they feel with each other; and through it they have mercy on each other; and through it, the wild animal feels for its offspring. And God has delayed ninety-nine mercies through which he will have mercy on his servants on the Day of Judgement. (*Sahih Muslm, Kitab Al-Tawbah;* 2109/4; no. 2752; see also *Sahih Bukhari, Kitab Al-Riqaq,* no. 6469)

love, for God says in the Holy Qur'an: *Lo! those who believe and do good works, the Infinitely Good will appoint for them love* (*Maryam*, 19:96).

The words: *and He hath power over all things*, remind Muslims that they must be mindful of God's Omnipotence and thus fear God.[9] God says in the Holy Qur'an:

> . . . [A]nd fear God, and know that God is with the God-fearing. / Spend your wealth for the cause of God, and be not cast by your own hands to ruin; and do good. Lo! God loveth the virtuous. . . . (*Al-Baqarah*, 2:194-95)

> [A]nd fear God, and know that God is severe in punishment. (*Al-Baqarah*, 2:196)

Through fear of God, the actions, might and strength of Muslims should be totally devoted to God. God says in the Holy Qur'an:

> . . . [A]nd know that God is with those who fear Him. (*Al-Tawbah*, 9:36)

> O ye who believe! What aileth you that when it is said unto you: Go forth in the way of God, ye are bowed down to the ground with heaviness. Take ye pleasure in the life of the world rather than in the Hereafter? The comfort of the life of the world is but little in the Hereafter. / If ye go not forth He will afflict you with a painful doom, and will choose instead of you a folk other than you. Ye cannot harm Him at all. God is Able to do all things. (*Al-Tawbah*, 9:38-39)

*   *   *

The words: *His is the sovereignty and His is the praise and He hath power over all things*, when taken all together, remind Muslims that just as every-

---

9. **Fear of God Is the Beginning of Wisdom**

The Prophet Muhammad ﷺ is reported to have said: *The chief part of wisdom is fear of God — be He exalted* (*Musnad al-Shahab*, 100/1; Al-Dulaymi, *Musnad Al-Firdaws*, 270/2; Al-Tirmidhi, *Nawadir Al-Usul*, 84/3; Al-Bayhaqi, *Al-Dala'il*, and Al-Bayhaqi, *Al-Shu'ab*; Ibn Lal, *Al-Makarim;* Al-Ash'ari, *Al-Amthal*, et al.). This evidently is similar to the Prophet Solomon's علیه السلام words in the Bible: The *fear of the LORD is the beginning of Wisdom* . . . (Proverbs 9:10); and: *The fear of the LORD is the beginning of knowledge* (Proverbs 1:7).

34

thing in creation glorifies God, everything that is in their souls must be devoted to God:

> All that is in the heavens and all that is in the earth glorifieth God; His is the sovereignty and His is the praise and He hath power over all things. (*Al-Taghabun*, 64:1)

For indeed, all that is in people's souls is known, and accountable, to God:

> He knoweth all that is in the heavens and the earth, and He knoweth what ye conceal and what ye publish. And God is Aware of what is in the breasts (of men). (*Al-Taghabun*, 64:4)

As we can see from all the passages quoted above, souls are depicted in the Holy Qur'an as having three main faculties: the mind or the intelligence, which is made for comprehending the truth; the will which is made for freedom of choice, and sentiment which is made for loving the good and the beautiful.[10] Put in another way, we could say that man's soul

10. **The Intelligence, the Will and Sentiment in the Holy Qur'an**
Thus God in the Holy Qur'an tells human beings to believe in Him and call on Him (thereby using the intelligence) with fear (which motivates the will) and with hope (and thus with sentiment):

> Only those believe in Our revelations who, when they are reminded of them, fall down prostrate and hymn the praise of their Lord, and they are not scornful, / Who forsake their beds to cry unto their Lord in fear and hope, and spend of that We have bestowed on them. / No soul knoweth what is kept hid for them of joy, as a reward for what they used to do. (*Al-Sajdah*, 32:15-17)

> (O mankind!) Call upon your Lord humbly and in secret. Lo! He loveth not aggressors. / Work not confusion in the earth after the fair ordering (thereof), and call on Him in fear and hope. Lo! the mercy of God is near unto the virtuous. (*Al-A'raf*, 7:55-56)

Likewise, the Prophet Muhammad ﷺ himself is described in terms which manifest knowledge (and hence the intelligence), eliciting hope (and hence sentiment) and instilling fear (and hence motivating the will):

> O Prophet! Lo! We have sent thee as a witness and a bringer of good tidings and a warner. (*Al-Ahzab*, 33:45)

> Lo! We have sent thee (O Muhammad) as a witness and a bearer of good tidings and a warner. (*Al-Fath*, 48:8)

knows through *understanding* the truth, through *willing* the good, and through virtuous emotions and *feeling* love for God. Continuing in the same chapter of the Holy Qur'an (as that quoted above), God orders people to fear Him as much as possible, and to listen (and thus to understand the truth); to obey (and thus to will the good), and to spend (and thus to exercise love and virtue), which, He says, is better for our souls. By engaging *everything* in our souls — the faculties of knowledge, will, and love — we may come to be purified and attain ultimate success:

> So fear God as best ye can, and listen, and obey, and spend; that is better for your souls. And those who are saved from the pettiness of their own souls, such are the successful. (*Al-Taghabun,* 64:16)

*   *   *

In summary then, when the entire phrase *He Alone, He hath no associate, His is the sovereignty and His is the praise and He hath power over all things* is added to the testimony of faith — *There is no god but God* — it reminds Muslims that their hearts, their individual souls and all the faculties and powers of their souls (or simply their *entire* hearts and souls) must be totally devoted and attached to God. Thus God says to the Prophet Muhammad 鑿 in the Holy Qur'an:

> Say: Lo! my worship and my sacrifice and my living and my dying are for God, Lord of the Worlds. / He hath no partner. This am I commanded, and I am first of those who surrender (unto Him). / Say: Shall I seek another than God for Lord, when He is Lord of all things? Each soul earneth only on its own account, nor doth any laden bear another's load. . . . (*Al-An'am,* 6:162-164)

These verses epitomize the Prophet Muhammad's 鑿 complete and utter devotion to God. Thus in the Holy Qur'an God enjoins Muslims who truly love God to follow this example,[11] in order in turn to be loved[12] by God:

---

11. **A Goodly Example**
The love and total devotion of the Prophet Muhammad 鑿 to God is for Muslims the model that they seek to imitate. God says in the Holy Qur'an:

36

Say, (O Muhammad, to mankind): If ye love God, follow me; God will love you and forgive you your sins. God is Forgiving, Merciful. (*Aal 'Imran*, 3:31)

Love of God in Islam is thus part of complete and total devotion to God; it is not a mere fleeting, partial emotion. As seen above, God commands in the Holy Qur'an: *Say: Lo! my worship and my sacrifice and my living and my dying are for God, Lord of the Worlds. / He hath no partner.* The call to be totally devoted and attached to God heart and soul, far from being a call for a mere emotion or for a mood, is in fact an injunction requiring all-embracing, constant and active love of God. It demands a love in which the innermost spiritual heart and the whole of the soul — with its intelligence, will and feeling — participate through devotion.

None Comes with Anything Better

We have seen how the blessed phrase: *There is no god but God, He Alone, He hath no associate, His is the sovereignty and His is the praise and He hath power over all things* — which is the best that all the prophets have said — makes explicit what is implicit in *the best remembrance (There is no god but God)* by showing what it requires and entails, by way of devotion. It remains to be said that this blessed formula is also in itself a sacred invocation — a kind of extension of the First Testimony of faith *(There is no god but God)* — the ritual repetition of which can bring about, through God's grace, some of the devotional attitudes it demands, namely, loving and be-

---

Verily in the messenger of God ye have a goodly example for him who hopeth for God and the Last Day, and remembereth God much. (*Al-Ahzab*, 33:21)

The totality of this love excludes worldliness and egotism, and is itself beautiful and loveable to Muslims. Love of God is itself loveable to Muslims. God says in the Holy Qur'an:

And know that the messenger of God is among you. If he were to obey you in many matters, ye would surely fall into misfortune; but God hath made the faith loveable to you and hath beautified it in your hearts, and hath made disbelief and lewdness and rebellion hateful unto you. Such are they who are the rightly guided. (*Al-Hujurat*, 49:7)

12. This "particular love" is in addition to God's universal Mercy *which embraceth all things (Al-A'raf*, 7:156); but God knows best.

ing devoted to God with all one's heart, all one's soul, all one's mind, all one's will or strength, and all one's sentiment. Hence the Prophet Muhammad ﷺ commended this remembrance by saying:

> He who says: "There is no god but God, He Alone, He hath no associate, His is the sovereignty and His is the praise and He hath power over all things" one hundred times in a day, it is for them equal to setting ten slaves free, and one hundred good deeds are written for them and one hundred bad deeds are effaced, and it is for them a protection from the devil for that day until the evening. And none offers anything better than that, save one who does more than that.[13]

13. *Sahih Al-Bukhari, Kitab Bad' al-Khalq, Bab Sifat Iblis wa Junudihi; Hadith* no. 3329.
Other Versions of the Blessed Saying
This blessed saying of the Prophet Muhammad's ﷺ, is found in dozens of *hadith* (sayings of the Prophet Muhammad ﷺ) in differing contexts in slightly varying versions.

The one we have quoted throughout in the text *(There is no god but God, He alone. He hath no associate. His is the sovereignty, and His is the praise, and He hath power over all things)* is in fact the shortest version. It is to be found in *Sahih al-Bukhari: Kitab al-Adhan* (no. 852); *Kitab al-Tahajjud* (no. 1163); *Kitab al-'Umrah* (no. 1825); *Kitab Bad' al-Khalq* (no. 3329); *Kitab al-Da'awat* (nos. 6404, 6458, 6477); *Kitab al-Riqaq* (no. 6551); *Kitab al-I'tisam bi'l-Kitab* (no. 7378); in *Sahih Muslim: Kitab al-Masajid* (nos. 1366, 1368, 1370, 1371, 1380); *Kitab al-Hajj* (nos. 3009, 3343); *Kitab al-Dhikr wa'l-Du'a'* (nos. 7018, 7020, 7082, 7084); in *Sunan Abu Dawud: Kitab al-Witr* (nos. 1506, 1507, 1508); *Kitab al-Jihad* (no. 2772); *Kitab al-Kharaj* (no. 2989); *Kitab al-Adab* (nos. 5062, 5073, 5079); in *Sunan al-Tirmidhi: Kitab al-Hajj* (no. 965); *Kitab al-Da'awat* (nos. 3718, 3743, 3984); in *Sunan al-Nasa'i: Kitab al-Sahw* (nos. 1347, 1348, 1349, 1350, 1351); *Kitab Manasik al-Hajj* (nos. 2985, 2997); *Kitab al-Iman wa'l-Nudhur* (no. 3793); in *Sunan Ibn Majah: Kitab al-Adab* (no. 3930); *Kitab al-Du'a'* (nos. 4000, 4011); and in *Muwatta' Malik: Kitab al-Qur'an* (nos. 492, 494); *Kitab al-Hajj* (no. 831).

A longer version including the words *yuhyi wa yumit* — (There is no god but God, He alone. He hath no associate. His is the sovereignty, and His is the praise. He giveth life, and He giveth death, and He hath power over all things.) — is to be found in *Sunan Abu Dawud: Kitab al-Manasik* (no. 1907); in *Sunan al-Tirmidhi: Kitab al-Salah* (no. 300); *Kitab al-Da'awat* (nos. 3804, 3811, 3877, 3901); and in *Sunan al-Nasa'i: Kitab Manasik al-Hajj* (nos. 2974, 2987, 2998); *Sunan Ibn Majah: Kitab al-Manasik* (no. 3190).

Another longer version including the words *bi yadihi al-khayr* — (There is no god but God, He alone. He hath no associate. His is the sovereignty, and His is the praise. In His Hand is the good, and He hath power over all things.) — is to be found in *Sunan Ibn Majah: Kitab al-Adab* (no. 3931); *Kitab al-Du'a'* (no. 3994).

The longest version, which includes the words *yuhyi wa yumit wa Huwa Hayyun la yamut bi yadihi al-khayr* — (There is no god but God, He alone. He hath no associate. His is the sovereignty, and His is the praise. He giveth life, and He giveth death. He is the Living,

In other words, the blessed remembrance, *There is no god but God, He Alone, He hath no associate, His is the sovereignty and His is the praise and He hath power over all things,* not only requires and implies that Muslims must be totally devoted to God and love Him with their whole hearts and their whole souls and all that is in them, but provides a way, like its beginning (the testimony of faith) — through its frequent repetition[14] — for them to realize this love with everything they are.

---

who dieth not. In His Hand is the good, and He hath power over all things.) — is to be found in *Sunan al-Tirmidhi: Kitab al-Da'awat* (no. 3756) and in *Sunan Ibn Majah: Kitab al-Tijarat* (no. 2320), with the difference that this latter *hadith* reads: *bi yadihi al-khayr kuluhu* (in His Hand is *all* good).

It is important to note, however, that the Prophet Muhammad ﷺ described only the first (shortest) version as: *the best that I have said — myself, and the prophets that came before me,* and only of that version did the Prophet ﷺ say: *And none comes with anything better than that, save one who does more than that.*

(These citations refer to the numbering system of *The Sunna Project's Encyclopaedia of Hadith [Jam' Jawami' al-Ahadith wa'l-Asanid],* prepared in cooperation with the scholars of al-Azhar, which includes *Sahih al-Bukhari, Sahih Muslim, Sunan Abu Dawud, Sunan al-Tirmidhi, Sunan al-Nasa'i, Sunan Ibn Majah,* and *Muwatta' Malik.*)

14. **Frequent Remembrance of God in the Holy Qur'an**

The Holy Qur'an is full of injunctions to invoke or remember God frequently:

> Remember the name of thy Lord at morn and evening. (*Al-Insan*, 76:25)

> So remember God, standing, sitting and [lying] down on your sides. (*Al-Nisa*, 4:103)

> And do thou (O Muhammad) remember thy Lord within thyself humbly and with awe, below thy breath, at morn and evening. And be not thou of the neglectful. (*Al-'Araf*, 7:205)

> . . . Remember thy Lord much, and praise (Him) in the early hours of night and morning. (*Aal 'Imran*, 3:41)

> O ye who believe! Remember God with much remembrance. / And glorify Him early and late. (*Al-Ahzab*, 33:41-42)

(See also: 2:198-200; 2:203; 2:238-239; 3:190-191; 6:91; 7:55; 7:180; 8:45; 17:110; 22:27-41; 24:35-38; 26:227; 62:9-10; 87:1-17, et al.)

Similarly, the Holy Qur'an is full of verses that emphasize the paramount importance of the Remembrance of God (see: 2:151-7; 5:4; 6:118; 7:201; 8:2-4; 13:26-28; 14:24-27; 20:14; 20:33-34; 24:1; 29:45; 33:35; 35:10; 39:9; 50:37; 51:55-58; and 33:2; 39:22-23 and 73:8-9 as already quoted, et al.), and the dire consequences of not practising it (see: 2:114; 4:142; 7:179-180; 18:28; 18:100-101; 20:99-101; 20:124-127; 25:18; 25:29; 43:36; 53:29; 58:19; 63:9; 72:17 et al.; see also 107:4-6). Hence God ultimately says in the Holy Qur'an:

God says in one of the very first revelations in the Holy Qur'an: *So invoke the Name of thy Lord and devote thyself to Him with a complete devotion* (*Al-Muzzammil*, 73:8). ✿

Love of God as the First and Greatest Commandment in the Bible

The *Shema* in the Book of Deuteronomy (6:4-5), a centrepiece of the Old Testament and of Jewish liturgy, says: *Hear, O Israel: The LORD our God, the LORD is one! / You shall love the LORD your God with all your heart, and with all your soul, and with all your strength.*[15]

Likewise, in the New Testament, when Jesus Christ, the Messiah ﷺ, is asked about the Greatest Commandment, he answers ﷺ:

> But when the Pharisees heard that he had silenced the Sadducees, they gathered together. Then one of them, a lawyer, asked Him a question, testing Him, and saying, "Teacher, which is the great commandment in the law?" Jesus said to him, "'You shall love the LORD your God with all your heart, with all your soul, and with all your mind.' This is the first and greatest commandment. And the second is like it: 'You shall love your neighbour as yourself.' On these two commandments hang all the Law and the Prophets." (Matthew 22:34-40)

And also:

> Then one of the scribes came, and having heard them reasoning together, perceiving that he had answered them well, asked him, "Which is the first commandment of all?" Jesus answered him, "The first of all the commandments is: 'Hear, O Israel, the LORD our God, the LORD is

---

> Has not the time arrived for the believers that their hearts in all humility should engage in the remembrance of God . . . ? (*Al-Hadid*, 57:16)
>
> . . . [S]lacken not in remembrance of Me. (*Taha*, 20:42)

and:

> Remember your Lord whenever you forget. (*Al-Kahf*, 18:24)

15. Herein all Biblical Scripture is taken from the New King James Version. Copyright 1982 by Thomas Nelson, Inc. Used by permission. All rights reserved.

one. And you shall love the LORD your God with all your heart, with all your soul, with all your mind, and with all your strength.' This is the first commandment. And the second, like it, is this: 'You shall love your neighbour as yourself.' There is no other commandment greater than these." (Mark 12:28-31)

The commandment to love God fully is thus the *First and Greatest Commandment* of the Bible. Indeed, it is to be found in a number of other places throughout the Bible including: Deuteronomy 4:29, 10:12, 11:13 (also part of the *Shema*), 13:3, 26:16, 30:2, 30:6, 30:10; Joshua 22:5; Mark 12:32-33 and Luke 10:27-28.

However, in various places throughout the Bible, it occurs in slightly different forms and versions. For instance, in Matthew 22:37 *(You shall love the LORD your God with all your heart, with all your soul, and with all your mind)*, the Greek word for "heart" is *kardia*, the word for "soul" is *psyche*, and the word for "mind" is *dianoia*. In the version from Mark 12:30 *(And you shall love the LORD your God with all your heart, with all your soul, with all your mind, and with all your strength)* the word "strength" is added to the aforementioned three, translating the Greek word *ischus*.

The words of the lawyer in Luke 10:27 (which are confirmed by Jesus Christ ﷺ in Luke 10:28) contain the same four terms as Mark 12:30. The words of the scribe in Mark 12:33 (which are approved of by Jesus Christ ﷺ in Mark 12:34) contain the three terms *kardia* ("heart"), *dianoia* ("mind"), and *ischus* ("strength").

In the *Shema* of Deuteronomy 6:4-5 *(Hear, O Israel: The LORD our God, the LORD is one! / You shall love the LORD your God with all your heart, and with all your soul, and with all your strength)*, in Hebrew the word for "heart" is *lev*, the word for "soul" is *nefesh*, and the word for "strength" is *me'od*.

In Joshua 22:5, the Israelites are commanded by Joshua ﷺ to love God and be devoted to Him as follows:

"But take careful heed to do the commandment and the law which Moses the servant of the LORD commanded you, to love the LORD your God, to walk in all His ways, to keep His commandments, to hold fast to Him, and to serve Him with all your heart and with all your soul." (Joshua 22:5)

What all these versions thus have in common — despite the language differences between the Hebrew Old Testament, the original words of Jesus Christ السلام عليه in Aramaic, and the actual transmitted Greek of the New Testament — is the command to love God fully with one's heart and soul and to be fully devoted to Him. This is the First and Greatest Commandment for human beings. ❋

In the light of what we have seen to be necessarily implied and evoked by the Prophet Muhammad's ﷺ blessed saying: *The best that I have said — myself, and the prophets that came before me — is: "There is no god but God, He Alone, He hath no associate, His is the sovereignty and His is the praise and He hath power over all things,"*[16] we can now perhaps understand the words: "The best that I have said — myself, and the prophets that came before me" as equating the blessed formula: *There is no god but God, He Alone, He hath no associate, His is the sovereignty and His is the praise and He hath power over all things,* precisely with the "First and Greatest Commandment" to love God, with all one's heart and soul, as found in various places in the Bible. That is to say, in other words, that the Prophet Muhammad ﷺ was perhaps, through inspiration, restating and alluding to the Bible's First Commandment. God knows best, but certainly we have seen their effective similarity in meaning. Moreover, we also do know (as can be seen in the notes) that both formulas have another remarkable parallel: the way they arise in a number of slightly differing versions and forms in different contexts, all of which, nevertheless, emphasize the primacy of total love and devotion to God.[17]

---

16. Sunan *Al-Tirmithi, Kitab Al-Da'wat, Bab al-Du'a fi Yawm 'Arafah, Hadith* no. 3934. *Op. cit.*

17. **In the Best Stature**
Christianity and Islam have comparable conceptions of man being created in the best stature and from God's own breath. The Book of Genesis says:

> So God created man in His own image; in the image of God He created him; male and female He created them. (Genesis 1:27)

And:

> And the LORD God formed man of the dust of the ground, and breathed into his nostrils the breath of life; and man became a living being. (Genesis 2:7)

And the Prophet Muhammad ﷺ said: *Verily God created Adam in His own image.* (*Sahih Al-Bukhari, Kitab Al-Isti'than,* 1; *Sahih Muslim, Kitab Al-Birr,* 115; *Musnad Ibn Hanbal,* 2: 244, 251, 315, 323 etc., et al.)

And We created you, then fashioned you, then told the angels: Fall ye prostrate

(II) Love of the Neighbour

Love of the Neighbour in Islam

There are numerous injunctions in Islam about the necessity and paramount importance of love for — and mercy towards — the neighbour. Love of the neighbour is an essential and integral part of faith in God and

---

before Adam! And they fell prostrate, all save Iblis, who was not of those who make prostration. (*Al-A'raf*, 7:11)

By the fig and the olive / By Mount Sinai, / And by this land made safe / Surely We created man of the best stature / Then We reduced him to the lowest of the low, / Save those who believe and do good works, and theirs is a reward unfailing. / So who henceforth will give the lie about the judgment? / Is not God the wisest of all judges? (*Al-Tin*, 95:1-8)

God it is Who appointed for you the earth for a dwelling-place and the sky for a canopy, and fashioned you and perfected your shapes, and hath provided you with good things. Such is God, your Lord. Then blessed be God, the Lord of the Worlds! (*Al-Ghafir*, 40:64)

Nay, but those who do wrong follow their own lusts without knowledge. Who is able to guide him whom God hath sent astray? For such there are no helpers. / So set thy purpose (O Muhammad) for religion as a man by nature upright — the nature (framed) of God, in which He hath created man. There is no altering (the laws of) God's creation. That is the right religion, but most men know not — / (*Al-Rum*, 30:29-30)

And when I have fashioned him and breathed into him of My Spirit, then fall down before him prostrate. (*Sad*, 38:72)

And when thy Lord said unto the angels: Lo! I am about to place a viceroy in the earth, they said: Wilt thou place therein one who will do harm therein and will shed blood, while we, we hymn Thy praise and sanctify Thee? He said: Surely I know that which ye know not. / And He taught Adam all the names, then showed them to the angels, saying: Inform Me of the names of these, if ye are truthful./ They said: Be glorified! We have no knowledge saving that which Thou hast taught us. Lo! Thou, only Thou, art the Knower, the Wise. / He said: O Adam! Inform them of their names, and when he had informed them of their names, He said: Did I not tell you that I know the secret of the heavens and the earth? And I know that which ye disclose and which ye hide. / And when We said unto the angels: Prostrate yourselves before Adam, they fell prostrate, all save Iblis. He demurred through pride, and so became a disbeliever . . . / And We said: O Adam! Dwell thou and thy wife in the Garden, and eat ye freely (of the fruits) thereof where ye will; but come not nigh this tree lest ye become wrong-doers. (*Al-Baqarah*, 2:30-35)

love of God because in Islam without love of the neighbour there is no true faith in God and no righteousness. The Prophet Muhammad 鑻 said: *"None of you has faith until you love for your brother what you love for your-self."*[18] And: *"None of you has faith until you love for your neighbour what you love for yourself."*[19]

However, empathy and sympathy for the neighbour — and even formal prayers — are not enough. They must be accompanied by generosity and self-sacrifice. God says in the Holy Qur'an:

It is not righteousness that ye turn your faces[20] to the East and the West; but righteous is he who believeth in God and the Last Day and the angels and the Scripture and the prophets; and giveth wealth, for love of Him, to kinsfolk and to orphans and the needy and the wayfarer and to those who ask, and to set slaves free; and observeth proper worship and payeth the poor-due. And those who keep their treaty when they make one, and the patient in tribulation and adversity and time of stress. Such are they who are sincere. Such are the pious. (*Al-Baqarah*, 2:177)

And also:

Ye will not attain unto righteousness until ye expend of that which ye love. And whatsoever ye expend, God is Aware thereof. (*Aal 'Imran*, 3:92)

Without giving the neighbour what we ourselves love, we do not truly love God or the neighbour.✿

Love of the Neighbour in the Bible

We have already cited the words of the Messiah, Jesus Christ 鑻, about the paramount importance, second only to the love of God, of the love of the neighbour:

18. *Sahih Al-Bukhari, Kitab al-Iman*, Hadith no. 13.
19. *Sahih Muslim, Kitab al-Iman*, 67-1, Hadith no. 45.
20. The classical commentators on the Holy Qur'an (see: *Tafsir Ibn Kathir, Tafsir Al-Jalalayn*) generally agree that this is a reference to (the last movements of) the Muslim prayer.

This is the first and greatest commandment. And the second is like it: 'You shall love your neighbour as yourself.' On these two command- ments hang all the Law and the Prophets. (Matthew 22:38-40)

And:

And the second, like it, is this: "You shall love your neighbour as your- self." There is no other commandment greater than these. (Mark 12:31)

It remains only to be noted that this commandment is also to be found in the Old Testament:

You shall not hate your brother in your heart. You shall surely rebuke your neighbour, and not bear sin because of him. You shall not take vengeance, nor bear any grudge against the children of your people, but you shall love your neighbour as yourself: I am the LORD. (Leviti- cus 19:17-18)

Thus the Second Commandment, like the First Commandment, de- mands generosity and self-sacrifice, and *On these two commandments hang all the Law and the Prophets.* ✳

(III) Come to a Common Word Between Us and You

A Common Word

Whilst Islam and Christianity are obviously different religions — and whilst there is no minimising some of their formal differences — it is clear that the *Two Greatest Commandments* are an area of common ground and a link between the Qur'an, the Torah and the New Testament. What pref- aces the Two Commandments in the Torah and the New Testament, and what they arise out of, is the Unity of God — that there is only one God. For the *Shema* in the Torah, starts: *Hear, O Israel: The LORD our God, the LORD is one!* (Deuteronomy 6:4). Likewise, Jesus ﷺ said: *The first of all the commandments is: "Hear, O Israel, the LORD our God, the LORD is one"* (Mark 12:29). Likewise, God says in the Holy Qur'an: *Say: He, God, is One. / God, the Self-Sufficient Besought of all* (*Al-Ikhlas,* 112:1-2). Thus the Unity of

God, love of Him, and love of the neighbour form a common ground upon which Islam and Christianity (and Judaism) are founded.

This could not be otherwise since Jesus الَّيْهِ said: *On these two commandments hang all the Law and the Prophets* (Matthew 22:40). Moreover, God confirms in the Holy Qur'an that the Prophet Muhammad ﷺ brought nothing fundamentally or essentially new: *Naught is said to thee (Muhammad) but what already was said to the messengers before thee* (*Fussilat,* 41:43). And: *Say (Muhammad): I am no new thing among the messengers (of God), nor know I what will be done with me or with you. I do but follow that which is Revealed to me, and I am but a plain warner* (*Al-Ahqaf,* 46:9). Thus also God in the Holy Qur'an confirms that the same eternal truths of the Unity of God, of the necessity for total love and devotion to God (and thus shunning false gods), and of the necessity for love of fellow human beings (and thus justice), underlie all true religion:

> And verily We have raised in every nation a messenger, (proclaiming): Worship God and shun false gods. Then some of them (there were) whom God guided, and some of them (there were) upon whom error had just hold. Do but travel in the land and see the nature of the consequence for the deniers! (*Al-Nahl,* 16:36)

> We verily sent Our messengers with clear proofs, and revealed with them the Scripture and the Balance, that mankind may stand forth in justice. . . . (*Al-Hadid,* 57:25)

Come to a Common Word!

In the Holy Qur'an, God Most High tells Muslims to issue the following call to Christians (and Jews — the *People of the Scripture*):

> Say: O People of the Scripture! Come to a common word between us and you: that we shall worship none but God, and that we shall ascribe no partner unto Him, and that none of us shall take others for lords beside God. And if they turn away, then say: Bear witness that we are they who have surrendered (unto Him). (*Aal 'Imran,* 3:64)

Clearly, the blessed words: *we shall ascribe no partner unto Him,* relate to the Unity of God. Clearly also, worshipping *none but God,* relates to being totally devoted to God and hence to the *First and Greatest Commandment.* According to one of the oldest and most authoritative commentaries *(tafsir)* on the Holy Qur'an — the *Jami' Al-Bayan fi Ta'wil Al-Qur'an* of Abu Ja'far Muhammad bin Jarir Al-Tabari (d. 310 A.H./923 C.E.) — *that none of us shall take others for lords beside God,* means "that none of us should obey in disobedience to what God has commanded, nor glorify them by prostrating to them in the same way as they prostrate to God." In other words, that Muslims, Christians and Jews should be free to each follow what God commanded them, and not have "to prostrate before kings and the like";[21] for God says elsewhere in the Holy Qur'an: *Let there be no compulsion in religion. . . . (Al-Baqarah,* 2:256). This clearly relates to the Second Commandment and to love of the neighbour of which justice[22] and freedom of religion are a crucial part. God says in the Holy Qur'an:

> God forbiddeth you not in regard to those who warred not against you on account of religion and drove you not out from your homes, that ye should show them kindness and deal justly with them. Lo! God loveth the just dealers. (*Al-Mumtahinah,* 60:8)

*   *   *

We thus as Muslims invite Christians to remember Jesus's ﷺ words in the Gospel (Mark 12:29-31):

> ". . . 'the LORD our God, the LORD is one. And you shall love the LORD your God with all your heart, with all your soul, with all your mind, and with all your strength.' This is the first commandment. And the second, like it, is this: 'You shall love your neighbour as yourself.' There is no other commandment greater than these."

As Muslims, we say to Christians that we are not against them and that Islam is not against them — so long as they do not wage war against Mus-

---

21. Abu Ja'far Muhammad Bin Jarir Al-Tabari, *Jami' al-Bayan fi Ta'wil al-Qur'an (Dar al-Kutub al-'Ilmiyyah,* Beirut, Lebanon, 1st ed., 1992/1412), *tafsir* of Aal-'Imran, 3:64; Volume 3, pp. 299-302.

22. According to grammarians cited by Tabari (op. cit.) the word "common" *(sawa')* in "a common word between us" also means "just," "fair" *(adl).*

lims on account of their religion, oppress them and drive them out of their homes (in accordance with the verse of the Holy Qur'an [*Al-Mumtahinah*, 60:8] quoted above). Moreover, God says in the Holy Qur'an:

They are not all alike. Of the People of the Scripture there is a staunch community who recite the revelations of God in the night season, falling prostrate (before Him). / They believe in God and the Last Day, and enjoin right conduct and forbid indecency, and vie one with another in good works. These are of the righteous. / And whatever good they do, nothing will be rejected of them. God is Aware of those who ward off (evil). (*Aal-'Imran*, 3:113-115)

Is Christianity necessarily against Muslims? In the Gospel Jesus Christ ﷺ says:

He who is not with me is against me, and he who does not gather with me scatters abroad. (Matthew 12:30)

For he who is not against us is on our side. (Mark 9:40)

. . . for he who is not against us is on our side. (Luke 9:50)

According to the Blessed Theophylact's[23] *Explanation of the New Testament,* these statements are not contradictions because the first statement (in the actual Greek text of the New Testament) refers to demons, whereas the second and third statements refer to people who recognised Jesus, but were not Christians. Muslims recognize Jesus Christ as the Messiah, not in the same way Christians do (but Christians themselves anyway have never all agreed with each other on Jesus Christ's ﷺ nature), but in the following way: . . . *the Messiah Jesus son of Mary is a Messenger of God and His Word which He cast unto Mary and a Spirit from Him* . . . (*Al-Nisa'*, 4:171). We therefore invite Christians to consider Muslims *not against* and thus *with them,* in accordance with Jesus Christ's ﷺ words here.

Finally, as Muslims, and in obedience to the Holy Qur'an, we ask

---

23. The Blessed Theophylact (1055-1108 C.E.) was the Orthodox Archbishop of Ochrid and Bulgaria (1090-1108 C.E.). His native language was the Greek of the New Testament. His *Commentary* is currently available in English from Chrysostom Press.

Christians to come together with us on the common essentials of our two religions . . . *that we shall worship none but God, and that we shall ascribe no partner unto Him, and that none of us shall take others for lords beside God . . . (Aal 'Imran, 3:64)*.

Let this common ground be the basis of all future interfaith dialogue between us, for our common ground is that on which hang *all the Law and the Prophets* (Matthew 22:40). God says in the Holy Qur'an:

> Say (O Muslims): We believe in God and that which is revealed unto us and that which was revealed unto Abraham, and Ishmael, and Isaac, and Jacob, and the tribes, and that which Moses and Jesus received, and that which the prophets received from their Lord. We make no distinction between any of them, and unto Him we have surrendered. / And if they believe in the like of that which ye believe, then are they rightly guided. But if they turn away, then are they in schism, and God will suffice thee against them. He is the Hearer, the Knower. (*Al-Baqarah*, 2:136-137)

Between Us and You

Finding common ground between Muslims and Christians is not simply a matter for polite ecumenical dialogue between selected religious leaders. Christianity and Islam are the largest and second largest religions in the world and in history. Christians and Muslims reportedly make up over a third and over a fifth of humanity respectively. Together they make up more than 55% of the world's population, making the relationship between these two religious communities the most important factor in contributing to meaningful peace around the world. If Muslims and Christians are not at peace, the world cannot be at peace. With the terrible weaponry of the modern world, with Muslims and Christians intertwined everywhere as never before, no side can unilaterally win a conflict between more than half of the world's inhabitants. Thus our common future is at stake. The very survival of the world itself is perhaps at stake.

And to those who nevertheless relish conflict and destruction for their own sake or reckon that ultimately they stand to gain through them, we say that our very eternal souls are all also at stake if we fail to sincerely make every effort to make peace and come together in harmony. God says in the

Holy Qur'an: *Lo! God enjoineth justice and kindness, and giving to kinsfolk, and forbiddeth lewdness and abomination and wickedness. He exhorteth you in order that ye may take heed* (Al Nahl, 16:90). Jesus Christ ﷺ said: *Blessed are the peacemakers . . .* (Matthew 5:9), and also: *For what profit is it to a man if he gains the whole world and loses his soul?* (Matthew 16:26).

So let our differences not cause hatred and strife between us. Let us vie with each other only in righteousness and good works. Let us respect each other, be fair, just and kind to another and live in sincere peace, harmony and mutual goodwill. God says in the Holy Qur'an:

> And unto thee have We revealed the Scripture with the truth, confirming whatever Scripture was before it, and a watcher over it. So judge between them by that which God hath revealed, and follow not their desires away from the truth which hath come unto thee. For each We have appointed a law and a way. Had God willed He could have made you one community. But that He may try you by that which He hath given you (He hath made you as ye are). So vie one with another in good works. Unto God ye will all return, and He will then inform you of that wherein ye differ. (*Al-Ma'idah,* 5:48)

> *Wal-Salaamu 'Alaykum,*
> *Pax Vobiscum.*

Loving God and Neighbor Together:
A Christian Response to
"A Common Word Between Us and You"

Original text as published in the New York Times
(November 2007)

with added commentary by

MIROSLAV VOLF, JOSEPH CUMMING, AND MELISSA YARRINGTON

This open letter, commonly referred to as the Yale Response, was originally published in the *New York Times* on November 18, 2007, only one month after "A Common Word," with the Arabic translation of the Yale Response released at a press conference in the United Arab Emirates shortly after. The drafters of the Yale Response were aware of the importance of timing, knowing that the Muslim signatories of "A Common Word" had risked extending their hand and that there is only so long a hand can remain outstretched in midair before the discomfort caused by hesitation changes the dynamic and colors future interactions negatively. A timely, considered, and bold response informed by deep Christian convictions was needed to pave the way for substantive interaction on difficult questions. In the eighteen months since the publication of the Yale Response, we have been delighted to witness extensive and fruitful face-to-face interactions between Muslim and Christian leaders in multiple formal events and innumerable informal interactions and to read various thoughtful responses given by different representatives of the worldwide Christian community.

The text of the Yale Response is reprinted below. In the commentary section that follows, we take the opportunity to give the reader, Christian and Muslim, insight into reasons underlying some of the potentially controversial wording of the Yale Response. The comments are written against the background of both actual debates concerning the Yale Response in the months after it was published and the ensuing dialogue between Christians and Muslims about the salient issues. They are, obviously, one intervention in a larger conversation, and while we seek to speak with integrity, we recognize and encourage others to participate vigorously.

The Text of the Yale Response

*In the name of the Infinitely Good God
whom we should love with all our being*⁴

Preamble

As members of the worldwide Christian community,⁴ we were deeply encouraged and challenged by the recent historic open letter signed by 138 leading Muslim scholars, clerics, and intellectuals from around the world. *A Common Word Between Us and You* identifies some core common ground between Christianity and Islam which lies at the heart of our respective faiths⁴ as well as at the heart of the most ancient Abrahamic faith, Judaism.⁴ Jesus Christ's call to love God and neighbor was rooted in the divine revelation to the people of Israel embodied in the Torah⁴ (Deuteronomy 6:5; Leviticus 19:18). We receive the open letter as a Muslim hand of conviviality and cooperation extended to Christians world-wide. In this response we extend our own Christian hand in return,⁴ so that together with all other human beings we may live in peace and justice⁴ as we seek to love God and our neighbors.

Muslims and Christians have not always shaken hands in friendship; their relations have sometimes been tense, even characterized by outright hostility.⁴ Since Jesus Christ says, "First take the log out of your own eye, and then you will see clearly to take the speck out of your neighbor's eye" (Matthew 7:5), we want to begin by acknowledging that in the past (e.g. in the Crusades) and in the present (e.g. in excesses of the "war on terror") many Christians have been guilty of sinning against our Muslim neighbors.⁴ Before we "shake your hand" in responding to your letter, we ask forgiveness of the All-Merciful One⁴ and of the Muslim community around the world.

Religious Peace — World Peace

"Muslims and Christians together make up well over half of the world's population. Without peace and justice between these two religious communities, there can be no meaningful peace in the world." We share the sentiment of the Muslim signatories expressed in these opening lines of their open letter. Peaceful relations between Muslims and Christians stand as one of the central challenges of this century, and perhaps of the whole present epoch.◄ Though tensions, conflicts, and even wars in which Christians and Muslims stand against each other are not primarily religious in character, they possess an undeniable religious dimension. If we can achieve religious peace◄ between these two religious communities, peace in the world will clearly be easier to attain. It is therefore no exaggeration to say, as you have in *A Common Word Between Us and You,* that "the future of the world depends on peace between Muslims and Christians."

Common Ground

What is so extraordinary about *A Common Word Between Us and You* is not that its signatories recognize the critical character of the present moment in relations between Muslims and Christians. It is rather a deep insight and courage with which they have identified the common ground between the Muslim and Christian religious communities. What is common between us lies not in something marginal nor in something merely important to each. It lies, rather, in something absolutely central to both: love of God and love of neighbor. Surprisingly for many Christians, your letter considers the dual command of love to be the foundational principle not just of the Christian faith, but of Islam as well.◄ That *so much* common ground exists — common ground in some of the fundamentals of faith — gives hope that undeniable differences◄ and even the very real external pressures that bear down upon us cannot overshadow the common ground upon which we stand together. That this common ground consists in *love* of God and of neighbor gives hope that deep cooperation between us can be a hallmark of the relations between our two communities.

Love of God

We applaud that *A Common Word Between Us and You* stresses so insistently the unique devotion to one God,◄ indeed the love of God, as the primary duty of every believer. God alone rightly commands our ultimate allegiance.◄ When anyone or anything besides God commands our ultimate allegiance — a ruler, a nation, economic progress, or anything else — we end up serving idols and inevitably get mired in deep and deadly conflicts.◄

We find it equally heartening that the God whom we should love above all things is described as being Love.◄ In the Muslim tradition, God, "the Lord of the worlds," is "The Infinitely Good and All-Merciful."◄ And the New Testament states clearly that "God is love" (1 John 4:8). Since God's goodness is infinite and not bound by anything,◄ God "makes his sun rise on the evil and the good, and sends rain on the righteous and the unrighteous," according to the words of Jesus Christ recorded in the Gospel (Matthew 5:45).

For Christians, humanity's love of God and God's love of humanity are intimately linked. As we read in the New Testament: "We love because he [God] first loved us" (1 John 4:19). Our love of God springs from and is nourished by God's love for us. It cannot be otherwise, since the Creator who has power over all things is infinitely good.

Love of Neighbor

We find deep affinities with our own Christian faith when *A Common Word Between Us and You* insists that love is the pinnacle of our duties toward our neighbors.◄ "None of you has faith until you love for your neighbor what you love for yourself," the Prophet Muhammad said. In the New Testament we similarly read, "whoever does not love [the neighbor] does not know God" (1 John 4:8) and "whoever does not love his brother whom he has seen cannot love God whom he has not seen" (1 John 4:20). God is love, and our highest calling as human beings is to imitate the One whom we worship.

We applaud when you state that "justice and freedom of religion are a crucial part" of the love of neighbor. When justice is lacking, neither love of God nor love of the neighbor can be present. When freedom to worship

54

God according to one's conscience is curtailed, God is dishonored, the neighbor oppressed, and neither God nor neighbor is loved.

Since Muslims seek to love their Christian neighbors, they are not against them, the document encouragingly states. Instead, Muslims are *with* them. As Christians we resonate deeply with this sentiment. Our faith teaches that we must be with our neighbors — indeed, that we must act in their favor — even when our neighbors turn out to be our enemies. "But I say unto you," says Jesus Christ, "Love your enemies and pray for those who persecute you, so that you may be children of your Father in heaven; for he makes his sun rise on the evil and on the good" (Matthew 5:44-45). Our love, Jesus Christ says, must imitate the love of the infinitely good Creator;⁴ our love must be as unconditional as is God's — extending to brothers, sisters, neighbors, and even enemies.⁴ At the end of his life, Jesus Christ himself prayed for his enemies: "Forgive them; for they do not know what they are doing" (Luke 23:34).

The Prophet Muhammad did similarly⁴ when he was violently rejected and stoned by the people of Ta'if. He is known to have said, "The most virtuous behavior is to engage those who sever relations, to give to those who withhold from you, and to forgive those who wrong you."⁴ (It is perhaps significant that after the Prophet Muhammad was driven out of Ta'if, it was the Christian slave 'Addas who went out to Muhammad, brought him food, kissed him, and embraced him.⁴)

The Task Before Us

"Let this common ground" — the dual common ground of love of God and of neighbor — "be the basis of all future interfaith dialogue between us," your courageous letter urges. Indeed, in the generosity with which the letter is written you embody what you call for. We most heartily agree. Abandoning all "hatred and strife," we must engage in interfaith dialogue⁴ as those who seek each other's good, for the one God unceasingly seeks our good. Indeed, together with you we believe that we need to move beyond "a polite ecumenical dialogue between selected religious leaders" and work diligently together to reshape relations between our communities and our nations so that they genuinely reflect our common love for God and for one another.⁴

Given the deep fissures in the relations between Christians and Muslims today, the task before us is daunting. And the stakes are great. The future of the world depends on our ability as Christians and Muslims to live together in peace. If we fail to make every effort to make peace and come together in harmony you correctly remind us that "our eternal souls" are at stake as well.⁴

We are persuaded that our next step should be for our leaders at every level to meet together and begin the earnest work of determining how God would have us fulfill the requirement that we love God and one another. It is with humility and hope that we receive your generous letter, and we commit ourselves to labor together in heart, soul, mind and strength for the objectives you so appropriately propose.

Commentary on the Yale Response

In the name of the Infinitely Good God whom we should love with all our being The drafters of the Yale Response chose to follow the long-standing Christian tradition of including an invocation at the beginning of their letter. Invocations are common in many liturgical traditions to open any gathering of God's people, and even translators of the Bible throughout history have been known to include an invocation at the start of each book. For example, the Peshitta Bible, which was in common use by the fifth century, included many invocations. Another interesting example is the earliest translation of the New Testament in Arabic, which is found in St. Catherine's Monastery in the Sinai Peninsula. In this translation, known as the Mount Sinai Arabic Codex 151 (867 CE), the translator includes a different invocation at the beginning of each of the books of the New Testament.

For the purpose of this response, various invocations were considered. It was desirable to begin with a strong affirmation of our worship of and reliance on the One True God. The particular phrase "Infinitely Good God" was chosen with verses such as Psalm/Zabūr 100:5 in mind, which verses are relevant to the topic of God's love: "For the LORD is good; his steadfast love endures forever, and his faithfulness to all generations." Similarly, Psalm/Zabūr 106:1 says: "Praise the LORD! O give thanks to the LORD for he is good, for his steadfast love endures forever!" From the perspective of the revelation of God in Jesus Christ and New Testament/Injīl passages such as 1 John 4:7-12, the mention of the *infinitely* good God was intended to signal the main theme of the response, which is at the same time the heart of the Gospel: the indiscriminate and unconditional nature of divine love as the most important feature of the Christian understanding of God.

As members of the worldwide Christian community The Yale Response does not claim to represent all Christians everywhere, but affirms that the signatories are members of the worldwide Christian community, a community in which there is much diversity regarding ecclesiastical structures as well as many beliefs and practices, but a community that historically and traditionally holds some core creedal affirmations. Most Christians would hold that the Bible is normative Scripture and that the Nicene Creed and Apostles' Creed faithfully express important Christian core convictions — convictions about the One True God, Creator of all there is, as well as about Jesus Christ, the Savior of the world. Such creeds are held to be accurate (and by some, authoritative) summaries of key teachings of the Scriptures as a whole, building on a wide variety of biblical texts, including the following: "In the beginning God created the heavens and the earth" (Genesis 1:1 in the Torah/Old Testament); "The LORD our God, the LORD is one" (Deuteronomy 6:4 in the Torah/Old Testament); "In the beginning was the Word, and the Word was with God, and the Word was God" (John 1:1 in the Injīl/New Testament); "The grace of the Lord Jesus Christ and the love of God and the fellowship of the Holy Spirit be with you all" (2 Corinthians 13:14 in the Injīl/New Testament); and "that Christ died for our sins in accordance with the Scriptures, that he was buried, that he was raised on the third day" (1 Corinthians 15:3-4 in the Injīl/New Testament).

core common ground between Christianity and Islam which lies at the heart of our respective faiths To say that something is "at the heart" of the Christian faith is not to say that it *is* the heart of the Christian faith. For the Christian, Jesus Christ is the undisputed heart of faith. The Bible in the Injīl/New Testament speaks of Jesus as the Messiah (Matthew 1:1), the Word of God (John 1:1), the Author of Life (Acts 3:15), the Image of God (2 Corinthians 4:4), the Light of the World (John 8:12), the Resurrection and the Life (John 11:25), the Son of David (Luke 18:39), the Son of God (John 1:49; the meaning of this title is discussed in detail by Miroslav Volf's chapter in this volume entitled "God Is Love"), and Savior (Ephesians 5:23), to name just a few of Jesus' important titles. To be a Christian means, above all, to be a follower of Jesus Christ and through Jesus to have access to God. However, it is quite accurate to say that loving God and loving neighbor lie *at* the heart of Christian faith, since Jesus himself named them as the first and second greatest commandments (Matthew 22:36-38). Similarly, to say that these commandments lie at the heart of the Christian faith is not to say that they are the only indispensable requirements for Christians. Faith, understood as utter trust in God, is also such a requirement (though many theologians, such as Martin Luther, understood faith to be the main form that love for God must take). "Without faith it is impossible to please God" (Hebrews 11:6).

as well as at the heart of the most ancient Abrahamic faith, Judaism The term "Abrahamic faith" is most often used to refer to Judaism, Christianity, and Islam, along with other faith traditions that trace their spiritual heritage to Abraham, who was called by the invisible God to leave his own people's polytheistic idol worship and to worship the One God. It is appropriate for Christians to understand theirs as an Abrahamic faith. In the Injīl/New Testament, Romans 4:16 says that those who believe in Christ "share the faith of Abraham," and Galatians 3:7 and 29 refer to believers in Christ as "children of Abraham." In the Gospel according to Matthew (1:1-17), the genealogy of Jesus Christ is traced back to Abraham. The Bible notes that Abraham's life pre-dates the giving of the Mosaic law and affirms that Abraham believed God and God counted Abraham's faith as righteousness (cf. Genesis 15:6 in the Torah/Old Testament; Romans 4:9; Galatians 3:6-7; and James 2:23 in the Injīl/New Testament). For Christians, using the designation "Abrahamic faith" not only is appropriate but also provides a useful starting point for discussion of similarities and differences in Jewish, Christian, and Muslim understandings of God and God's dealings with humanity.

the divine revelation to the people of Israel embodied in the Torah The designation "Torah" (as distinct from "Old Testament") is used because Muslims, to whom this response is addressed, are familiar with the term (as well as because it honors Judaism as the religious ancestor to both the Christian and Muslim faiths). The Qur'ān makes frequent reference to the "previous Scriptures," namely, the Law (Torah), the Psalms (Zabūr), and the Gospel/New Testament (Injīl) in verses like Sūra 5:68: "Say: 'O People of the Scripture, you have no basis until you observe the Torah and the Gospel and what was revealed to you from your Lord,'" and Sūra 4:163:

"We have sent thee inspiration, as We sent it to Noah and the Messengers after him: we sent inspiration to Abraham, Ismā'īl, Isaac, Jacob and the Tribes, to Jesus, Job, Jonah, Aaron, and Solomon, and to David We gave the Psalms." The New Testament calls "the Law and the Prophets," and sometimes simply "the Law," what Christians nowadays call the "Old Testament" (cf. 1 Corinthians 14:21, which refers to a quotation from Isaiah as "the Law").

In the first five centuries AH (seventh to eleventh centuries AD), Muslim commentators, theologians, and jurists usually dealt with the "previous Scriptures" assuming, on the basis of qur'anic references to these Scriptures, that the Law, Psalms, and New Testament were given by God but misinterpreted by Jews and Christians. Muslim-Christian dialogue during these centuries frequently involved reference to and debate about the proper interpretation of specific passages from the Bible. After the eleventh century, there is a noticeable shift in the character of the dialogue. From then on, Muslims more frequently believe that the actual text of the Bible has been intentionally corrupted and is therefore not trustworthy and cannot provide any basis for dialogue. Martin Accad has argued, "it can be demonstrated that until the time of Ibn Ḥazm in the eleventh century, the accusation of *taḥrīf* in the sense of 'intentional corruption of the Holy Scriptures' was virtually non-existent. Even where some grave and serious suspicions were raised against the integrity of the text, the accusation can certainly not be considered to have been a central or foundational element of the Muslim discourse against Christianity. If it has become the starting point of that discourse today, it is certainly worth knowing that it has not always been the case, and that it is therefore possible to think otherwise. Even after Ibn Ḥazm, as late as the fourteenth century, Ibn Taymiyya recognized that the Islamic position towards *taḥrīf* as textual corruption was still diverse and ambiguous."[1]

It is encouraging that the authors of "A Common Word" did such extensive exegesis of biblical texts. Since the Hebrew, Aramaic, and Greek manuscripts that now provide the basis for translations of the Bible predate the sixth century, perhaps Muslims and Christians will be able to re-

---

1. Martin Accad, "The Gospels in the Muslim Discourse of the Ninth to the Fourteenth Centuries," *Islam and Christian-Muslim Relations* 14/1 (2003): 67-91; see also Abdullah Saeed, "The Charge of Distortion of Jewish and Christian Scriptures: Tension between the Popular Muslim View and the Qur'ānic/Tafsir View," *The Muslim World* 92/3&4 (2002): 419-36.

turn to dialogue focusing on the interpretation of these texts rather than on questions of reliability. If we engaged in reading and interpreting our respective holy books together, polemics would decrease and Muslims and Christians would be able thoughtfully and considerately to seek truth together while fully respecting each other's core convictions and practices.

We receive the open letter as a Muslim hand of conviviality and cooperation extended to Christians world-wide. In this response we extend our own Christian hand in return The metaphor of a handshake implies a sense of goodwill toward our Muslim neighbors and a desire to work together with them toward greater peace and justice in the world in which we live. A handshake is like an "embrace" — not in the sense of *I'tināq* but as a gesture of openness to receive the other and be received by the other, a gesture that does not swallow the other or let oneself be swallowed by the other, a gesture that suggests willingness to listen to how things look from the perspective of the other as well as state one's own perspective.[2] The metaphor of a handshake does not imply that Christians are capitulating on core convictions, for instance by denying the triunity of the One God, divinity of Christ, or Christ's death and resurrection. Similarly, for Muslims the metaphor does not suggest that they have given up on any of their convictions. Handshaking is not about which convictions we hold to be true; it is about our attitude toward each other and each other's convictions.

A handshake also does not imply we believe that all issues that lead to conflict involving Christians and Muslims have been or will be so easily resolved. Rather, the extending of our hand symbolizes our willingness to work on resolving these conflicts through peaceful means and to work together whenever and however possible so as to live at peace with one another in justice as we share common space in this world.

so that together with all other human beings we may live in peace and justice Several explicit commands in the New Testament/Injīl demand of Christians to pursue peace, such as: "Repay no one evil for evil, but give thought to do what is honorable in the sight of all. If possible, so far as it depends on you, live peaceably with all" (Romans 12:17-18), and the words spoken by Jesus, "Blessed are the peacemakers, for they will be called children of

---

2. Cf. Miroslav Volf, *Exclusion and Embrace: Theological Exploration of Identity, Otherness, and Reconciliation* (Nashville: Abingdon, 1996).

God. Blessed are those who are persecuted because of righteousness, for theirs is the kingdom of heaven" (Matthew 5:9-10). The Bible also calls on believers to pursue justice: "Let justice roll down like waters and righteousness like an ever-flowing stream" (Amos 5:24 in the Prophets of the Old Testament), and "You have neglected the weightier matters of the law, justice and mercy and faith" (Matthew 23:23 in the Injīl/New Testament).

Muslims and Christians have not always shaken hands in friendship; their relations have sometimes been tense, even characterized by outright hostility While there have been some moments of peaceful coexistence throughout the fourteen centuries of Muslim-Christian relations, clearly much of this history has been marked by tension and strife, and the list of grievances on both sides is long and real. Conquest and reconquest of territory and sacred space, persecution of religious minorities, curtailing of religious freedoms, discrimination or oppression based on gender/faith/ethnicity, disrespecting sacred symbols, persecution of religious converts, acts of violence done in the name of God, and inadequate public censure of unjustified violent acts — these are only some of the categories of grievances felt between Christians and Muslims. In the light of such enormous indictments, the challenges before these two communities are immense. Affirmation of each other as neighbors who believe God calls us to love one another opens the possibility of peaceful coexistence, even if, given the long history of violence, living in the light of this affirmation will be enormously difficult.

Since Jesus Christ says, "First take the log out of your own eye, and then you will see clearly to take the speck out of your neighbor's eye" (Matthew 7:5), we want to begin by acknowledging that in the past (e.g. in the Crusades) and in the present (e.g. in excesses of the "war on terror") many Christians have been guilty of sinning against our Muslim neighbors This simple paragraph was a complicated one to draft, requiring knowledge of history and theology as well as cultural and spiritual sensitivity. The drafters were aware that the request for forgiveness would be controversial — that responses to it would range from spirited defense to vigorous opposition — and recognize that Christians from different backgrounds may have varied understandings of this issue. It was felt, though, that the paragraph was demanded by the main thrust of the Yale Response as a whole — namely, the emphasis on unconditional love even for enemies. The paragraph names one aspect of what it means for Jesus' followers to have a genuinely Christian posture of unconditional love when engaging with the Muslim world.

The original text of the Yale Response explicitly states the chief reason for the apology, namely, that Jesus in Matthew 7:5 in the Injīl/New Testament taught that when we are in conflict with others and wrongs have been committed on both sides, Jesus' followers must take the initiative of apologizing first. This initiating does not ignore wrongs committed by the other party, and indeed Jesus said that if we apologize first we will "see more clearly" to help others understand where they have wronged us. Muslims and Christians through the centuries and today have committed terrible wrongs in both directions, but Jesus says that his followers must apologize first whether or not the others apologize.

One question some have raised regarding this paragraph is the appropriateness of "representative repentance." Can and should Christians seek forgiveness from God and their neighbors for wrongdoing that members of their community have committed, rather than they themselves? In the Bible, Daniel (Daniel 9:1-19 in the Prophets of the Old Testament), Ezra (Nehemiah 9:1-37), and others did explicitly repent before God of sins committed by their people, though they themselves had not personally committed these sins. Even if one accepts the idea of representative repentance, it has been argued that it is inappropriate in this particular case because only some of the signatories can trace ancestry to Crusaders and because Christians are not responsible for excesses perpetrated by secular governments and military regimes today.

Also, many Christians today do not consider themselves part of anything like "Christendom," but followers of Jesus Christ living in a variety of nations, cultures, and civilizations or, in the language of Revelation 5:9 in the Injīl/New Testament, a people "ransomed for God from every tribe and language and people and nation." If we were to ask forgiveness on behalf of "Christendom" or "Christian nations" or even "all Christians" for wrongdoing committed against Muslims in the course of the Crusades or in the course of the "war on terror," it would perpetuate civilizationally defined communalism instead of moving beyond those conflict-inducing self-identifications. Thus, the critical distinction in the Yale Response is that as Christians we "acknowledge" that "many Christians" have sinned against Muslim neighbors. The drafters of the Yale Response (who themselves can trace their heritages to both perpetrators and victims) are grateful to those

Christian signatories who represent victims of the Crusades and excesses of the "war on terror," especially Arab and Eastern Orthodox Christians, for the generosity of their gesture in joining this expression of sorrow.

Those involved in peacemaking and reconciliation between Christians and Muslims recognize that events such as the Crusades and the "war on terror" are a stumbling block for Muslim trust of Christians and their ability to envisage peaceful coexistence. Part of the goal of the drafters of the Yale Response was to express that many (and hopefully the vast majority of) Christians in the world today are deeply disturbed that the most sacred symbol of their faith — the cross of Jesus Christ — has become to many Muslims (and, for that matter, to many Jews) not a symbol of good news, self-sacrifice, and salvation, but of military conquest and oppression. By offering an apology, the drafters and signatories express regret for actions done by others who identified themselves by the name of Jesus (or are misidentified by others as belonging to that name), and who have so tragically misrepresented Jesus' teachings and person by their actions. Asking forgiveness, then, is not so much representative repentance as it is acknowledgment of the seriousness of these wrongdoings in God's eyes and in the eyes of our Muslim neighbors. It is vitally important for the Muslim audience of this letter to understand that, far from condoning violence inappropriately perpetrated under the banner of Christianity, the signatories of this letter believe that Jesus marks the path to genuine peace for *all* people regardless of generation, race, or religion. The positive response from both Muslim participants and the Muslim public to this paragraph from the moment the Yale Response was published, as well as at the Yale conference, and the frequency with which this particular paragraph was cited, indicates that the authors of the Yale Response correctly anticipated one of the principal obstacles Muslims face in trusting Christians. First, Muslims around the world were deeply moved by this paragraph and felt that it was "unprecedented" (though of course Pope John Paul II and the Reconciliation Walk are examples of other similar gestures that perhaps received less coverage in the Muslim press). Second, a number of Muslim bloggers called on their leaders to respond in kind by apologizing for wrongs done toward Christians and Jews.

Clearly Christians also face obstacles in trusting Muslims, and it is our hope that acknowledgment of Christian wrongdoing will prompt Muslims to acknowledge Muslim wrongdoing against Christians. This hope brings us to another significant issue that was considered as the paragraph was drafted, namely, the unilateral character of this Christian request for forgiveness. We could well imagine that some Christians would object, wanting to ask for forgiveness only as they hear Muslims ask for forgiveness of Christians for the wrongs Muslims have perpetrated against them. The argument would then be that it makes sense to ask for forgiveness only if both sides are willing to do so. But from the Christian standpoint, such a requirement would show a mistaken understanding of repentance and the request for forgiveness. For in the Christian account of how things are, repentance and forgiveness are not part of an economy of equal exchange, so that I repent as much as I see you repenting in return, or that I forgive as much as I see you forgiving in return. We don't barter with forgiveness and repentance. Instead, we grant forgiveness and we repent, because God in whom we believe requires us to forgive before the wrongdoer has repented and to repent for our wrongdoing irrespective of whether the others have repented for theirs. God forgave, and so we forgive — and that has nothing to do with what the other person does. God asks us to repent when we have sinned, and so we repent — and that has nothing to do with what the other person does.

we ask forgiveness of the All-Merciful One Mercy is undoubtedly one of God's principal attributes, with the following verses being only a few of many references found in the Bible: "The LORD, the LORD, a God **merciful** and gracious, slow to anger, and abounding in steadfast love and faithfulness" (Exodus 34:6 in the Torah/Old Testament); "For the LORD your God is a **merciful** God; he will not abandon or destroy you or forget the covenant with your forefathers" (Deuteronomy 4:31 in the Torah/Old Testament); "Remember your **mercy**, O LORD, and your steadfast love, for they have been from of old" (Psalm/Zabūr 25:6); "to give knowledge of salvation to his people in the forgiveness of their sins, because of the tender **mercy** of our God, whereby the sunrise shall visit us from on high to give light to those who sit in darkness and in the shadow of death, to guide our feet into the way of peace" (Luke 1:77-79 in the Injīl/New Testament); and "But God, being rich in **mercy**, because of the great love with which he loved us, even when we were dead in our trespasses, made us alive together with Christ — by grace you have been saved" (Ephesians 2:4-5 in the Injīl/New Testament). As we were aware that the Yale Response would be translated into Arabic (and other languages of the Muslim world), words were carefully chosen in view of terms to be used in the various translations, in order to ensure accurate communication of key concepts.

Peaceful relations between Muslims and Christians stand as one of the central challenges of this century, and perhaps of the whole present epoch Humanity faces other major challenges in the twenty-first century, including environmental issues, ethics of life, economic issues, world hunger, etc. But it is not an exaggeration to say that Muslim-Christian relations pose one of the central challenges as a chief component in so many of these other major issues. The religious dimension of many conflicts should be neither underplayed nor overplayed; it is always just one factor, not necessarily the decisive factor.

If we can achieve religious peace It is important to specify what is meant by "religious peace." There is a warning in Holy Scripture we should heed — a warning about false prophets of old who "healed the wound of my people lightly, saying, 'Peace, peace,' when there is no peace" (see Jeremiah 6:13-16 and Ezekiel 13:1-16 in the Prophets of the Old Testament). We have to be realistic and modest about what we can hope to achieve. For Christians, what we mean by peace and how we go about making peace is governed by the understanding of how Christ has reconciled human beings to God. This is the root of our motivation for the work of reconciliation: It is because God has reconciled humanity that we are called to "make every effort to live in peace with all people and to be holy" (Hebrews 12:14 in the Injīl/New Testament). God's reconciliation of human beings, who were God's enemies, provides a model for what it means for humans to reconcile. Thus to "achieve religious peace" means to transform a relationship of possible enmity into one of friendship. And to be a friend does not mean to deny differences but rather to understand each other accurately, to treat each other with respect, and to share with one another.

your letter considers the dual command of love to be the foundational principle not just of the Christian faith, but of Islam as well A fundamental question for both "A Common Word" and any Christian response to it, including the Yale Response, is whether Muslims and Christians mean the same thing by "love of God" and "love of neighbor," and indeed whether they mean the same thing by "God" and "neighbor." What is meant by these terms when used by a Christian may be partially or even radically different from what is meant when used by a Muslim. Moreover, popular understandings of these terms may differ from the accounts of theologians and scholars in each faith community. Finally, even among Muslims and among Christians, whether they are scholars of their faith or lay people, there are major differences as to how these terms are understood. Clarifying what we mean by these terms and determining the extent of overlap as well as disagreement is an essential part of the ongoing discussion between the Muslims and Christians who are part of this dialogue. This goal of clarification is really what the papers in this volume attempt to do, and, in addition to exploring the practical consequences of "A Common Word," it is also what engaged the participants of the 2008 Yale conference on the "A Common Word."

That *so much* **common ground exists . . . gives hope that undeniable differences** The Yale Response speaks here of undeniable differences because the Muslim and the Christian participants in the dialogue initiated by "A Common Word" recognize that each community holds some mutually exclusive truth claims regarding the nature of God, the way of salvation, etc. These differences may be not only undeniable but also irreducible. In "On 'A Common Word Between Us and You'" (the first chapter in this volume) H.R.H. Prince Ghazi bin Muhammad bin Talal has expressed the same thought starkly but accurately: "'A Common Word' does *not* signal that Muslims are prepared to deviate from, or concede one iota of, any of their convictions in order to reach out to Christians — and we expect the reverse is also true. Let us be crystal clear: 'A Common Word' is about equal peace, not about capitulation." The same can be said of the Yale Response. What lies behind this affirmation of the convictions of each community in the context of engagement in a dialogue is the belief that faith convictions are not subject to negotiation and compromise in the way, for instance, that a business deal or a political settlement may be subject to negotiation and compromise. The reason for this is simple: in addition to many other things that faith is about, faith is always also about truth. Islam and Christianity contain convictions that make truth claims about God and God's relation to the world. One cannot strike a deal about these convictions in an interfaith encounter — "I'll give up a bit of what I believe and you'll give up a bit of what you believe, and so we'll agree." Instead, in an interfaith encounter we can come to deeper understanding of our own and the other's convictions and discover that we already agree on more than we originally thought.

We applaud that *A Common Word Between Us and You* **stresses so insistently the unique devotion to one God** Much of the Yale Response presupposes that Muslims and Christians, along with Jews, all seek to worship the One True God. For some today, this is a controversial claim. But throughout the history of Christianity, Christians have for the most part believed that Muslims seek to worship the "same" God as Christians and Jews. Thomas Aquinas and Martin Luther held this view, to name just two examples of seminal theologians from two different streams of Christianity. Even if it is true that Muslims and Christians seek to worship the One True God, they often deeply disagree about the nature and attributes of that One God. An analogy may help — inadequate but still useful: Muslim and Christian disagreements about the nature and attributes of God may be compared to how members of two political parties describe a president of a country. They are speaking about the same person, but they may have very different descriptions and understandings of that person.[3]

God alone rightly commands our ultimate allegiance That God deserves and commands our ultimate allegiance above all other devotions is a common theme throughout the Bible: "It is the LORD your God you shall fear. Him you shall serve and by his name you shall swear" (Deuteronomy 6:13 in the Torah/Old Testament, also quoted by Jesus in Matthew 4:10 and Luke 4:8 in the Injīl/New Testament), "All the nations you have made shall come and worship before you, O Lord, and shall glorify your name. For you are great and do wondrous things; you alone are God. Teach me your way, O LORD, that I may walk in your truth; unite my heart to fear your name. I give thanks to you, O Lord my God, with my whole heart, and I will glorify your name forever. For great is your steadfast love toward me" (Psalm/Zabūr 86:9-13), and "seek first the kingdom of God and his righteousness" (Matthew 6:33 in the Injīl/New Testament).

When anyone or anything besides God commands our ultimate allegiance — a ruler, a nation, economic progress, or anything else — we end up serving idols and inevitably get mired in deep and deadly conflicts It has been a consistent temptation of all religious people, Christians included, to fuse, or confuse, devotion to God and devotion to their social group (clan, kingdom, or nation). When such confusion occurs, mundane agendas of a social group take on a religious hue, and, in extreme situa-

---

3. See "Answers to Frequently Asked Questions Regarding the Yale Response to 'A Common Word Between Us and You,'" in this volume, pp. 182-85.

tions, war ends up "sacralized." Devotion to the One God of all people — which is by definition what the One God is — serves to counter tendencies to claim God only for oneself.

We find it equally heartening that the God whom we should love above all things is described as being Love The Yale Response did not raise some central Christian convictions on which Christians and Muslims differ (such as the triunity of the One God, God's incarnation in Jesus Christ, or Jesus' death on the cross), not because the drafters considered these convictions unimportant, but because they were not the immediate subject matter of "A Common Word," nor did "A Common Word" deny them; love of God and love of neighbor were the subject matter, and "A Common Word" remained silent about the Trinity, incarnation, and cross. The Yale Response, therefore, concentrated on the account of the love of God and of neighbor. But decisively informing what the Yale Response said about the love of God and neighbor were convictions about the Trinity, the incarnation, and the cross.

For Christians, a proper understanding of God's love and therefore also of human love for God and for neighbor, which are derived from God's love, is intimately linked to the doctrines of the Trinity, the incarnation, and the cross. Regarding the Trinity, Christians in no way compromise the absolute uniqueness and singularity of God. Without going deeply into technical matters of the Christian doctrine of the Trinity, it is important to note that for the great mainstream of Christians throughout the centuries there is only one numerically identical divine "essence" shared by the three divine modes of subsistence. That is why it would be as idolatrous for Christians as it is for Muslims to affirm that "God has an associate." At the same time, many great Christian thinkers believe that it is the doctrine of the Trinity which makes it possible to understand God as love. God does not merely love creation, something outside God's own being. God is love in God's own very being, and it is for this reason that God loves creation. Further, for God to *be* love apart from God's relation to creation implies that love is given and received within the Divine Being, which is what Christians believe happens between the persons of the Trinity. The claim that the One God is the God of love and the claim that the absolutely unique God is triune belong together.

It is this same love in God's own being that Christians believe they see as manifest in the incarnation, in God's self-opening and self-giving love

68

toward us in receiving our nature into God's own self. God loves us enough to give God's own self to us and for us, by coming among us as one of us (see John 1:14; 17:23-26; Philippians 2:1-11; and Hebrews 2:14-18; 4:12-16 in the Injīl/New Testament).

Because God *is* love in God's own being, and because God gives of God's own being to and for humankind, God's love for humanity is as unconditional and indiscriminate as the sun's rays, which warm both the evil and the good (Matthew 5:45 in the Injīl/New Testament). It is this unconditional love, rooted in the very being of God, that is demonstrated in the self-giving death and resurrection of Jesus Christ. On the cross, Jesus Christ voluntarily and intentionally stretched out his arms to embrace humans, who by their actions and attitudes demonstrate themselves to be enemies of God. "God shows his love for us in that while we were still sinners, Christ died for us. Since, therefore, we have now been justified by his blood, much more shall we be saved by him from the wrath of God. For if while we were enemies we were reconciled to God by the death of his Son, much more, now that we are reconciled, shall we be saved by his life. More than that, we also rejoice in God through our Lord Jesus Christ, through whom we have now received reconciliation" (Romans 5:8-11 in the Injīl/New Testament); therefore, on the cross we see the eternal divine love turned toward finite and sinful humanity for the sake of humanity's redemption.

In the Muslim tradition God, "the Lord of the worlds," is "The Infinitely Good and All-Merciful" Many Christians believe that Muslims do not see love as one of the main attributes of God. Inherent in any endeavor at effective communication across cultural and linguistic boundaries (as is certainly the case in Muslim-Christian relations) is the challenge of defining words and uncovering the subtle differences in their meaning. Certainly the word "love" carries vastly different connotations to different audiences, depending on language, context, generation, etc. Christians who speak English and have studied the Scriptures can automatically identify with this dilemma, and they frequently utilize the original Greek and Hebrew words when exegeting particular texts, in order to understand truthfully the meaning of the sacred Scriptures.

An important aspect of this dialogue is for Muslim scholars to explicate relevant terms and ideas found in the Qur'ān and for Christian scholars to explicate relevant terms and ideas found in the Bible regarding the nature of God's love. For Muslims, Arabic terms such as *al-Wadūd* and

Rahma are central to this discussion. Some Muslim scholars argue that *al-Wadūd* can indeed be understood as similar in meaning to the Greek word *agapē*. Further discussion about what the texts truly convey in using these terms is central to this dialogue. Regarding the Arabic word *Rahma*, which is often translated in English as "mercy," there are parallels to the Hebrew term *Ḥesed*. Interestingly, in Yemen (South Arabia), pre-Islamic Christian inscriptions in an older dialect of Arabic have been found that use the trinitarian formula "in the name of *Rahmān-ān,* and his Messiah, and the Holy Spirit."[4]

When discussing God's mercy as an aspect of God's love, it is important to keep in mind connotations of the word in various religious cultures. Most Christians today, if asked to describe the mercy of God, would likely refer to ideas such as forgiveness and the withholding of deserved punishment. Most Muslims, if asked to describe the *Rahma* of God, would likely refer to ideas related to God's provision of food and drink and other material needs, ideas demonstrating that God *cares* for humans. But in the Christian Scriptures and tradition, God's care for humans is a very prominent, indeed, essential feature of God's mercy. And in Islam, God is certainly thought of as forgiving. As Muslims and Christians dialogue about these important concepts, we hope that gaining a more accurate understanding of one another's perspectives will stimulate us to retrieve the forgotten, submerged, and/or "backgrounded" aspects of our respective traditions.

Since God's goodness is infinite and not bound by anything A crucial aspect of the claim that God's love is not bound by anything is the claim that God's love is unconditional. This claim follows for Christians directly from the conviction that God *is* love. The consequence is that God's love is not reactive, dependent on the character of the object of love. Martin Luther has expressed this view in a most radical way in his *Heidelberg Disputation.* The last thesis of the disputation, which in many ways sums up the whole of it and the whole of his theology, reads as follows: "The love of God does not find, but creates, that which is pleasing to it. The love of man comes into being through that which is pleasing to it."[5] The contrast is between sovereignly creative divine love, which is independent of what it "finds"

---

4. Cf. Joan Copeland Biella, *Dictionary of Old South Arabic* (Chico, Calif.: Scholars, 1982), 280.

5. Martin Luther, *Luther's Works* (Philadelphia: Fortress Press, 1957), vol. 31, p. 57.

and instead makes everything to which it directs itself to be loveable, and reactive human love, which is dependent on what it "finds" — on the pleasing character of the object of love — and therefore expects the objects to become loveable before it can love them.

love is the pinnacle of our duties toward our neighbors For Christians, the nature of God's love informs the proper character of love of neighbor, including how Christians are to love their Muslim neighbors. First, since God's love is unconditional and indiscriminate, human beings ought to love all their neighbors, the ones who belong to their "group" (whether familial, cultural, or religious) as well as those who do not, and those who are friendly to them as well as those who are not. Second, as demonstrated on the cross, God's love is sacrificial. The cross of Jesus Christ represents the path of self-denial, of giving up one's life so that others might live. If this symbol of sacrifice, atonement, and redemption is to be cleansed from the corrupt image placed on it through the Crusades and current media depictions of hatred, greed, and immorality, then Christians must live out its message of love, service, and sacrifice in their daily lives with their Muslim neighbors. For "this is how we know what love is: Jesus Christ laid down his life for us. And we ought to lay down our lives for our brothers and sisters" (1 John 3:16 in the Injīl/New Testament).

Our love, Jesus Christ says, must imitate the love of the infinitely good Creator In this same passage where Jesus tells his followers to love their enemies, he goes on to say, "For if you love those who love you, what reward do you have? Do not even the tax collectors do the same? And if you greet only your brothers and sisters, what more are you doing than others? Do not even the Gentiles do the same? You therefore must be perfect, as your heavenly Father is perfect" (Matthew 5:46-48 in the Injīl/New Testament). Similarly, in 1 Peter 1:13-16 in the Injīl/New Testament, Christians read the following series of commands: "Therefore, preparing your minds for action, and being sober-minded, set your hope fully on the grace that will be brought to you at the revelation of Jesus Christ. As obedient children, do not be conformed to the passions of your former ignorance, but as he who called you is holy, you also be holy in all your conduct, since it is written, 'You shall be holy, for I am holy.'" Similarly, as recorded in Luke 6:36 in the Injīl/New Testament, Jesus admonishes his followers to "Be merciful, just as your Father is merciful."

71

our love must be as unconditional as is God's — extending to brothers, sisters, neighbors, and even enemies Following the teaching of the whole New Testament rooted in the example of Jesus, Christians have affirmed through the centuries that showing love for enemies is the pinnacle of Christian moral behavior. Thomas Aquinas (1225-74 CE), for instance, writes: "That man should actually do so, and love his enemy for God's sake, without it being necessary for him to do so, belongs to the perfection of charity. For since man loves his neighbor, out of charity, for God's sake, the more he loves God, the more does he put enmities aside and show love towards his neighbor."[6] Protestant reformer Martin Luther (1483-1546 CE) insisted that "the continual forgiveness of the neighbor" — a basic form of love for one's enemy — is "the primary and foremost duty of Christians, second only to faith and the reception of forgiveness."[7] Even more, he argued, following Romans 12:21 in the Injīl/New Testament, that love does more than simply not count the offenders guilty and not press charges against them; he insisted that one should "load" the enemy "with kindness so that, overcome with good, he will be kindled with love for you."[8] In the same vein he wrote that those who follow Christ "grieve more over the sin of their offenders than over the loss or offense to themselves. And they do this that they may recall those offenders from their sin rather than avenge the wrongs they themselves have suffered. Therefore they put off the form of their own righteousness and put on the form of those others, praying for their persecutors, blessing those who curse, doing good to the evildoers, preparing to pay the penalty and make satisfaction for their very enemies that they may be saved. This is the Gospel and the example of Christ."[9] Metropolitan John Zizioulas argues that the Eastern Orthodox tradition sees love of enemies as a direct consequence of the Christian understanding of freedom and grace: "No other form of love is freer than this, and no other form of freedom is more suitable to be identified with love for enemies. . . . Love which does not expect reciprocity is truly 'grace,' namely freedom."[10]

---

6. Thomas Aquinas, *Summa Theologica*, trans. Fathers of the English Dominican Province (New York: Benziger Brothers, 1947), 1292.

7. *Luther's Works*, vol. 21, p. 149.

8. *Luther's Works*, vol. 45, p. 283.

9. *Luther's Works*, vol. 31, p. 306.

10. John Zizioulas, "Sickness and Therapy in Orthodox Theology," in *Theology and Psychiatry in Dialogue*, trans. Vasilios Thermos (Athens: Apostoliki Diakonia, 1999), 133-56.

In the Christian tradition, to practice love of enemy does not imply lack of concern for justice. There is a rich tradition of reflecting on the relationship between the two. Elsewhere in this commentary, in the discussion of wrongs done by Muslims and Christians to one another, we have touched on the relationship between love and justice.[11]

The Prophet Muhammad did similarly The Yale Response shows respect for Muslims by using the word "Prophet" when referring to Muhammad. This use does not mandate agreement concerning the nature and implications of this title, a subject on which Christians and Muslims have differing views. By using the title "Prophet," the Yale Response is simply seeking to honor Muslims and the way they relate to the founder of their religion as well as to employ the polite manner with which "A Common Word" itself was written. "A Common Word" repeatedly refers to Jesus by using his title "Christ" without thereby implying that Muslims affirm everything Christians mean by the title "Christ" — including the affirmation of his death as atoning sacrifice ("For there is one God and one mediator between God and human beings, Christ Jesus, himself human, who gave himself as a ransom for all people," 1 Timothy 2:5-6 in the Injīl/New Testament).

The Prophet Muhammad . . . is known to have said, "The most virtuous behavior is to engage those who sever relations, to give to those who withhold from you, and to forgive those who wrong you" The biography of the Prophet Muhammad relates this episode, which took place six centuries after Jesus taught his followers to love their enemies, and we affirm this time as one in which an application of Jesus' teaching is apparent in the Prophet Muhammad's life. Since Muslims everywhere hold the Prophet Muhammad to be the one they most desire to emulate in conduct, it is fitting to highlight this particular incident.

after the Prophet Muhammad was driven out of Ta'if, it was the Christian slave 'Addās who went out to Muhammad, brought him food, kissed him, and embraced him Christians might find it interesting that 'Addās was a refugee from the city of Nineveh (northern Iraq), a city associated with the prophet Jonah, whom God notably called to love his enemies.

---

11. For more on this relationship, see Miroslav Volf, *Exclusion and Embrace*, 193-231.

Abandoning all "hatred and strife," we must engage in interfaith dialogue The term "interfaith dialogue" is widely used and has many different meanings, depending on the goals of those engaged in the dialogue and the participants' understanding of their own respective faiths. Different approaches to interfaith dialogue serve different functions in peacemaking, and many of these approaches can be complementary. Some believers worry that the term implies a renunciation or downplaying of fundamental faith convictions in order to reach a lowest common denominator of lifeless platitudes. But it need not necessarily be understood in that way. Instead, the Yale Response proposes to go beyond "a polite ecumenical dialogue" and is written with the assumption that faith matters profoundly for the way Christians and Muslims understand the world and seek to live in the world, indeed that faith claims the ultimate loyalties of those who embrace it. The goal of interfaith dialogue under these conditions is to understand our respective faiths better, to communicate with each other more effectively, to identify ways in which our convictions overlap, and to seek ways in which, all the differences notwithstanding, we can live together in peace.

our common love for God and for one another As is evident from the whole Yale Response, whose main thrust is to underscore how Christians understand both divine and human love and invite Muslims to reflect on whether and to what extent they understand love in similar ways, the use of the phrase "common love" does not imply that by "love" Muslims and Christians mean the same thing. Indeed, the closing paragraphs of the Yale Response are an invitation to dialogue about those very questions. Rather, the sentence in which the phrase occurs simply acknowledges our common commitment to loving God and neighbor, however we understand the meaning of that love, and it encourages Muslims and Christians alike to seek to put that love into practice.[12]

"our eternal souls" are at stake as well The claim, formulated as an echo of a statement in "A Common Word" that "our eternal souls" are at stake in pursuing the path of peace, underscores that (1) the pursuit of peace is

---

12. See also the comments on the phrase "your letter considers the dual command of love to be the foundational principle not just of the Christian faith, but of Islam as well" (pp. 65-66 above).

an essential duty of every Christian and (2) how humans live is not irrelevant to the state of their eternal souls. It is a basic Christian conviction that salvation is not gained through works, but is the gift of God made possible by the death and resurrection of Jesus Christ: "For by grace you have been saved through faith. And this is not your own doing; it is the gift of God, not a result of works, so that no one may boast." The same verse continues by underscoring that even if salvation is "not a result of works" it still must issue in good works. "For we are his workmanship, created in Christ Jesus for good works, which God prepared beforehand, that we should walk in them" (Ephesians 2:8-10 in the Injīl/New Testament). As verse 10 illustrates, for Christians the human capacity to love neighbors is made possible by the God who creates people anew in Jesus Christ. The Bible also tells us that those who think they know Jesus Christ but refuse to follow Jesus' model of love are self-deceived and do not know him (1 John 2:4-6, 9-11; 3:10, 15 in the Injīl/New Testament). In the language of Galatians 2:20 in the Injīl/New Testament, Christ lives in and through those united with him by faith, and they are therefore obliged to imitate Christ, to live as he lived — to love God, love neighbors, love enemies, and therefore vigorously pursue peace. Prejudice, hostility, active animosity, or outright violence on the part of a Christian toward anyone, including any individual Muslim or any Muslim community, is not an option for a follower of Jesus Christ and may in fact be an indicator that, notwithstanding loud protestations to the contrary, one is in fact not an authentic follower of Jesus Christ.

PART II

Muslim Perspectives

Loving God and Loving Neighbor

HABIB ALI AL-JIFRI

May God's peace, mercy, and blessings be upon you. All praise belongs to God. May the blessings of God be upon our Master Muhammad ﷺ and upon his forefathers and brothers the prophets of God, including our Masters Adam, Noah, Hūd, Abraham, Moses, Jesus and all the prophets sent between them. May blessings also be showered upon his family, companions, successors, and those who followed after them in doing good deeds until the last day.

Imām Ahmad [ibn Hanbal] narrates in his *Musnad* [collection of Hadīth] and al-Bukhārī in his *al-Adab al-Mufrad*, a sound Hadīth in which the Prophet Muhammad ﷺ said, "Whoever does not thank people has not thanked God." For that reason we thank the honorable professor, my dear friend Miroslav Volf, and his team for their positive response to "A Common Word." And [we thank them for] the fruit of their efforts [evident] in this historic conference, which we hope and pray to God will mark the beginning of a transformation in the world in which we live.

Last night was the night of Isrā' and Mi'rāj[1] (the twenty-seventh night of the month of Rajab). On the same night fourteen centuries ago, the

1. This marks the Prophet Muhammad's ﷺ miraculous night Journey from Mecca to Jerusalem and his heavenly ascent from Jerusalem to the Divine Presence.

Transcribed from the keynote address given by Habīb 'Alī al-Jifrī during the Yale Common Word Conference, July 2008; translated by Jeff Hayes and Joseph Cumming, and edited by Wael Zubi, March 2009.

Prophet Muḥammad ﷺ was transported to the *al-Aqṣā*[2] Mosque (which I pray that God will hasten to liberate). There he met with all of the Prophets and Messengers. And among them he encountered our Master Jesus Christ عليه السلام twice in the course of the same night, the first encounter taking place at the *al-Aqṣā* Mosque and the second encounter taking place in the second heaven. One of the factors that made me sense the spirituality of our gathering at Yale (where followers of our Master Muḥammad ﷺ are meeting those seeking to follow our Master Jesus Christ عليه السلام) is that it reminds us of the encounter on that night fourteen centuries ago between our Master Prophet Muḥammad and our Master Christ عليه السلام. God, may He be praised and exalted, says

> And when your Lord said to the angels, "I am appointing on earth a vicegerent,"[3] they said, "What, will You appoint therein one who will do corruption therein and shed blood, while we glorify You with praise and sanctify You?" He said, "Assuredly, I know what you know not."[4]

Humanity is God's vicegerent *(khalīfa)* on earth. And God *(al-Ḥaqq),*[5] may He be glorified and exalted, did not deny the possibility that humanity would sow corruption. But He also affirmed His Wisdom in choosing to place humanity in this world. With this thought in mind, I want to begin by reminding us of the ultimate goal of meetings such as this one. This conference of ours and its purposes can be summarized in the following three points:

(1) We recognize that the world in which we live appears to be a world that has sunk into corruption[6] and bloodshed just as the Angels feared; the taking of lives has become a widespread phenomenon and something which people do without much thought, as has the exploitation of the weak and the poor, and the total disregard of their rights. Humankind is greedy for wealth. We pursue wealth, rank, status, dom-

---

2. المسجد الأقصى literally means "the farthest place of prostration/prayer" and refers to the Noble Sanctuary/Temple Mount in Jerusalem.

3. Literally *khalīfa*, which means vicegerent or designated representative.

4. Qur'an, Sūrat al-Baqara (2): 30, Royal Aal al-Bayt Institute translation.

5. The Arabic word *al-Ḥaqq* is one of the names of God in the Qur'an, and it is variously translated as "The Truth," "The Real One," or "Ultimate Reality."

6. *Fasād*, the full breadth of anything rotten, harmful, or evil.

ination, power, and hegemony. Tons of wheat are thrown into the sea in order to influence the market price of wheat, while thousands die of hunger. The environment is in crisis; the earth upon which we were placed as vicegerents and stewards cries out to God against our destruction and failure as stewards. Humanity's innate nature *fiṭra*[7] (which is divinely bestowed) laments man's destructiveness. Because moral principles have been replaced with a system of absolute relativism, there are no longer any guideposts or fixed points[8] for our moral compass, for our *fiṭra*. This absence of guideposts has led to the problems we see in the world around us.

(2) The second point is that religion, which came from God (may He be praised and exalted) to guide humanity and resolve its problems, has become part of the problem; therefore let us use these conferences to reestablish the role of religion so it becomes a means for the solution and not part of the problem.

(3) The third point, which is in reality a continuation of the second point, is that we need to form an alliance with one another, while respecting our differences. Let us call this the alliance of virtuous people against vice.

These three points are what one of the greatest scholars who signed "A Common Word," Sheikh ʿAbdallāh bin Bayyah,[9] exhorted me to bring up in the beginning of my remarks.

So now let us reflect a bit on love of God and love of neighbor. The human soul usually loves because of some kind of need or lack. It is difficult for human beings to love for reasons other than a need or cause. Unless a human being is elevated in perspective, the causes of love in the human soul are usually beauty, because God gave human beings an innate nature *(fiṭra)* that loves beauty — beauty of sound, beauty of form, beauty of meaning. A number of great spiritual masters said that the secret of humankind's attraction to beauty — indeed its essence — is God. When God gathered together all created beings in the world of the spirits, before He gave them bodies, he made a covenant with them, the covenant of

---

7. *Fiṭra* refers to innate human nature, which is understood (in Islam) as the inherently good and uncorrupted nature that instinctively recognizes the unity of God, etc.

8. *Thawābit.*

9. A leading Muslim scholar, born in Mauritania, who currently teaches at King Abdulaziz University in Saudi Arabia.

tawḥīd,[10] saying "'Am I not your Lord?' They said, 'Indeed you are, and we bear witness.'"[11] Each one of us heard God when God addressed us in the world of the spirit. And every spirit was enraptured with the love of God when it heard the beauty of God's address. He is the Creator of beauty, may He be praised and exalted, which is why humankind is moved by every kind of beauty. So the root of humankind's inclination toward beauty is love.

The second reason that moves human beings to love is the benevolence *(iḥsān)* one being receives from another. Souls are fashioned by the One who acted with benevolence toward them. And the nature of the human soul is that it loves the one who is good to it.

The third reason is perfection. The shortcoming and defects of the human soul cause it to be drawn to beauty and perfection when it encounters them. These three reasons are therefore the steps we climb to arrive at the unconditional love of God, may He be praised and exalted. We love God because God is beautiful and He loves beauty. Beauty is a creation of God because beauty is an outward manifestation of the self-revelation *(tajalliyyāt)* of God. So we love God because He is uniquely characterized by absolute perfection in this existence. We love God also because God is the One who is good to us and is the original source of goodness.

So God is beautiful, and real beauty (beauty that reminds us of God) is the highest way to the knowledge of Him. To the degree that a human soul is receptive to goodness and elevated in its ability to taste beauty, it is prepared to love and know God. And to the degree that a human soul is weak in its ability to perceive true beauty, to that degree the soul's knowledge and love of God (may He be praised) is also weak. Perfection bears the fruit of our *tanzīh*[12] of God, mighty and majestic is He. Our *tanzīh* of Him is our acknowledgement that He is above every comparison, anthropomorphism, description, and partner, that He cannot be divided up, that he does not become incarnate *(ḥulūl),*[13] and that He is transcendent, not dwelling in time or place in any way.

---

10. *Tawḥīd* is the affirmation of divine unity.

11. Qur'an: Sūrat al-Aʿrāf (7): 172.

12. Acknowledgement of God's incomparability, transcendence, and purity — that God is far above all created things.

13. *Ḥulūl* literally means "indwelling" or "descent," but in Arabic Christian theology (and in Islamic discussions of that theology) it is a technical term for "incarnation." In Islamic theology it is also used in debates over whether or not God had *ḥulūl* in the burning bush (in the story of Moses).

We have appreciated the fact that some of our Christian brothers and sisters have shed light on the Christian philosophy of the Trinity during this time at Yale. Now perhaps they would also like to hear our belief on this matter, since we differ with them on this issue. We do not believe that God, mighty and majestic is He, can be divided, nor do we believe in divine incarnation *(ḥulūl)* or hypostatic union *(ittiḥād)*.

And we do not believe that the way to the knowledge of God can be reduced to rationalizations, but rather we are supposed to be elevated to the love of God. God's goodness is exemplified by the fact that God created us *ex nihilo*. We believe that God's love for us is evident in the fact that he created us with a beautiful and pure natural disposition *(fiṭra)*. We do not believe in original sin, rather we believe He created us in a way that was honored. As the Qur'an says, "We created man with the best *taqwīm*."[14]

One of God's greatest graces toward us is the grace of *imhāl*:[15] whenever we make mistakes, He covers our mistakes; despite our deserving punishment, He still gives us time to put things right. Even though faults stem from us, He does not expose them. Were He to expose us for everything we did, it would be difficult for us even to sit before each other. The degrees of ascension toward goodness/excellence/refinement have no end. The degrees of spiritual ascension in the love of God bear fruit, whether we love beauty or perfection or benevolence. For whatever reason we love, God is the One who ultimately deserves our love. Rābiʿa al-mʿAdawiyya,[16] that knower of her Lord and lover of her Lord, said, "I love Thee with two loves, love of my *hawā*,[17] and perfect love, to love Thee as is Thy due." As for the love of *hawā*, it is related to preoccupation with remembering You (God), and forgetting everything else but loving You and remembering You, loving nothing more than You. The love that You are deserving of is the love of a lover who has had the veil lifted by his beloved. This comes from the fruit of love when the Beloved shows Himself to the lover so that he will witness His light.

The love of God will elevate one to one's true station, the station of the human spirit, which is the element that truly makes us human. Humankind will see that the soul's passions, its greed, anger, love of status, and

14. Qur'an: Sūrat al-Tīn (95): 4. *Taqwīm* is form, arrangement, or stature.

15. Not punishing us promptly.

16. Rābiʿa al-ʿAdawiyya al-Qaysiyya was a prominent woman Ṣūfī saint who lived in the eighth century CE/second century AH.

17. *Hawā* is passion, fancy, capricious desire, or personal inclination.

pride, and every other inclination toward transient things is a veil that a human being has to get rid of so he can return to his true home, the abode of the spirit. The spirit is trapped in the physical body. It is a test from God, and we need to rise above and be elevated in our rank of getting close to God.

One of the great scholars, Sheikh Muḥammad Saʿīd al-Būṭī, said in his message to all the attendees of this conference (please pay close attention to this), there is a difference between an action and an attribute. God describes the people of Divine love in the Qurʾan with, "He loves them and they love Him"[18] — the love of God for his creation is an action, and love is an attribute of God Himself. God loves, but we cannot say according to Muslim belief that God is love, because love is an attribute. The problem can be solved thus: The attributes of God are eternal, and they do not change with the changing states of people. What stems from our love of God is love of neighbor. A human could love another being with the love of natural inclination totally devoid of loving for the sake of God, but this form of love will be susceptible to change. I might love a neighbor because of his proximity to me or because of his generosity or some other likeable attributes I find in him, but these things can change and therefore that love might change. But the true understanding of love of neighbor, for which we came to this "Common Word" conference, is a type of love of neighbor that emerges from a great tree, the tree of the love of God. Love of God will lead us to love the creation of God. If you love the Creator, you will love what He created. The love of the Creator will lead to love of the creation. I love my neighbor because God chose my neighbor for me.

Let me speak now of the deep meaning of a human being and his relations with those around him. There are two types of relationships. There are those relations that a human being has freedom to choose, and there are relationships that are not of his choosing. If you have an acquaintance or friend, you are the one who chooses him as a friend, and you can make another choice and move on. You do not have to take a particular individual as a friend, and if you have differences with one another you can part. You are not obligated to keep up the friendship. Thus it is very natural to find that someone who has a friend of bad character leaves off that friendship and chooses another friend. He has a choice.

However, our true faith is shown when we do not have a choice. We do

---

18. Qurʾan: Sūrat al-Māʾida (5): 54.

not generally choose our neighbors. We are forced into situations. One can move from one house to another, but it is harder to move from one city to another; and even if one manages to move from one city to another, he cannot leave the earth to live on a different planet. One is forced to have relationships with one's neighbors. Who chooses your neighbors for you? It is God who does the choosing, and anything your Beloved (God) chooses for you should also be beloved to you. Anything that God chooses, you should love; we should love what God has chosen for us, and we should be good to all those whom God has chosen to be our neighbors. I should not act well toward my neighbor to get something in return: I should be good because I love God's choice for me. It is on this basis that love of neighbor will become something profound.

The great Imām Abū Ḥanīfa[19] had a bad neighbor who used to trouble him. Whenever the great Imām was about to teach his students, the neighbor would start doing something to disturb the lesson. Among the things he did was to sing loudly while playing a musical instrument. On one occasion this became very annoying; the Imām's students left because the neighbor was disturbing them by reciting poetry in an annoying way.

The students asked Abū Ḥanīfa why he had not reported him to the authorities. Abū Ḥanīfa said: "This is my neighbor, and the Prophet ﷺ is reported to have said: 'Gabriel continually told me to take care of my neighbor to the extent that I thought he was going to make him my heir.'[20] Even if he harms me, I will never harm my neighbor."

One night Abū Ḥanīfa and his students did not hear the neighbor, and the students asked him: "Why do we not hear your neighbor today?" Some people you miss because of their benevolence, and some people's absence is noticed because of the bad they do. This prompted the Imām to say also, "Where is my neighbor?" and his students started laughing. Imām Abū Ḥanīfa asked, "Why are you laughing?" They said, "God has relieved you of him." The Imām asked, "Has he been harmed in some way?" They said, "He has been in some sort of trouble, and the police have imprisoned him." He said, "I must intercede." He went at night to the

---

19. Abū Ḥanīfa Nuʿmān ibn Thābit (d. 150 AH/767 CE), acclaimed *al-Imām al-Aʿẓam* (the Great Imām) is credited as the founder of one of the four major Sunnī schools of Islamic jurisprudence — the Ḥanafī school, which bears his name. He lived in Kūfa and is said to have met a number of the companions of the Prophet Muḥammad ﷺ.

20. Narrated by our Master ʿAbdallāh ibn ʿUmar ﷺ and our Lady ʿĀʾisha ﷺ and cited in the Ḥadīth collections of Bukhārī and Muslim.

door of the Caliph, which no one ever did unless he was called. He told the doorkeeper to call the Caliph: "I want to see the Caliph." The doorkeeper said that the Caliph was sleeping and had retired to his private quarters with his family. He said, "Then go get him." The doorkeeper was amazed that Abū Ḥanīfa had come, because he never came even on a normal day let alone in the middle of the night. His love of God and the love of his neighbor compelled him, and the lack of it would have been a weakness, which would have spoiled his love. The Caliph woke up and came out to Abū Ḥanīfa, who said, "My neighbor has been imprisoned. If my neighbor has defrauded someone of his right, I will take care of it. If he oppressed other people, I will take care of it." [The Caliph] said, "Tomorrow." Abū Ḥanīfa replied, "No, tonight, O Commander of the Faithful." So the Caliph gave orders that Abū Ḥanīfa's neighbor be released. Abū Ḥanīfa left immediately and did not wait for his neighbor to thank him, for anyone who loves God will be benevolent to and love his neighbor without seeking gratitude in return. This neighbor became one of the Imām's students and became a scholar of great repute.

I could tell story after story, but I do not want to take too long. I want to call for a beautiful neighborliness and for dealing with everyone around us on the basis of loving God. Our love of God should lead us to love our neighbor.

People out there are asking about these conferences, saying, "We have heard many beautiful things said. Dialogue has been going on for thirty years. What is the result? These religious dialogues have been taking place for a long time." The reason people are making such remarks is that the results of these conferences are not reaching the public. I think that the first benefit that took place with this conference was the positive response among all the participants. All of us have a responsibility to spread the message, and many of us attending this conference have schools or followers, churches or mosques.

What is the role for each of us toward those around us in enlightening them as to why we came together? I want to give thanks and laud to my dear friend Miroslav, who when he first came to Abu Dhabi announced that there were five hundred American signatories of the Yale Response. He also informed me that he was teaching the "Common Word" initiative in his lectures. This is a beautiful example for us all to follow. Every teacher present should teach this "Common Word" to his students, let them hear its beauty, let it reach out there, because until now it has mostly remained in our circle. Let us take it outside our circle, because beauty stems ultimately from the Creator.

So let us spread this beauty, let us use the media. The greater danger is not in a dog's biting a man, but a man's biting a dog. The media can seduce those in it into only broadcasting things that will excite people, but getting people excited should not be the goal of the media; it is only a means. The world needs to be guided. The media has a responsibility to make a positive contribution in spreading this awareness and understanding. All of us are able (by the will of God) to make this "Common Word" a living reality. I ask God Almighty to choose us and you people who take part to spread His light in existence in the days that are before us. I am absolutely certain that these are the days when God is going to manifest His light in this existence, and His light is going to shine on every house on earth. The question is not whether or not this will happen, for it surely will. The true question is, Will God choose you, will God choose me? May God choose us all to be agents of truth.

O You (God) who gave divine success to the people of good, bless us and make us people of good. As You gaze upon us, let your light shine in our hearts so we can continually ascend in Your love.

God, "The Loving"

Reza Shah-Kazemi

This article addresses the question, "To what extent can God be described as 'The Loving' in the Islamic tradition?" Quite apart from its intrinsic importance in terms of the Islamic conception of God, it is a question that has acquired extrinsic, quasi-political dimensions in the light of the recent discussions surrounding the historic "A Common Word" initiative launched in Amman in 2007,[1] inviting Christians to engage in dialogue on the basis of love of God and love of neighbor. This principle of love was deemed to constitute the indisputable common ground of Islam, Christianity, and, indeed, all revealed religions. However, among the Christian voices critical of this initiative, one encountered the following objection: Muslims do not place love at the center of their faith as we Christians do; they do not see God primarily as love, as we do; the God in whom Muslims believe is a God of anger, not love. According to this caricature, all too prevalent in the West, the very notion of a loving God in Islam is a contradiction in terms: *Allāh* is conceived by Muslims as utterly remote and aloof from his creation, so it is argued, his inaccessibility being the very ransom of his absoluteness. Thus *Allāh* is but a transcendent lawgiver at best, an arbitrary dictator at worst. This caricature is then contrasted with the God in whom Christians believe, a God whose love is so clearly enunciated in the

---

1. See www.acommonword.com for the document itself, and the responses thereto by a large number of Christian scholars, leaders, churches, and organizations.

This is an abridged version of a paper presented at the conference "Loving God and Neighbor in Word and Deed," Yale Center for Faith & Culture, July 25, 2008.

famous words of St. John's Gospel: "For God so loved the world, that He gave His only-begotten Son, that whosoever believeth in him should not perish, but have everlasting life" (John 3:16). Whereas God's love is seen as absolute and unconditional in Christianity, it is seen by Muslims — if it is deemed to be seen by them at all — as strictly conditional: *Allāh* only loves those who submit to him.

In addressing the theme of God as "The Loving" in Islam, then, this critique outlined above will also be addressed, albeit indirectly. The first part of the paper will look at the question of divine love from the point of view of theology and on the basis of a *prima facie* reading of the Qur'ān. The second moves from theology to spirituality, addressing the theme of divine love through the discourse of Sufism. In the third section the mystical speculations of the Sufis will be seen to be grounded in a spiritual assimilation of the message of the Qur'ān; here it will be made clear that the deepest nature of God is articulated by the principle of *rahma* — loving compassion, or compassionate love; the "heart" of God pulsates with *rahma*, attracts through *rahma*, delivers through *rahma*.

The Theological "Problem" of Love

God is described in the Qur'ān as "The Loving," *al-Wadūd,* and as such He is qualified by the quality of love *(hubb)* in the Qur'ān. First, as regards the attribute *al-Wadūd,* we have the following two verses:

And He is the Forgiving, the Loving. (85:14)

Ask forgiveness of your Lord, then turn to Him repentant. Truly my Lord is Merciful, Loving. (11:90)

It is important to note that in both places the quality of divine love is linked with that of mercy and forgiveness. As will be seen in the following parts of this paper, this interpenetration of love and mercy is of utmost significance in the Islamic conception of God's love for His creation.

Although the name "The Lover," *al-Muhibb,* is not normally given as one of the ninety-nine names of God, the Qur'ān refers to God as "loving" *(yuhibbu)* in many places and in several respects. Thus Fakhr al-Dīn al-Rāzi, one of the most important of the classical commentators, states in his comment on *al-Wadūd* in 85:14 that the meaning of this name is *al-Muhibb,* and observes that a majority of the commentators hold this view.[2] He adds that ascribing this quality of love *(hubb)* to God as *al-Wadūd* is based on intellectual evidence: God loves that which is good, and good is that which is required essentially; evil, on the other hand, is but accidentally required. Every good thing is thus beloved by God on account of its essentiality.[3]

Al-Tabarī, in his seminal commentary, likewise refers to the principle of *mahabba,* "love," joining it with that of *maghfira* ("forgiveness"), as an explanation of the meaning of God as *al-Wadūd.* He also refers to an interpretation according to which the two names in 85:15, *al-Ghafūr, al-Wadūd,* together mean *al-Ḥabīb,* "The Beloved."[4]

In respect of God's love as *hubb,* we find that God is described as loving *(yuhibbu)* eight types of people: the virtuous (2:195 et passim); those who are repentant (2:222); those who purify themselves (2:222); the pious (3:76 et passim); those who have patience (3:146); those who trust in Him (3:159); the just (5:42 et passim); and those who fight for His sake (6:14).[5] By contrast He is described in many verses as "not loving" disbelievers, the rebellious, the vicious, the proud, and so on.

This initial view of God as "The Loving" reveals but a superficial apprehension of divine love, for the love in question appears not very different from human love: God, just like us, loves those who are good and does not love those who are bad. He promises to love those who follow the Prophet: "Say [O Prophet]: If you love God, follow me. God will love you" (3:31).

It is on such a casual perusal of the qur'ānic view of divine love that the outside observer might infer that for Muslims, God's love is condi-

2. Fakhr al-Dīn al-Rāzī, *al-Tafsīr al-kabīr,* vol. 11 (Beirut: Dār Iḥyā' al-Turāth al-'Arabī, 2001), 114.

3. He also states that *al-Wadūd* can be understood in the passive sense, as the verbal noun *faʿʿūl* can be understood in the sense of a *mafʿūl* (passive) form; he gives as examples the word *rakūb,* meaning "mount" (that which is mounted), from the root *rakiba,* "to ride"; and *halūb,* a "cow" (that which is milked), from the root *halaba,* "to milk." The meaning of *al-Wadūd* can thus also be "The Beloved": God is beloved by His righteous slaves, according to al-Rāzī, "who love Him on account of what they know of His perfections, those pertaining to His Essence, His Qualities, and His Acts."

4. *Jāmiʿ al-bayān* (vol. 30; Beirut: Dār Iḥyā' al-Turāth al-'Arabī, 2001), 169.

5. A verse much commented on by the Sufis refers to God's bringing forth "a people whom He loves and who love Him" (5:54).

tional, contingent upon particular human acts and qualities, rather than
being an essential aspect of God, manifested in a manner at once universal
and unconditional. God's love appears to be given as a reward for the righteous and denied as a punishment to the sinners. While this picture cannot
be disputed on its own level, it certainly does not exhaust the nature of the
Islamic conception of divine love. The surface or immediate meaning of
the verses cited pertains, in like fashion, to the surface or immediate manifestations of divine love within the created order. What remains to be dis-
covered, beneath the surface of these verses, is what the true nature of divine love is, and how it is related, not just to specific manifestations of
God's love, but rather to the very substance of manifestation itself — the
whole of the created realm.

If the classical commentaries are consulted on these verses, the picture
of divine love that emerges is not, however, substantially altered, for the
commentators as a rule focus on the moral imperatives which flow from
these verses, and they stress the need for each individual to shed all blame-
worthy qualities and adopt the praiseworthy ones in order to become worthy recipients of divine love.

The problem becomes even more complicated if one consults the
works of the Muslim theologians. For a major strand of Muslim theology
has difficulty with ascribing love to God, even if He describes Himself as
al-Wadūd in the Qur'ān. Such theological schools as the Jahmiyya,[6] the
Mu'tazila, and the dominant school of *kalām* in Islam, the Ash'ariyya,
identified God's "love" with His will. For example, the Mu'tazilite Abū 'Alī
al-Jubbā'ī (d. 303/915), in common with the rest of his school, sees a near-
equivalence between God's love and His will *(irāda)*: God's love for His
creatures is only an expression of His will to reward and honor them in the
hereafter.[7] Abū Hasan al-Ash'arī (d. 324/935), erstwhile disciple and then
opponent of al-Jubbā'ī and founder of the most influential school of theology in Islam, is largely at one with his former teacher in regard to the
meaning of God's love; he states that, in addition to willing or desiring to
reward His creatures in the hereafter, God's "love" also consists in willing

---

6. According to Ibn Taymiyya, it was the teacher of al-Jahm b. Ṣafwān (d. 128/745-46),
al-Ja'd b. Dirham (d. 105/723-24), who is regarded as the first theologian to deny that God
loves His creatures. See his *Kitāb majmū'at fatāwā*, vol. 1 (Cairo: Matba'at Kurdistān al-
'Ilmiyya, 1326-29/1908-11), 207-8. Cited by Joseph N. Bell, *Love Theory in Later Hanbalite Islam* (Albany, N.Y.: State University of New York, 1979), 60, 233 n. 93.

7. Daniel Gimaret, *Les Noms divins en Islam* (Paris: Les Editions du Cerf, 1988), 424-25.

them to be believers — even though He knows from all eternity who will be and who will not be a believer.[8] For al-Ashʿarī, God's compassion *(rahma)*, His approval *(riḍā)*, and His love are alike aspects of His beneficent will *(irādat al-inʿām)*. He differs from the Muʿtazilites, however, in his occasional references to these attributes of God as being *identical* with His will, not just aspects or forms assumed by His will. Thus for al-Ashʿarī everything that God wills is also, by definition, "loved" and "approved" by Him, including even bad actions: one has to define, however, the precise manner in which His love and approval are exercised.[9]

Despite this reservation, al-Ashʿarī's doctrine led to such impasses as the following: if God wills everything, and thus loves everything, how can the Qurʾān describe Him in good logic as not loving those things willed by Him, such as the immoral acts of the disbelievers? Although, as will be seen below, the gnosis of the Sufis as a whole transcended this volitive perspective on God, within the realm of theology it fell to the neo-Hanbalite school to rectify this inordinate and massive stress on the will by the Ashʿarites. The equivalence between will and love was strongly opposed within the domain of scholastic theology by, for example, Ibn Taymiyya, who asserted not only that God's love is real and is not reducible to His will, but also that this will itself presupposed love: "Every will necessarily requires a love, for everything willed is willed only because it is loved or because it is a means to something loved. If love is assumed not to exist, then will is an impossibility."[10]

Another immensely influential Ashʿarite theologian, al-Bāqillānī (d. 404/1013), asserts forcefully that such emotional qualities as love and anger can only be ascribed to God as indications of divine recompense for good and evil, respectively. Divine love can only mean "God's will to reward those with whom He is satisfied, whom He loves and befriends"; and His anger means simply His will "to punish those with whom He is angered, whom He hates and to whom He shows enmity. Nothing else!" If one tries to define love and anger in terms of anything other than His will to do good or harm, then one will fall into anthropomorphism: one will be

---

8. Gimaret, *Les Noms divins*, 425.

9. See Daniel Gimaret, *La Doctrine d'al-Ashʿarī* (Paris: Les Éditions du Cerf, 1990), 195.

10. Bell, *Love Theory*, 65. One should also note that there were Sufis who upheld Ashʿarism on the theological plane while transcending its precepts on the plane of gnosis *(maʿrifa)*. Despite his critique of theology generally, al-Ghazzālī himself is still referred to as an "Ashʿarite theologian."

ascribing to God "an aversion and a change arising in His nature when He is angered, and a tenderness, inclination, and tranquility in His nature when He is pleased" — which is impossible for God.[11]

As is evident, the theologians of Islam exercise extreme caution when speaking about love in relation to God. They do so because of their acute need to stress above all else God's transcendence, His incomparability *(tanzīh)*. This stress on divine transcendence, in turn, is based on the definitive credal principle of *tawhīd*, the affirmation of Divine Unity. For God's uniqueness (that is, the transcendent one-and-only character of ultimate reality) strictly requires a denial of any comparability between Him and His creation: "There is nothing like Him" (42:11). If there were anything comparable to Him, then that "thing" would undermine the absolute uniqueness of God, it would be a "partner" with God; and to ascribe a partner to God constitutes the cardinal sin in Islam, that of *shirk* — idolatry, polytheism. If no thing is like Him, it follows that He is not like any thing: any attribution to God of a quality, such as love, which appears to bring Him into a mode of comparability with His creatures blurs this fundamental distinction between the Absolute and the relative and thus is seen by the theologian as undermining the principle of *tawhīd*.

Most theologians, then, find themselves compelled to engage in a kind of implicit or explicit reductionism in relation to the divine name and attribute "The Loving" to ensure that divine "love" had nothing in common with what is normally understood as love on the human plane. If love is described in humanly familiar terms as a kind of longing *(tahannun)* or a passionate desire *('ishq)* or even as an inclination *(mayl)*, seeking a consummation as yet unrealized, then, on several theological counts, it cannot be ascribed to God. Where and how and can such a love be ascribed to a transcendent Reality that possesses absolute uniqueness, infinite perfection, utter immutability, and eternal synchronicity? Absolute uniqueness means there is no peer or like or partner or consort God could love; infinite perfection means that there can be no state or quality lacking in God that He might lovingly aspire to realize; utter immutability means that God cannot in any sense be said to undergo change, moving from one state to another, such as is presupposed by love; eternal synchronicity means that whatever God is now, He has always been and will always be, thus precluding any possibility of attaining, through love, an object as yet

---

11. Bell, *Love Theory*, 56.

unattained. In short, to quote al-Juwaynī: "The Lord utterly transcends everything which indicates temporal contingency or deficiency."[12]

Against this theological background, it is not hard to see why many in the West arrived at the caricature described in the introduction to this article. Whereas the principle "God is Love" is at the core of Christian theology, this principle, it is argued, is either non-existent in Islam or else derivative, having been borrowed apologetically from Christianity, whose very essence is defined in terms of the overflowing love of God: "For God so loved the world, that He gave His only begotten Son, that whosoever believeth in him should not perish, but have everlasting life" (John 3:16).

Given this *a priori* Christian conception of divine love in terms of a fatherly love for the creation, on the one hand, and given the centrality of scholastic theology within Christian thought on the other, it was altogether natural for early Christian investigation of Islam first to focus on Islamic theology, and second to look for something analogous to the Christian conception of a loving God within that theology. This initial orientation predetermined the ensuing stereotype; for, as seen above, Muslim theologians, far from describing God in terms of love, debated the very legitimacy of ascribing love to God in any essential manner. But this is only one side of the story, a fragment of a discourse and a fraction of a universe vibrant with divine love, a universe in which God's love for creation constitutes both the context and the content of one's life and thought as a spiritually sensitive Muslim. Moving from a narrow theological view of divine love to a broader spiritual perspective helps us to debunk the stereotype of a love-less God in Islam.

From Theology to Spirituality

To debunk the stereotype, then, it should be clearly stated, first, that theology — *kalām* — does not play anything like the determinative role within Islam as it does within Christianity. The inner life and spiritual sensibility of the Muslim is not determined by theological doctrines, to say the least. The great "renewer" *(mujaddid)* of Islam, al-Ghazzālī (d. 1111), puts the case very forcefully in his *The Book of Knowledge,* volume one of his magis-

---

12. *Kitāb al-lumaʿ fī qawāʾid Ahl al-Sunna,* in Michel Allard, *Textes apologétiques de Guwainī: Textes arabes traduits et annotés* (Beirut: Dar el-Machreq, 1968), p. 149.

terial and immensely influential *Ihyā' 'ulūm al-dīn* ("Enlivening the sciences of religion"): the theologian, *al-mutakallim,* knows only the outward aspects of the creed *(al-'aqīda),* and these pertain to the external aspects of the heart and of speech. As regards knowledge *(ma'rifa)* of God, His qualities and His acts, one must know that "this spiritual knowledge cannot be attained by the science of theology." Rather, he asserts, theology is almost like "a veil" *(hijāb)* obscuring this knowledge, and "a barrier" against it. The sole means of attaining true knowledge of God and His qualities is through the grace of luminous guidance granted by God — a grace described as being preceded by another grace, that of spiritual discipline, struggle against the faults of one's soul *(mujāhada).* "The only way to attain this knowledge is through spiritual struggle, which God has established as the prelude to Guidance."[13]

Thus, in order to appreciate the deepest meaning of the nature of divine reality within the Islamic universe of discourse, and to arrive at a more profound understanding of the meaning of God as "The Loving," it is not to the theologians that one should look in the first instance, but rather to those who made this spiritual struggle *(mujāhada)* the foundation of their lives; and this means focusing on the works of the Sufis. One of the key premises of this paper is that the spiritual perspectives of the Sufis had, and to some extent still have, a much greater resonance with grass-roots Muslims than do the abstruse concepts of the theologians or the legalistic precepts of the jurists. So when we turn our attention to the mystics of Islam, we should not think that we are departing from the mainstream of Muslim society; rather, the Sufis raised to their highest pitch, and plumbed to their deepest implications, the spiritual values of the Islamic revelation, which defined the spiritual impulses radiating throughout Muslim society; and their influence over the whole of society — in terms of arts, crafts, literature, and the sciences, from one end of the Muslim world to the other — cannot be fully accounted for in the absence of this spiritually "leavening" role.

Thus, if we wish to appreciate the meaning of God's love within Islam,

---

13. *Ihyā' 'ulūm al-dīn* (Beirut: Dār al-Jīl, 1992), 34; see the English translation of Nabih Amin Faris, *The Book of Knowledge* (Lahore: Sh. Muhammad Ashraf; repr. 1970), 55, which I have not followed. Also to be noted here is the following: "All that theology offers in the way of useful evidence is contained in the Qur'ān and Hadith. Whatever evidence is not contained therein is either reprehensible argumentation, or mere wrangling over distinctions set up by opposing sects." *Ihyā',* 33 (Faris trans., 53).

Sufi doctrines and perspectives can be investigated without fear of drifting from the moorings of Islamic society. To speak of the doctrines of the Sufis is to speak about the deepest spiritual values of the Islamic revelation — the Qur'ān and the Sunna — not about some extraneous and luxuriant speculations of a mystical minority isolated from the wider community of Muslims. On the contrary, it is precisely because of their fidelity to the spiritual values of the revelation that the Sufis were able to resonate so deeply with the aspirations and sensibilities of ordinary Muslims.[14]

Nonetheless, there still remains the suspicion in Western academic circles that the Sufis may not be altogether representative of the specifically Islamic revelation; theories still abound that the mystical doctrines of the Sufis originated out of various Christian or Buddhist or Hindu influences. Nowadays this suspicion is being dispelled by scholars who have, following Massignon,[15] shown the qur'ānic roots of the central concepts employed by the Sufis in the elaboration of their mystical perspectives.

When we turn to the Sufis we are overwhelmed by the sheer exuberance of their proclamation of love, human and divine. For the Sufis, love is at the very heart of being; the whole cosmos vibrates and pulsates with that

14. It would not be out of place to support this contention by citing the following anecdote from a recent important work by Seyyed Hossein Nasr. After making a pilgrimage to the shrine of the Sufi saint Mian Mir on the outskirts of Lahore in the 1960s, he recalls taking a horse-drawn carriage (a *tonga*) back to the city. It was driven by a poor, scantily dressed man who, upon discovering that his passenger was Persian, began reciting line after line of Sufi poetry from Rūmī, Hāfiz and 'Attār: "That example — riding in the carriage that night under the starry sky of the Punjabi countryside listening to an illiterate *tonga* driver reciting some of the most sublime mystical love poetry ever written, reciting both from memory and from the center of his heart — shows how universal the living reality of the love for God is in the Islamic spiritual universe." He then adds this important point: "This love uses the sublime language of the Sufi poets, but this poetry speaks for all those Muslims, technically Sufi and non-Sufi alike, who are aware of God's love for His creation" (Seyyed Hossein Nasr, *The Heart of Islam: Enduring Values for Humanity* [New York: HarperCollins, 2002], 215).

15. See his pioneering work, *Essai sur les origins du lexique technique de la mystique musulmane* (Paris: Librairie Philosophique J. Vrin, 1968). For a view of this theme from within the Sufi tradition, see Martin Lings, *What Is Sufism?* (Cambridge: Islamic Texts Society, 1993), and Abū Bakr Sirāj ad-Dīn, *The Book of Certainty* (Cambridge: Islamic Texts Society, 1992), both of which are excellent works disclosing the extent to which the essence of Sufism is rooted in the Qur'ān; see also M. Lings, "The Nature and Origin of Sufism" (223-38), and S. H. Nasr, "The Qur'ān as the Foundation of Islamic Spirituality," in *Foundations*, vol. 1 of *Islamic Spirituality*, ed. S. H. Nasr (London: Routledge & Kegan Paul, 1987), 3-10.

love which eternally flows from the very heart of God. Many books could be filled with this kind of "love mysticism" expressed by the Sufis. It suffices for our purposes here to give a few brief "tastes" of this view of God's love, using passages from two great Sufis, Rūmī and Ibn 'Arabī, by way of illustration of this rich vein of Islamic spirituality.[16]

Jalāl al-Dīn Rūmī

In one simple line of his *Mathnawī*,[17] Rūmī addresses and transcends the theological reservation about speaking of God in terms of love: "Love is one of the attributes of that divine reality which needs nothing."[18] God has no need of anything, and yet love is indeed one of His attributes, and not just love in the sense connoted by the divine name *al-Wadūd* or even *al-Muhibb*, but love in the passionate sense implied in *'ishq*, the word Rūmī uses in this line. While *wudd* or *hubb* might be tolerated by the theologian as a quality of God, the ascription of *'ishq* to God was severely censured, as this ascription most emphatically appeared to endow God with a need, the need of the passionate lover for the beloved. Rūmī thus seems to be delib-

16. See S. H. Nasr, "Compassion and Love, Peace and Beauty," in *The Heart of Islam — Enduring Values for Humanity,* ed. Seyyed Hossein Nasr (New York: HarperCollins, 2002), 201-36, for a succinct presentation of these fundamental themes in the Islamic tradition; Gai Eaton, "Truth and Mercy," in *Islam and the Destiny of Man* (Albany, N.Y.: Islamic Texts Society/George Allen & Unwin, 1985), 52-69, for a profound and eloquent exposition of these two dominant motifs in Islamic spirituality; Annemarie Schimmel, *Mystical Dimensions of Islam* (Chapel Hill, N.C.: University of North Carolina Press, 1975), for a comprehensive overview of mystical traditions within Islam, with particular accent on the theme of love within Sufism; Margaret Smith, *Rabi'a the Mystic and Her Fellow Saints in Islam* (Cambridge: Cambridge University Press, 1928), for an account of the doctrines of the great female saint Rābi'a al-'Adawiyya, often described as the pioneer of love-mysticism in Islam. The early development of this love-oriented mysticism is well presented in the essay by Carl Ernst, "The Stages of Love in Early Persian Sufism, from Rābi'a to Rūzbihān," in *Classical Persian Sufism from Its Origins to Rumi (700-1300),* vol. 1 of *The Heritage of Sufism,* ed. Leonard Lewisohn (Oxford: Oneworld, 1999), 435-55.

17. The *Mathnawī* is often referred to in Persia as a poetic commentary on the Qur'ān. Indeed, as Corbin notes, it is "meditated and practised as the 'Persian Qur'ān' (*Qur'ān-i Fārsī*)" (*En Islam iranien* III [Paris: Gallimard, 1971], 216-17).

18. *Mathnawī-i ma'nawī* (Tehran: Bihzād, 1371 Sh.), bk. 6, l. 974, p. 965; see Nicholson's translation, *The Mathnawi of Jalaladdin Rumi* (London: Luzac, 1934), bk. 6, l. 971, p. 312, which I have not followed.

erately and provocatively juxtaposing the two elements — the theological concept of a God beyond all need, and an ascription to God, not just of love, but of a passionate love. It is as though, in this single line, he is calling for a spiritual act of recognition of two apparently contradictory notions, and the intellect is unable to reconcile the two, for:

> Whatever I say in exposition and explanation of love, when I come to Love itself, I am ashamed of all that. . . .
> In expounding it [love], the intellect lay down [helplessly], like an ass in the mire; it was Love alone that uttered the explanation of love and loverhood.[19]

It is only by means of love that divine love can be understood, love being "the astrolabe of the mysteries of God."[20] One needs to plumb the depths of love within one's own heart in order to understand the love that God is by His deepest nature; here, Rūmī is but poetically expressing a key qur'ānic principle: "We shall show them Our signs on the horizons and in their own souls, until it be clear to them that He is the Real" (*Fuṣṣilat,* 41:53). The word for "signs" is the same as the word for verses of the revelation, *āyāt* (sing. *āya*), and the implication here is that the revelation of God's reality is given not just by the verses of scripture, but also by that outward revelation of His nature which the whole cosmos is, and that inward revelation constituted by intellectual apprehension and contemplative assimilation. Rūmī's lines here express the need to gauge the divine mysteries by means of the "astrolabe" of love, for love alone deciphers the signs and reveals its own divine essence: "The proof of the sun is the sun."[21]

Ibn ʿArabī

The twelfth-century Spanish mystic Muhyiddīn Ibn al-ʿArabī is known by the epithet of "the Greatest Master" (al-Shaykh al-Akbar), on account of the sheer scope and depth of the doctrines expounded by him and the in-

---

19. *Mathnawī-i maʿnawī,* bk. 1, l. 115 (identical reference in *Mathnawī,* Persian original).
20. *Mathnawī-i maʿnawī,* bk. 1, l. 110.
21. *Mathnawī-i maʿnawī,* bk. 1, l. 116.

fluence of these doctrines on the subsequent development of Sufism. Love is described by him as the very principle or root *(aṣl)* of Being *(kitāb al-mahabba)*. He writes in his most commented work, *Fuṣūs al-hikam:* "That movement constituted by the very being of the cosmos is a movement of love."[22] It is not just that everything which occurs in life is a cosmic dance of love; the very process by which being emerges from nonbeing is described by Ibn al-ʿArabī as a movement initiated, sustained, and consummated by God's love. In common with many Sufis he cites the famous *hadīth qudsī* or "divine saying," transmitted by the Prophet: "I was a hidden treasure and I loved to be known, so I created the creation in order to be known,"[23] and adds, "If it were not for this love, the world would never have appeared in this concrete existence. In this sense, the movement of the world from nonexistence toward existence was a movement of Love."[24]

In Ibn ʿArabī's complex cosmogony, the love of God to be known is linked with the mercy of God in the most surprising manner: for God has "mercy" upon His own names and qualities, which are yearning to be known in outward existence. God's love to be known stems from that aspect of the divine reality or "treasure" which wishes to manifest its properties. So, however contradictory it may sound, God has mercy upon Himself, "breathing" upon His own names and qualities and thus bringing them into existence through loving compassion. The "breath of the Compassionate" *(nafas al-Rahmān)* is the existentiating force behind the cosmos in its entirety:

> Do you not see how the Absolute breathed out and relieved the Divine Names of (the pain of compression) which they had been feeling because of the nonappearance of their effects, in an entity called the world? This happened because the Absolute loves relaxation [*rāha*]. And relaxation was only to be obtained through the existence of forms.

---

22. *Fusus al-hikam* (Cairo: al-Matbaʿa al-Maymaniyya, 1321/1903), 256. See the translation by Caner Dagli, *The Ringstones of Wisdom* (Chicago: Kazi Publications, 2004), 261, which I have not followed.

23. This saying is one of the cornerstones of Sufi metaphysics. However, it is not regarded by scholars of Ḥadīth as having an authentic chain of transmission, though the same scholars accept its meaning and message by reference to the verse, "And We only created the jinn and mankind in order that they might worship Me," and to the comment on this by Ibn ʿAbbās: the phrase "that they might worship Me" means "that they might know Me."

24. *Fusus*, 256; cf. Dagli trans., 261-62.

Thus is it patent that movement is caused by love, and that there can be no movement in the world but that it is motivated by Love.[25]

This stress on the inseparability of love and mercy within the divine nature and thus within this world, which is nothing but the manifestation of that nature "loving to be known," leads us back to the Qur'ān. For Ibn 'Arabī's perspective, in spite of its complex metaphysical elaborations, arises organically out of the spiritual principle of loving mercy or compassionate love, which is inscribed in the heart of the qur'ānic revelation.

Revelation Revisited: *Rahma* as All-encompassing Love

Many might be of the opinion that the exalted view of divine love expressed by such mystics has little if anything to do with the Qur'ān.[26] But this view is contradicted by the mystics themselves, who assert that whatever inspiration they may have received is but the fruit of their assimilation of the message of the Qur'ān and the Prophet. Ibn 'Arabī cites this saying of Abū Madyan (d. 1198), the seminal Maghribi spiritual authority from whom many Sufi orders claim descent: "The spiritual aspirant [*al-murīd*] is not a true aspirant until he finds in the Qur'ān everything to which he aspires."[27]

25. *Fusus*, 256. It is interesting to note that Ibn Sīnā — and following him, most of the Muslim philosophers — had a similar vision of an *'ishq* that is at one with the very nature of being, penetrating and directing all existence. God's wisdom and governance "plant into everything the general principle of love"; and since "the good is loved in its very essence," on the one hand, and since God is the supreme good, on the other, it follows that all things love and tend toward God as the supreme object of love. Ibn Sīnā also defines the divine Essence in terms of love: "The highest subject of love is identical with the highest object of love, namely Its [God's] high and sublime Essence. . . . And because there is no distinction among the divine qualities of Its Essence, love is here the Essence and Being purely and simply. . . . In all beings, therefore, love is either the cause of their being, or being and love are identical with them" (see E. L. Fackenheim's translation of Ibn Sīnā's *Risāla fī'l-'ishq*, "A Treatise on Love by Ibn Sīnā," *Mediaeval Studies* 7 [1945]: 213-14).

26. Binyamin Abrahamov surveys the theme of love in the Qur'ān and Hadith in fewer than two pages and concludes: "It is obvious that such scanty material, at least concerning the plain meaning of the Qur'ānic verses, could not be the source of the great theories of divine love which were developed later in Islam" (*Divine Love in Islamic Mysticism: The Teachings of Al-Ghazali and Al-Dabbagh* [London/New York: RoutledgeCurzon, 2003], 14).

27. Ibn al-'Arabī, *al-Futūhāt al-Makkiyya* (vol. 3; Cairo, 1329 AH), 94, l. 2. Cited by Michel Chodkiewicz, *Un océan sans rivage — Ibn Arabî, le livre et le loi* (Paris: Éditions du

We might go further and say that, as regards divine love, it is not just the Sufis but also every sensitive Muslim who concretely feels the all-embracing love of God, this, in the very measure of their receptivity to the spiritual substance of the qur'ānic revelation. This love may be indefinable in its ultimate essence, but it is undeniable as regards its penetrating presence; it is evasive conceptually, but all-pervasive existentially; it is disclosed by everything beautiful, yet enclosed by nothing; expressed by every loving subject and lovable object, yet exhausted by none. This is so because the Muslim does not view God's love only through the prism of the divine Name *al-Wadūd*, nor, still less, through the spectacles of theology; rather, the love of God is perceived and received as an all-embracing quality of creative being, and not simply conceived as an anthropomorphic emotion writ large and superimposed on God.

Divine love is seen and felt as a quality streaming forth in innumerable outpourings of the Divine Spirit — in the form of the beauty of virgin nature, in the beauty and wisdom of divine guidance through the scriptures and through heavenly messengers, in the sanctity of the saints, indeed, in every conceivable and perceivable form of love, goodness, beauty, and beatitude that can be found around us and within us, surging up from the primordial, God-given nature of the human soul: "We shall show them Our signs on the horizons and in their own souls so that it be clear to them that He is the Real" (*Fuṣṣilat* 41:53).

These outpourings of the spirit of love are designated, and at the deepest level constituted,[28] by the names and attributes and acts of God. Just as on the human plane love assumes several forms — conjugal, filial, parental, sibling, etc. — while being reducible to none of them, so, *a fortiori*, divine love assumes a panoply of self-manifestations, while being reducible to none of them. A dazzling configuration of divine qualities is summoned up before the Muslim devotee when reading the Qur'ān, qualities that are infused with love, radiate love, and generate love. In addition to *al-Wadūd*, we have such names as *al-Rahmān*, The Lovingly Compassionate; *al-Rahīm*, The Lovingly Merciful; *al-Laṭīf*, The Loving-Kind; *al-Walī*, The Loving

---

Seuil, 1992), 47. In this same passage, Ibn al-'Arabī asserts that when the Qur'ān truly "descends" upon the heart, and not just the tongue, the result is a sweetness *(halāwa)* beyond all measure, surpassing all delight *(ladhdha)*.

28. "By Thy Names, which have filled the foundations of all things," as Imam 'Alī says in verse 4 of his famous supplication titled *Du'ā' Kumayl*, in *Supplications: Amīr al-Mu'minīn*, trans. W. C. Chittick (London: Muhammadi Trust, 1995).

Friend; *al-Karīm*, The Generous; *al-Barr*, The Benevolent; *al-Halīm*, The Gentle; *al-Ra'ūf*, The Kind; *al-Wakīl*, The Absolutely Trustworthy; *al-Ghafūr*, The Forgiver; *al-'Afū*, The Effacer of Sin; *al-Tawwāb*, The Relenting; and so on. Each of these qualities is felt to be a manifestation of love according to a particular modality; the totality of these names and qualities — and the acts that manifest them — does not just bestow a sense of the effusion of love from God to creation, but also, in their very diversity, this configuration of qualities expresses something of the infinite and thus ultimately transcendent essence of God's love. This love both penetrates and reintegrates the whole of creation, a reintegration or "making one" — the essence of *tawhīd* — with the One, whose very infinitude defies definition; hence the love in question is both inescapable in its manifestations and ungraspable in its essence — both immanent and transcendent.

In addition to these specific divine names is a whole set of acts and descriptions which express loving qualities, but from which divine names in the theological sense are not classically derived:

"He is of tremendous bounty," we are told repeatedly in the Qur'ān;

"Every single good thing you have is [a grace] from God" (16:53);
God's graces are boundless, and thus innumerable: "Were you to count the graces of God, you could not number them" (14:34);[29]
His gracious gifts are showered on both those who reject Him and those who strive for Him: "Unto each, the former and the latter, do We extend the gracious gift of thy Lord. And the gracious gift of thy Lord can never be enclosed" (17:20);
"Do you not see how God hath made serviceable to you whatever is in the skies and on earth, and has lavished His blessings upon you, both outwardly and inwardly?" (31:20).

All these descriptions of God's acts, attributes, and nature are brought together in a myriad of combinations, associations, and implications, and are apprehended by the Muslim as so many mutually illuminating stars in a veritable constellation of divine love: "Light upon light," *nūr 'alā nūr*, as the Qur'ān says in one of its most graphic symbols of the divine mystery, telling us that God is the Light of the Heavens and the earth.[30]

29. Note the gifts of creation in the two verses preceding this one.
30. For Sufi commentaries on the famous "verse of light" (24:35), see Kristin Zahra

The question will of course be raised, What of the opposite kind of names of qualities — those of anger, wrath, chastisement, and so on? These are certainly found and found in abundance in the Qur'ān, but they cannot alter the conception of God as primarily, overwhelmingly, inherently, and essentially loving. It is of the utmost importance to understand that this constellation of loving qualities (referred to in terms of *lutf,* "lovingkindness," or *jamāl,* "beauty") is viewed as being much more indicative of the core of the divine nature — closer to the "pole" of ultimate reality — than is the constellation of wrathful qualities (pertaining to *qahr,* "all-conquering power," or *jalāl,* "majesty"). For these rigorous qualities are to be seen in the light of the loving qualities, which brilliantly overshadow them. What are the bases of this assertion?

As regards the qur'ānic basis for the assertion that God is inherently and overwhelmingly loving, one should focus first of all on the two names for mercy: *al-Rahmān* and *al-Rahīm.*[31] Every chapter of the Qur'ān except one begins with the phrase, *Bismi'Llāh al-Rahmān al-Rahīm,* which could be translated, "In the Name of God, The Lovingly Compassionate, The Lovingly Merciful," for the quality expressed by both of these names for mercy is *rahma,* and this quality is understood as combining both mercy and love. In other words, the word is close to the meaning of *caritas* in Latin and *agapē* in Greek, and can be translated as "charity" in the strictly etymological sense of the word, and not in the reduced sense that has become conventional today.[32] Just as love is the inherent, defining reality of charity, so *rahma* is to be understood primarily in terms of a love that gives of itself: what it gives is what it is, transcendent beatitude, which creates out of love

---

Sands, *Ṣūfī Commentaries on the Qur'ān in Classical Islam* (London/New York: Routledge, 2006), 110-35.

31. It is to be noted that al-Ghazālī, in his commentary on the divine names, refers to *al-Wadūd* as being close in meaning to *al-Rahīm,* but whereas the latter requires an object in need of mercy, *al-Wadūd* bestows its graces from the outset upon all, not requiring any such object, this being among the consequences of the quality of love *(al-in'ām 'alā sabīl al-ibtidā' min natā'ij al-wudd).* See his *The Ninety-Nine Beautiful Names of God (al-Maqṣad al-asnā fī sharh asmā' Allāh al-husnā),* trans. D. B. Burrell, N. Daher (Cambridge: Islamic Texts Society, 1999), 119; also Al-Ghazālī, *Al-Maqṣad al-asnā fī sharh asmā' Allāh al-husnā,* Arabic text, ed. Fadlou A. Shehadi (Beirut: Dar El-Machreq, 1971), 132.

32. The King James translation of *caritas/agapē* as "charity," in the moving letter of St. Paul to the Corinthians, where charity is described as greater than hope and faith, is quite correct, since the primary meaning of the word, even according to the Oxford English Dictionary today, is "love."

and, upon contact with Its creation, assumes the nature of loving compassion, mercy, and the whole myriad of qualities mentioned earlier.

In the following saying of the Prophet, God's transcendent *rahma* is alluded to in terms of the most striking expression of *rahma* on earth — that expressed by a mother who, after searching frantically for her baby, clutches it to her breast and feeds it: "God is more merciful to His servants than is this woman to her child."[33] In English, one speaks of a mother's love for her child in such a context, rather than her mercy or compassion; thus the quality of *rahma* is far better translated into English as "loving mercy" or "merciful love," "loving compassion" or "compassionate love," than simply as "mercy" or "compassion." The clear implication is that mercy/compassion flow forth from infinite love, and are inseparable from it.

The Jewish scholar Ben-Shemesh goes so far as to translate the *basmala* as "In the Name of God, the Compassionate, the Beloved" to bring home this key aspect of love proper to the root of *rahma*.[34] He argues that in both Arabic and Hebrew the meaning of love is strongly present in the root *r-h-m* and gives the following compelling evidence: Psalm 18 contains the phrase, *Erhamha Adonay* — "I love thee my Lord."[35] In Aramaic/Syriac, the root *r-h-m* specifically denotes love, rather than "compassion." One can thus feel the resonance of this Syriac connotation within the Arabic *rahma*. Moreover, there is epigraphic evidence that early Christian sects in southern Arabia used the name *Rahmānan* as a name of God, and this name would probably have been understood as "The Loving."[36]

Rahma, as loving compassion/compassionate love, is thus invoked in two forms at the very beginning of every chapter of the Qur'ān, and is the formula of consecration *par excellence* of Islam uttered prior to initiating every important activity. It is recited seventeen times each day, at least, by every practicing Muslim in the canonical prayers. Al-Ghazzālī in his commentary on the divine Names, *al-Maqsad al-asnā,* asserts that the name *al-Rahmān* is close to the name *Allāh* and cites the all-important verse, "Call upon *Allāh* or call upon *al-Rahmān;* whichever you call upon, unto

---

33. Bukhārī, *Sahīh, kitāb al-adab, bāb* 18, *hadīth* no. 5999 (Bukhari summarized: p. 954, no. 2015); Muslim, *Sahīh, kitāb al-tawba, hadīth* no. 6978.

34. See A. Ben-Shemesh, "Some Suggestions to Qur'ān Translators," *Arabica* 16/1 (1969): 82.

35. Ben-Shemesh, 82.

36. See Albert Jamme, "Inscriptions on the Sabaean Bronze Horse of the Dumbarton Oaks Collection," *Dumbarton Oaks Papers* 8 (1954): 232ff.

Him belong the most beautiful names" (17:110). It should be noted in this verse that all the names are described as "most beautiful," including therefore all the names of rigor as well as those of gentleness, this being another sign of the predominance of divine love and over divine anger.[37] But the most important point to note here is that the name *al-Rahmān* is practically coterminous with the name *Allāh*, indicating that the quality of loving mercy takes us to the very heart of the divine nature. Indeed, al-Ghazzālī explains the meaning of *al-Rahmān* in terms of a loving inclination, for he says: "[*al-Rahmān*] is He who is lovingly inclined towards His creatures, first by creating them; second, by guiding them to faith and to the means of salvation; third by making them happy in the next world; and fourth by granting them contemplation of His noble Face."[38]

But to remain with the name *al-Rahmān* in qur'ānic context, consider the following verses:

(1) "He has prescribed mercy for Himself" (6:12): The word *kataba*, "he wrote," is used in this verse, so the literal meaning is, "He wrote *rahma* upon His own soul," implying that *rahma* is a kind of inner law governing the very *nafs*, the Self or Essence of God. The use of the image of "writing" here can be seen as a metaphor for expressing the metaphysical truth that *rahma* is, as it were, "inscribed" within the deepest reality of the divine nature. God's "inscription" *upon* Himself is thus God's description *of* Himself. These considerations help us to see why the Names of love and mercy overshadow those of wrath and rigor within the divine nature.

(2) In the chapter titled "*al-Rahmān*" (Sūra number 55), it is *al-Rahmān* who "taught the Qur'ān, created man, taught him discernment" (verses 1-3). The whole of this chapter evokes and invokes the reality of this essential quality of God, at once creative and redemptive. Indisputably among the most sublime in the Qur'ān, its majestic meaning and magical musicality combine to produce a rhythm that sets in motion a transformative reverberation of creative love, a marvelously

---

37. It should be noted that in the central canonical prayer of the Qur'ān, the *Fātiha*, it is mercy, compassion, and lordship that are ascribed to God, and not anger; the penultimate verse *ghayri'l-maghḍūbi 'alayhim*, "not the path of those upon is anger," does not explicitly refer to God as the subject of anger. See my *My Mercy Encompasses All: The Koran's Teachings on Compassion, Peace and Love* (Emeryville, Calif.: Shoemaker and Hoard, 2007), 8-9.

38. *The Ninety-Nine Beautiful Names*, 54 (translation modified); Arabic text, 66-67.

interiorizing melody that absorbs the contemplative soul of the reciter and directs its gaze toward the Paradises so irresistibly described.[39] The blessings of Paradise are not restricted, however, to the next life, for the glories, beauties, and harmonies of God's entire cosmos, including all the wonders of virgin nature, are also described in verses of supernal beauty, which are musically punctuated by the refrain, "so which of the favors of your Lord can you deny?" For, as already stressed above, there is no beauty, no harmony, no delight in the whole realm of creation that is not the grace or the favor of a loving Lord. In this chapter named after al-Rahmān, then, we are invited to contemplate the various levels at which *rahma* fashions the substance of reality: the *rahma* that describes the deepest nature of the divine; the *rahma* that is musically inscribed into the very recitation of the chapter; the *rahma* that creates all things; the *rahma* that reveals itself through the Qur'ān and through all the signs *(āyāt)* of nature. One comes to see that God has created not only *by rahma*, and *from rahma* but also *for rahma*: ". . . except those upon whom God has mercy: for this did He create them" (11:119); and *within rahma*: "My *rahma* encompasses all things" (7:156).

Al-*Rahmān* is normally used to refer to the creative power of *rahma*, and al-*Rahīm* to the salvific power of *rahma*. Combining these two properties of loving compassion, the creative and redemptive, or the existential and salvational, we see why it is that ultimately nothing can escape or be separated from God's all-embracing *rahma*.

The question remains unanswered, Where is the place and what can be the role of the wrathful attributes of God? The clearest possible articulation of the relationship between the qualities of love and those of anger is expressed in the well-attested saying of the Prophet, referring to what is inscribed on God's Throne: "My mercy precedes My wrath."[40] In Tirmidhī's

---

39. For an illuminating exegesis of this *sūra*, and especially of the "two paradises" mentioned therein, see Frithjof Schuon, "The Two Paradises" in his *Form and Substance in the Religions* (Bloomington, Ind.: World Wisdom, 2002), 253-55. For Schuon's profound exposition of the message of the Qur'ān in general, see the chapter "The Qur'ān" in his *Understanding Islam* (Bloomington, Ind.: World Wisdom, 1994), 39-94.

40. Bukhārī, *Sahīh*, II, *kitāb* (no. 63) *al-khalq*, *bāb* 1, *hadīth* no. 3022; Muslim, *Sahīh*, IV, *kitāb* (no. 49) *al-tawba*, *bāb* 4, *hadīth* no. 2751.

collection, the word "prevails" *(ghalabat)* is used: "My mercy prevails over My wrath."[41]

Mercy's preceding or prevailing over wrath can be understood as an expression of the supereminence of love and all associated qualities, which are deemed to be indicative of the essential nature of ultimate reality; the opposed qualities are to be seen as peripheral and accidental — their operation is to bring about a restoration of a ruptured equilibrium, so their goal is to bring things back to *rahma,* and not to punish for the sake of inflicting pain. Love thus has a principial or ontological priority within the divine nature. Understanding this principle helps one to cast in a different light the following verses:

> And We have tied every man's augury to his own neck, and We shall bring forth for him on the Day of Judgment a book which he will find open wide. [It will be said to him:] Read your book. Your own soul suffices this day unto you as a reckoner. (17:13)

> Whatever good comes to you is from God, and whatever evil comes to you is from your own soul. (4:79)

It is goodness, compassion, peace, and love that emanate from God to humans; whatever else they experience is solely the result of their own deeds, attitudes, and dispositions. It is not difficult to see why the mystics of Islam refer to God's "anger" as being nothing but the extrinsic consequence of a lack of receptivity on the part of man to the mercy of God.[42] Divine wrath is seen here as contingent, not essential: contingent in the sense of being called forth by contingent action — human sin — and thereby defined in terms of a disequilibrium that must be rectified.

Let us return to the divine name, *al-Wadūd,* and consider two sayings of the Prophet that al-Ghazzālī cites as examples of the attitudes which conform to this divine name:

> The Messenger of God said, when his teeth were broken and his face

---

41. Tirmidhī, *Sunan,* V, *bāb* no. 109, *hadīth* no. 3611.

42. *Fusus,* 222, especially Kāshānī's comment, as noted and explored fully by Toshihiko Izutsu, *Sufism and Taoism: A Comparative Study of Key Philosophical Concepts* (Berkeley/Los Angeles/London: University of California Press, 1983), 117 et passim.

was struck and bloodied: "Lord, guide my people, for they do not know."[43]

The second saying is:

> He commanded 'Alī: "If you want to precede the ones brought nigh, then be united with those who broke with you, give to the ones who excluded you, and forgive the ones who wronged you."[44]

Indeed, the theme of loving forgiveness is to be found concretely embodied in the Prophet's character and actions. This presentation can be concluded with a brief consideration of the way in which the Prophet reflects the *rahma* of God. First, we find him described in the Qur'ān as a *rahma* to the whole of creation: "We sent you not [O Prophet] save as a mercy for all the worlds" (39:53). Similarly, "It was through the mercy of God that you [O Prophet] were gentle with them. For if you had been harsh and hard-hearted they would have fled from you. So pardon them, and pray that they be forgiven" (3:159).

The Prophet is described in terms of divine qualities, *ra'ūf, rahīm*, kind and merciful: "There hath come unto you a messenger from yourselves, for whom whatever burdens you is grievous to him, full of concern for you, kind and merciful to the believers" (9:128).

The Prophet is named *al-habīb*, "the beloved," or *habību'Llāh*, "the beloved of God," meaning that he is the perfect model of a lovable human being: "If you love God, follow me. God will love you" (3:31), as cited earlier; but now it should be clearer that following his example means ensuring that mercy, love, and gentleness prevail within our souls, this being our way of mirroring the predominance of the same qualities within Ultimate Reality. It follows that entering into the mould of the prophetic love is to enter into the realm of the Real, and herein lies the fundamental aim not just of the Prophet's mission, but of all prophecy, in all ages and all places. In the chapter titled "The Poets" (*al-Shu'arā'*, Sūra 26) we are given an allusion to this basic aim of all the prophets of God. After mentioning the stories of Moses, Abraham, Noah, Hūd, Sālih, Lot, and Jethro, there is this refrain, which is like a summing up of the essence of the prophetic mes-

---

43. *Allāhumma'hdi qaumī fa-innahum lā ya'lamūn.*
44. *Al-Maqsad*, 119.

sage: "Truly thy Lord, He is indeed The Gloriously Mighty, The Lovingly Merciful *(al-'Azīz, al-Rahīm)*." Here the combination of God's saving mercy, on the one hand, and His glorious inaccessibility, on the other, is stressed: the manifestation of love, and the eternally unknowable essence of love.

To conclude, calling upon *Allāh* is tantamount to calling upon *al-Rahmān;* all things are created by *rahma,* for the sake of *rahma,* and are encompassed by *rahma;* thus God's *rahma* refers not only to mercy or compassion but also, and fundamentally, to the infinite love and overflowing beatitude of Ultimate Reality.

The Word of God:
The Bridge Between Him, You, and Us

SEYYED HOSSEIN NASR

Say, O People of the Book! Come to a word common between us and
you, that we shall worship none but God, and shall not associate
aught with Him, and shall not take one another as lords apart from
God.

Qur'ān, 3:65

The "common word" to which the chapter of the Qur'an "The House of
'Imrān" refers, and from which the title of the document "A Common Word
Between Us and You" has been taken, has been interpreted by such major
traditional commentators as Zamakhshahrī, Fakhr al-Dīn al-Rāzī, and Ibn
'Arabī as referring to Divine Unity or *al-Tawhīd*. Surely this is its basic meaning, as the Unity of the Divine Principle is what is common between all the
"usses" and all the "yous" who follow the sacred teachings at the heart of all
authentic religions. The "common word" means not only the acceptance of
Divine Unity but also attachment to the One with our whole being, and
therefore including love of the One and, further, love of His creation — or
the neighbor, for the neighbor comes from the One and returns to It. The
common word stated in the Qur'ān therefore contains within itself implicitly the two commandments of Christ announced in chapter 12 of the Gospel
of Mark in the New Testament. The consequence of our realization of our
ontological dependence on the One as absolute, regarding Him and also regarding what issues from Him in light of the ontological dependence on
Him of all creation, cannot but include His two commandments.

110

There is, furthermore, a second possible interpretation of the "common word" that can bring you and us, or more particularly Christians and Muslims, even closer together by embracing the instrument, or the means by which, the One has revealed Himself to all of us, Christian and Muslim alike. The second interpretation has to do with the meaning of the term "word" itself. In the original Arabic of the verse from "The House of 'Imrān" the term that is used is *kalimah*. Now the Noble Qur'an is known among Muslims as *kalām Allāh* or *kalimat Allāh,* meaning literally Word of God, while the term is also used in connection with Moses and Jesus. It is precisely this term that corresponds to the word *logos* in Christian Greek sources. Contrary to what some have claimed, the doctrine of the *logos* exists as much in Islam as it does in Christianity, albeit with different interpretations resulting from the different receptacles for which a religion is meant and also the diversity of Divine manifestations. As Islamic sources assert, *kullu yawmin Huwa fī'l-sha'n,* that is, "every day He manifests Himself in a different state." Furthermore, while the Gospel of John asserts that it was by the Word that all things were made, the chapter *Yā Sīn* in the Qur'ān exclaims that God said "be!" *(kun),* and there was. There is therefore again a similarity of cosmogonic function in the two religions as far as the Word is concerned.

Consequently, one can say not only that Divine Unity is a common word between us and you but that there is also a single *kalimah* or Logos in its principial reality in which we believe jointly, except that for Christians the Word is identified with Christ and for Muslims with the Qur'ān. It would bring us closer to each other if we realized that we are bound together not only by the doctrine of the One but also by the "doctrine of the Word," if we fix our gaze on the metahistorical and principial Word/Logos and not on one of its particular historical manifestations. There *were,* however, particular manifestations of this reality. Hence the creation of Christianity and Islam, as well as other religions, especially Judaism, if we confine ourselves within the Abrahamic family of religions — religions in which there are universal elements that unify and bind, and formal aspects and particularities that separate. Needless to say, different understandings of *kalimah* or *logos* have existed also within each tradition, as we see in the formulation of different types of Christology and also different understandings of the meaning of the Qur'ān as the Word of God.

*　　*　　*

Obviously, the "common word" as related to Divine Unity, followed by the Word as *kalimah* or *Logos*, in its metaphysical sense, and the resulting love of God and neighbor are the most important elements that unify and bind us together. The traditional Catholic credo begins with *credo in unum Deum*, which conveys the same meaning as *lā ilāha illa'Llāh*. Furthermore, we both accept the revelatory agency of the Word, however different might be our understanding of the form the Word has taken in this world and our interpretation of the process of revelation itself. From this similarity of doctrine issues the role played by Christ in Christianity as the perfect model to emulate, hence *imitatio Christi*, and the similar role played by the Prophet, the recipient of the Divine Word in Islam and the most perfect of men for Muslims, though not considered divine.

The list of similarities that bind us on the basis of these basic doctrines and that bring Christians and Muslims close together are too many to enumerate here. But let me mention a few: acceptance of sacred scripture; belief in the reality and preeminence of the Spirit within and in the spiritual world beyond our subjectivism; the immortality of the soul; the efficacy of prayer and other religious rites; the necessity for humans of ethical character here on earth and its consequences for life after death; ultimate judgment by God and eschatological realities; the reality of good and evil; interplay of the mercy and justice of God; the reflection of the wisdom of God in His creation; and the existence of a path in this life to march toward God, as seen in the mysticism of the two religions. Even in matters of the relation of faith to reason, Christianity and Islam have developed many parallel doctrines. In fact, in contrast to what some Christian sources have asserted, there is a Muslim parallel for practically *every* Christian position on the issue, from Tertullian, St. Augustine, Anselm, and St. Thomas to Calvin and Luther and more recently Barth and Tillich, and vice versa. When one ponders even this incomplete list of shared elements, one becomes aware of how many basic doctrines and practices do indeed unite us, especially if our religions were to be compared to what is held to be central in secular society. Nor can one side legitimately accuse the other of being opposed to the use of reason in matters of religion or lacking in love.

*   *   *

Of course, there are also walls that separate us. Otherwise Islam and Christianity would not have survived as separate religions as they have done providentially; rather, the two seas would have commingled into a single ocean. God's will seems to have commanded otherwise. In the *Mathnawī* of Jalāl al-Dīn Rūmī God addresses Moses and says, "Thou hast come to unify and not to separate." Surely our task today and tomorrow is to follow this command, but we cannot simply neglect the differences by pretending they do not exist. We hope that the common word between us and you will bring us closer together, not because differences do not exist, but in spite of their existence. As Frithjof Schuon once said, "Accord between religions is not possible in the human atmosphere but only in the Divine stratosphere." Our hope is that while being aware of the human atmosphere where different religious ideas and forms do exist as willed by God, we can ascend through the love and knowledge of God — and also sapience — to the stratosphere, where we can reach accord.

Meanwhile in this human atmosphere where we reside, we see such apparently insurmountable differences as the emphasis of Islam on Divine Unity and the negation of Trinity (at least as understood in the Qur'an), and the Christian emphasis on the Trinity, which is even transposed into the domain of Unity itself. We disagree on the episodes at the end of the life of Christ, and of course his divinity in contrast to his being a major prophet of God. We do not see eye to eye about the relation between canonical law and secular law, on the one hand, and *al-Sharīʿah* and *al-qānūn*, on the other. While much of our ethics is similar, we do hold different views concerning sexuality and its relation to original sin, the doctrine of which is central to much of Christian thought but rejected by Islam.

In this context of similarities and contrasts we each follow the teachings of a religion that claims to have a universal message for the whole of humanity, and this claim has played no small role in the long history of animosity between the two religions. It has led to religious wars, crusades, coercive missionary activity, and much else that has colored and still colors the relation between the two religions. Christians accuse Muslims of violence without paying attention to their own history and to what the Native Americans of New England would likely have said about the relation of Christianity to violence, had they survived to attend this conference. Muslims accuse Christians of not paying enough attention to the social teachings of religion based on justice, while not pointing out sufficiently the unjust practices that go on in parts of the Islamic world. A number of people on both sides also tend to paint the other as an extremist fringe, Christians using terrorism and Muslims using blasphemy against Islam, the Qur'ān, the Prophet, and what has come to be known more generally as Islamophobia. Needless to say, both terrorism in the Islamic world and Islamophobia do remain real, but they do not determine the whole reality of Islamic-Christian understanding. Meanwhile, both sides accuse the other of not practicing what they preach.

Yes, these and many other impediments have to be confronted head on and not simply ignored. On the social and political levels, the two religions have also to be self-critical of their own societies and not simply surrender to the political forces of the two worlds in which they form a majority. On the theological level, there must be in-depth dialogue if more external issues are to be solved. Without truth, religious dialogue becomes simply political expediency, and it is then better to leave it in the hands of diplomats rather than committed scholars of religion and theologians. Deep theological dialogue does not necessarily mean the surrender of one side to the other; it does, however, mean better understanding of the other and greater mutual respect. At least one can agree to disagree rather than making blanket statements that the other side is anathema. Of course, the ideal would be to transcend the formal order altogether to reach the transcendent truth of which theological doctrines are so many crystallizations. That truth resides in the world of meaning beyond forms, in what Rūmī calls the "spiritual retreat of God." But until we get there we must be able to come together, to know each other, to love one another, and to face together the many challenges posed by a world based on the forgetfulness of God. And it is precisely in this situation that a common word between us and you can play such a crucial role if there is sincerity and correct intention on both sides.

*   *   *

In the light of a long history of contentions and confrontations, of theological differences irreducible on the theological level and the need to realize this fact, and of the unprecedented global crisis in which accord or discord between religions has become crucial, it becomes clear why a common word between us and you is of such significance. Surely the "common word" is a most efficacious way to bring about amity between Christianity and Islam without either side's sacrificing the truth upon which it stands. And what can be more important to a religion than truth, without which religion divorces itself from its very source? Did not Christ call himself the Truth? And is not reference made to God in the Qur'an as *al-Ḥaqq,* the Truth? It is of the utmost importance for us to realize that the "common word" we are asked to accept and share does not at the same time demand of us to forgo the truth or to relativize it in the name of religious accord, as happens in so much of today's prevalent but shallow ecumenism that is willing to sacrifice truth for the sake of expediency.

The necessity of acceptance of the two commandments of the love of God and neighbor on the basis of the saying of Christ, and hence Christian truth, is evident to Christians. As for Muslims, the two principles are mentioned in the Qur'an and *Ḥadīth,* and their acceptance is therefore necessary and is moreover seen by Muslims to be based solidly on Islamic teachings. Furthermore, it must be remembered that, according to Islamic beliefs, what has been brought by an earlier prophet and not explicitly abrogated by a later revelation still stands as an expression of truth and God's commandment to and will for Muslims. In the light of this belief, the two commandments of Christ are also commandments for Muslims, even if they had been neither confirmed nor abrogated in the Qur'ān and *Ḥadīth.* Christ is after all not only the founder of Christianity, but also a major Islamic prophet.

*   *   *

Coming now to the meaning of the two commandments, three related issues come to mind and need to be explained: the meaning of God, the meaning of love, and the meaning of the love of God and neighbor. Without some accord on these issues, we would be attacked by those who stand against mutual harmony and comprehension on the subject of the very terms we are using in "A Common Word." There are already those on the Christian side who assert that the Christian God is not the same as Allah, who is an Arabic lunar deity or something like that. Such people who usually combine sheer ignorance with bigotry should attend a Sunday mass in Arabic in Bethlehem, Beirut, Amman, or Cairo and hear what Arabic term the Christians of these cities use for the Christian God. Nor is God simply to be identified with one member of the Christian Trinity, one part of three divinities that some Muslims believe wrongly that Christians worship. Allah, or God, is none other than the One God of Abraham, Isaac, Ishmael, Moses, Jesus, and Muhammad. In speaking of the love of God, let us not accuse each other of referring to different gods. How can one study the Bible, including both the Old and the New Testaments, and the Qur'ān without accepting that we are all breathing throughout all the worlds created by these sacred scriptures within the same universe of Abrahamic monotheism? What could be more insidious or even demonic than trying to undercut the binding effect of Christ's two commandments by claiming that Christians and Muslims are referring to two different gods and not the single God "whose mercy embraces all," as the Qur'ān asserts?

As for love, it is a reality that transcends whatever one writes about it. As Rūmī said, when it came to love the pen broke and the ink dried. And yet so much has been written about the subject. One can either write nothing, or fill libraries about love, but finally one must experience love to know what it is. Love attaches the lover to the beloved, carries the lover through dales and valleys of joy and sorrow, and finally leads to a union that is also a kind of death, for *amor est mors.* The love of God is not only the highest form of love, but also in reality the only love of which all other loves are but shadows. To love God fully is to give ourselves wholly to Him, body, soul, and mind, not to mention will and intelligence. We must give up our limited ego as that which defines us. The end of such love is what the Christian mystics call mystical union and to which Sufis refer, in a somewhat different language but concerning the same reality, as being consumed by the fire of love as a moth is immolated by the divine flame of the divine candle.

For the purpose of our present discourse, in the same way that it is unnecessary to engage in contentious theological discussions about the nature of God, it is also unnecessary to engage in analysis of the modes, stages, and states of love. Let us love God and leave the mystery of this attachment of each soul to its Creator to the Creator Himself. At all costs we should avoid considering our love of God to be superior to the love of the other for God. Such an illusory contention arises from our mistaking our own understanding of love for God as that love itself, and from absolutizing that understanding and thereby inflating our egos in the guise of religious devotion and righteousness. Let us love God and leave it for Him to decide on the intensity and sincerity of our loves, as well as of our differing views of Him. The Qur'ān invites Muslims explicitly to live at peace with followers of other religions and let God decide on the Day of Judgment concerning the truth or falsehood of their points of difference.

As for the love of neighbor, this command has been understood in a different manner over the ages. Today, it cannot include for Muslims only

Muslim neighbors, for Christians only Christian neighbors, or for Jews only Jewish neighbors. It must also include followers of other religious communities, even nonreligious communities, and especially the nonhuman world. In fact, if Muslims and Christians, not to speak of other groups, do not extend their love of neighbor to the natural world, the consequences of the environmental crisis caused in fact by the lack of love of neighbor, in its larger reality, will make other efforts more or less irrelevant.

The Qur'ān asserts that God created all humanity from a single soul *(nafs wāḥidah)*. Nevertheless, strife even within a single family, not to mention between religions and nations, continues to manifest itself. One might say that as a result of what Muslims call the fall *(hubūṭ)* and Christians original sin, the state of confrontation and strife is endemic to the human condition. But God has also given us the means of transcending the abode of strife for one of peace, of overcoming that religious and ideological exclusivism, which now endangers human existence, in favor of that inclusivism, out of which we gathered here are partisans.

It is not, however, enough to speak of "A Common Word Between Us and You" or even to accept its tenets with our tongue. We must also have the correct intention and live these commandments within ourselves, while setting examples for others. Let us love God with all our being, which means also to accept His Unity and the unity of His Word, which unite us. And let us love the neighbor, and more specifically our Muslim and Christian neighbors, not on the basis of mere sentimentality, which can weaken or strengthen in time, but on the never-changing foundation of the Truth.

To live fully as a Muslim or Christian does not require anything less of us than loving the neighbor, whether he or she be Muslim or Christian, and it requires us not to ask, "Is he or she one of us?" but to recognize that "He or she is one of His."

The Concept of Loving Neighbor
in the Qur'an and Hadith

His Excellency Judge Bola Abdul Jabbar Ajibola

It is reported on the authority of Abu Huraira that the Messenger of Allah (may peace be upon Him) observed: He who believes in Allah and the Last Day should either utter good words or better keep silence; and he who believes in Allah and the Last Day should treat his neighbor with kindness and he who believes in Allah and the Last Day should show hospitality to his guest.

Recorded by Bukhari and Muslim[1]

The Hadith quoted above, narrated by Abu Huraira (may Allah be pleased with him), is a succinct exposition of many verses of the Holy Qur'an that border on good neighborliness and the upholding of the common good. The Prophet of Islam, Muhammad (peace and blessings be upon him) did not qualify his statement on generosity to neighbors, and by implication the Hadith is meant for universal application.

The world today stands precariously on the precipice of confusion and conflicts. Suspicion and hatred have befogged the reasoning of human beings and restrained them from the observance of divine instructions on love, peace, tolerance, endurance, and compassion for fellow beings. Even the adherents of Abrahamic faiths — Islam, Christianity, and Judaism — have continued to spin the thread of hatred, violence, and armed conflict

1. See Sahih Bukhari, vol. 8, bk. 73, nos. 47 and 158; Sahih Bukhari, vol. 8, bk. 76, no. 482; and Sahih Muslim, bk. 1, nos. 75-78.

within and among themselves, with dire consequences against the safety and peace of the human race.

This situation arises from human misjudgments, and it is not the wish of God (SWT) that human beings should continue to live in endless strife. God says,

> O mankind! We have indeed created you from a male and a female, and made you nations and tribes that you may come to know one another. Truly the noblest of you in the sight of God is the most God-fearing among you. Truly God is Knower, Aware.[2]

Calling to faith and belief in God is a task for every Muslim, but the verse of the Holy Qur'an quoted above suffices a believer to live in the plurality of a multi-race, multi-faith, and multi-creed world. The multiplying effect of everyone's being kind and considerate to his neighbor does not only manifest in abounding love but also in societal peace and tranquility. This duty is so incumbent on us that the Prophet Muhammad ﷺ was narrated by Aisha and Ibn Umar to have said:

> Gabriel kept on recommending me about treating the neighbors in a kind and polite manner, so much so that I thought that he would order (me) to make them (my) heirs.[3]

Loving one's neighbors presumes kindness and generosity, which God (SWT) has decreed as an ordinary obligation from an individual to all and sundry people. It follows that this obligation is even more mandatory in the case of a neighbor. God says,

> And worship God, and associate nothing with Him. Be kind to parents, and near kindred, and to orphans, and to the needy, and to the neighbor who is near, and to the neighbor who is a stranger, and to the friend at your side, and to the wayfarer, and to what your right hands own. Surely God loves not the conceited, and the boastful.[4]

---

2. Qur'an: Sura al-Hujurat 49:13, Royal Aal al-Bayt Institute Translation.
3. See Sahih Bukhari, vol. 8, bk. 73, no. 44, and Sahih Muslim, bk. 32, no. 6354.
4. Al-Qur'an: Sura an-Nisa' 4:36, Royal Aal al-Bayt Institute Translation.

Several Hadith of the Prophet Muhammad ﷺ point to the rights that are due to a neighbor and the care that is due in dealing with him. The Prophet is reported to have said that "the first two opponents on the Day of Judgment are two neighbors."[5] He would frequently admonish his companions that when they made broth, they should add water to it and give it to members of the neighbors' households. And it is narrated by Abdullah bin Amr bin Al-As (may God be pleased with him) that once when a ewe was slaughtered and cooked in the house of the Prophet, he asked his household, "Did you give a part of it as present to our Jewish neighbor?"

The foregoing verses of the Qur'an and sayings of the Prophet Muhammad ﷺ clearly demonstrate the stance of Islam regarding the rights of the neighbor. Loving one's neighbor is not a matter of privilege but a divinely ordained duty. Even with the burden of a cantankerous neighbor, the Prophet once stated, "There is not to be any causing of harm, nor is there to be any reciprocating of harm."[6] This instruction demonstrates how accommodating God and His Prophet want us to be with regard to our neighbors.

A graphic illustration is taken from a particular experience of the Prophet Muhammad ﷺ himself. He had a neighbor who was in the habit of pelting him with objects and throwing things in his way whenever he went out for his five daily prayers. It so happened that one day the Prophet passed by the home of this neighbor, but he was not pelted with objects as usual. The man was not even there. Upon enquiry the Prophet learned that the man was sick, and he went into the man's home to wish him well. The neighbor was very surprised, as he had never thought he could be a recipient of the Prophet's good wishes. Then and there, he embraced Islam.

Islam does not foreclose the establishment of good relations with people whose disposition and attitudes may even appear inimical to our interests. God (SWT) says,

God does not forbid you in regard to those who did not wage war against you on account of religion and did not expel you from your homes, that you should treat them kindly and deal with them justly. Assuredly God loves the just.[7]

---

5. Recorded by Ahmad ibn Hanbal in al-Musnad, no. 4/151.
6. Recorded in Imam Malik's Al-Muwatta, no. 31.
7. Al-Qur'an: Sura al-Mumtahanah 60:8, Royal Aal al-Bayt Institute Translation.

The events of September 11, 2001, have continued to influence the attitude of Western nations and their citizens against persons from Islamic countries or those having Muslim identities. This negative attitude is not merely hearsay; I have myself experienced less-than-dignifying treatment from overzealous security operators at an airport near Washington, D.C. And many Muslims are stigmatized and avoided like plagues in their neighborhoods. For the actions of some miscreants, a whole faith, a revealed religion, and its adherents continue to be exposed to ridicule, hatred, and contempt. It is in the light of this situation that one can see the necessity of the "Common Word" initiative at this point in time.

Directives abound from the Holy Qur'an and the Hadith of the Holy Prophet which serve to guide the affairs of a Muslim in his interaction with his Lord, with fellow Muslims, with people of other revealed religions, and with polytheists and atheists. God (SWT) says in the Holy Qur'an 6:38 that nothing was left untouched in the Book. The actions of a few who follow their own whims and caprices should therefore not be foisted on Islam or its peace-loving adherents.

I enjoin us all as stakeholders in this initiative to approach all the issues with an open heart and ample courage to state the truth on the basis of righteous values and principles. May it please God that the intractable conflicts between people of our two faiths will now see some landmark solutions, ushering in a new era of harmonious co-existence among all peoples, with us as witnesses.

PART III

Christian Perspectives

God Is Love:
Biblical and Theological Reflections on a Foundational Christian Claim

MIROSLAV VOLF

For Christians, the statement "God is love" comes as close as any three words can to giving a "definition" of God. The phrase is short, but the "object" it describes is immense — infinite as well as related to every finite thing and to all finite things together. How does one write anything meaningful on such an enormous topic in the space of a few short pages? The challenge is increased given that I am writing in the context of dialogue between Muslims and Christians about the "Common Word" initiative, which is to say in a tension-filled theological space of wrestling to understand and articulate similarities of as well as differences between these two faiths with regard to what it means to love God and neighbor. To avoid overloading these pages with dense elaborations, I will limit myself to a few brief and inescapably inadequate remarks.

What do Christians mean when they say that God is love? To answer this question briefly it is best, I believe, to go back to the scriptural text in which that phrase originally occurs: 1 John 4:7-12.

> Beloved, let us love one another, because love is from God; everyone who loves is born of God and knows God. Whoever does not love does not know God, for God is love. God's love was revealed among us in this way: God sent his only Son into the world so that we might live through him. In this is love, not that we loved God but that he loved us and sent his Son to be the atoning sacrifice for our sins. Beloved, since God loved us so much, we also ought to love one another. No one has

125

ever seen God; if we love one another, God lives in us, and his love is perfected in us.

Differences and Stumbling Blocks

Properly understood, this text sums up the whole of the Christian faith. As it turns out, it also names a number of Christian convictions on which there are major differences between Christians and Muslims. Some may suggest that it is unwise to discuss in an interfaith setting a text which mentions these controversial Christian convictions in such a blunt way. But failing to discuss them will not make them disappear from the Scriptures or from the hearts of its Christian readers. Sweeping the distinctiveness of our respective faiths under the rug is mostly a form of (unintentional) falsehood and (well-meaning) dissimulation. Nothing good can come of it. Instead, motivated by care for those of other faiths as well as for the common good, we should bring those differences (as well as similarities) into the open, work to understand them accurately, present them without unnecessary stumbling blocks, and learn from each other.

Admittedly, the very designation of Jesus Christ as "the Son" and the description of God as sending "his only Son" is a major stumbling block to Muslims. The Qur'ān considers anyone who calls Jesus the "offspring of God" to resemble *kāfirs* (infidels) from the past (Surat al-Tawba 9:30). Most Muslims hear in the phrase "Son of God" a blasphemous claim that Jesus Christ was the offspring of a carnal union between God and a woman and that he is therefore an "associate" of God.

From the Christian point of view, this is a major misunderstanding — but unfortunately one whose force many Muslims feel at a psychologically deep level. Christians unambiguously and emphatically reject any notion that Jesus Christ, let alone the eternal Son, is the offspring of a carnal union between God and a creature, and they reject equally the notion that the eternal Son is God's "associate." In the Scriptures, "the Son" (as in "the Son of God") is a *metaphor* for the particular closeness of Jesus Christ, the incarnate Word, to God and his special status as revealer of God (see Matthew 11:25-27; John 14:9). In later tradition, "the Son" (as in "God, the Son") is again a *metaphor* expressing the conviction that the Word, which was with God from eternity (John 1:1), is not some lesser divinity associated with God but is of the same "substance" with God and therefore belongs to the very being of the one and unique God. The irony of this particular stumbling block is that Christians not only don't mean by "Son of God" what most Muslims fear they do mean, but that Christians actually use the phrase to oppose what most Muslims fear it expresses!

The comments on 1 John 4:7-12 that follow will be robustly theological rather than strictly exegetical; they are informed by an overarching reading of the Scripture as a whole, as well as by a set of Christian convictions developed by great Christian teachers on the basis of such an overarching reading of the Scripture. They are less in line with approaches of modern exegetes operating with a historical-critical method than they are with the style of interpreting that ancient commentators and church leaders such as St. Augustine (354-410) and Martin Luther (1483-1546) practiced.

Divine Being

The pivot of our text and the pivot of the whole of the Christian faith is the simple claim that God is love,[1] or, as St. Gregory of Nazianzus puts it more poetically, that God's "name is love."[2] Both the author of 1 John and his readers embrace this claim with such powerful conviction that he can introduce it in a mere subordinate clause (though he will repeat it again in a main clause only a few sentences later [v. 16]). To say "God is love" is not a static way of saying that God loves. Clearly, the author affirmed that God does love; he states so explicitly twice in our text (vv. 10, 11) and many times in the whole epistle! Indeed, a major thrust of our text is that God loves — actively (God is engaged with humanity so that "we may live" [v. 9]) and abundantly (out of love God sends "his only Son" [v. 9], which is to say God's own very self).

The claim that God *is* love says more, however, than only that God loves. It names the character of God's being, not merely the nature of God's activity toward the world. It describes the divine Fountain from which the river of divine love flows. God's very being is love — so much so

1. For a recent (2005) account of the whole of the Christian faith through the lens of the statement that "God is love," see the first encyclical letter of Pope Benedict XVI, *Deus Caritas Est* (http://www.vatican.va/holy_father/benedict_xvi/encyclicals/documents/hf_ben-xvi _enc_20051225_deus-caritas-est_en.html).

2. St. Gregory of Nazianzus, *Select Orations*, trans. Martha Vinson (Washington, D.C.: The Catholic University of America Press, 2003), 40.

that the great church father St. Augustine could, maybe a bit too daringly, invert the claim and write: "Love is God."[3] Not just any kind of love, of course, and not love as mere inter-human activity, as though Augustine had anticipated Ludwig Feuerbach, the great nineteenth-century critic of religion whose method consisted in transmuting all claims about God into claims about humanity.[4] But love properly understood *is* God and God *is* properly understood love.

The relationship between God's being and God's activity is a complicated matter — in one important sense "God is" and "God loves" are identical[5] — and does not need to occupy us here. It will suffice to note one momentous consequence of the claim that God's active loving of humanity is rooted in God's being as love. Since the eternal God *is* love, God loves irrespective of the existence or nonexistence of creation; as the Gospel of John puts it, God loved the "Son" before the world began (17:24). If God's love were in any way tied to the creation, then the creation would be necessary for God to be love. But creation is not necessary for God, and God does not become love with creation's coming into being. Instead, the contingent world is created *by* a God who always is love and *just because* God is love.

Commenting on 1 John 4:9, the Protestant reformer John Calvin (1509-64) writes:

> If you ask why the world has been created, why we have been placed in it to rule over the earth, why we are preserved in life to enjoy innumerable blessings, why we are endued with light and understanding, no other reason can be given except the free love of God.[6]

3. See Saint Augustine, Bishop of Hippo, *Homilies on the Gospel According to St. John, and His First Epistle*, vol. 29, Library of Fathers of the Holy Catholic Church (Oxford: J. H. Parker, 1848), homily 7, notes 4-5, p. 1182. Karl Barth, probably the greatest twentieth-century theologian, issues a warning: "If we say with 1 John 4 that God is love, the obverse that love is God is forbidden until it is mediated and clarified from God's being and therefore from God's act what the love is which can and must be legitimately identified with God" (Karl Barth, *Church Dogmatics* [hereafter *CD*] II/1, trans. T. H. L. Parker et al. [Edinburgh: T&T Clark, 1957], 276).

4. Ludwig Feuerbach, *The Essence of Christianity*, Great Books in Philosophy (Buffalo, N.Y: Prometheus Books, 1989).

5. So Karl Barth (*CD* II/1, 283) from the perspective of understanding God's being as act (257-72).

6. John Calvin, *1 John*, The Crossway Classic Commentaries (Wheaton, Ill.: Crossway Books, 1998), 79.

Similarly, the great Christian mystic Julian of Norwich (1342-1416) grounds creation in God's love:

> And in this love he has done all his works, and in this love he has made all things profitable to us, and in this love our life is everlasting. In our creation we had beginning, but the love in which he created us was in him from without beginning. In this love we have our beginning, and all this shall we see in God without end.[7]

The whole creation — everything that is not God — comes into existence on account of and within an already existing field of God's love, which defines the very being of God. As a character of God's being, God's love is as eternal as God is.

So God is love, and consequently God loves creatures; God is love, and consequently God's love is prior to there being any creature. But who is it that God loves prior to creation? The object of God's pre-creation love cannot be different from God's own very self. But is God's love — God's self-love — then still properly to be called *love?*

Divine Differentiation

Many Christian theologians through the centuries have seen a close connection between the claim that God *is* love and the claim that God is the Holy Trinity. Love implies, indeed requires, an object; "to love" is a transitive verb. If love is an essential attribute of God independent of the existence of everything that is not God, how could God be love if God were not, precisely as One God, somehow also differentiated in God's own being? Our text gestures at divine differentiation in that it names two actors in the drama of God's love for the world: God and God's Son (for Christians *not* an "offspring" or an "associate," as I have said earlier and as will be clear also from what I say below). Our text itself is pre-Trinitarian, but to make proper sense of it we need to presuppose that God is the Holy Trinity — in relation to the world as well as in God's own being apart from the world.

---

7. Julian of Norwich, *Showings,* trans. Edmund Colledge and James Walsh (New York: Paulist, 1978), 342-43.

Before exploring the relation between love and the triunity of the One God, it is important, especially in the context of a dialogue between Muslims and Christians, to state plainly what Christians do and do not mean when they say that God is triune. First, God is *uncompromisingly one.* For Christians to affirm God's triunity is *not* to deny God's unity. In the first Christian centuries, all the intense and intricate debates about the Trinity were carried on precisely because the church fathers refused to compromise on the unity of God. Jesus, after all, affirmed the signature confession of his own Jewish people: "The Lord our God, the Lord is one" (Mark 12:29). Either God is one, or there is no God. By definition, anything of which there can be two, or three, or more cannot be God in the proper sense of that term. Because God's oneness was so important to the great Christian thinkers, many of them insisted that the three divine "hypostases" subsist in a single, numerically identical and non-multipliable divine essence.

Second, God is *utterly unique.* God alone is God. All else that exists is non-God. Moreover, there is a categorical, not merely a quantitative or even qualitative, difference between God and the world. God is not a member in a common household of being with other entities in the world. The text we are considering expresses this thought with a simple claim: "No one has ever seen God" (1 John 4:12). The reason why no one has seen God isn't that people have not looked hard enough or that they could not get to a place from which it would be possible to spot God; rather, God is such that God cannot be seen with physical eyes at all. As St. Augustine says, "not with the eye but with the heart must He be sought";[8] and the condition of seeing God with the eye of the heart is a transformation of the whole person to be "like God" (1 John 3:2).

Third, God is *beyond number.*[9] This affirmation follows from God's categorical uniqueness. It is impossible to count God as one among many other things that can be counted — all different things in the world plus one more object, maybe the biggest of them all and containing them all, called God. So when we say that there is only one God, we don't mean it in the same sense as when we say that there is only one sun or even only one

8. Augustine, *Homilies,* homily 7, note 10, p. 1186.

9. See Denys Turner, "The 'Same' God: Is There an 'Apophatic' Solution, or, Who's to Know?" (paper presented at God and Human Flourishing Consultation, Yale Center for Faith & Culture, New Haven, Conn., 2009).

universe. Similarly, great theologians of the past believed that it is impossible, strictly speaking, to count *in* God — naming one after another, as discrete "objects," all the different "things" that are in God. So when we say that there are "three" hypostases in God, we don't mean it in the same way as when we say that Jesus took three disciples with him to the mount of Transfiguration. All human language about God, including language about God's oneness and triunity, is inadequate. Both the talk of "one" and of "three" is analogous when applied to God.

If the One God is utterly unique and beyond number, why do Christians then speak of divine triunity? Christians believe that the Word was made flesh in Jesus Christ (see John 1:1-18; 1 John 4:2-3). From this belief, it follows that the one, utterly unique God, who is beyond all counting, is internally differentiated as the Speaker, the Word, and the Breath (as we might express the divine triunity on the basis of John 1:1, which reads: "In the beginning was the Word, and the Word was with God, and the Word was God"). In speaking about God's sending God's Son, our text employs names more usual in the New Testament and in the tradition: "Father" and "Son," to which "Holy Spirit" is added on the basis of other texts and weighty dogmatic considerations. The designations may differ, but what they designate remains the same: They name the internal differentiation of the One God, who is beyond number and categorically different from everything else, which is not God.

How is the internal differentiation of the One God related to the claim that God is love? If God's being were *not* internally differentiated, how would we be able to say (1) that God *is* love in God's own eternal being, and (2) that God loves apart from God's relation to the world (because the world is contingent rather than necessary)? We could not. Without internal differentiation, God would love simply God's own self and be more properly described as Self-Love than as Love. As an incomparable and unique unity, however, God is an internally differentiated unity: there is "other" in the One God. And because there is "other" in God, there can be genuine love — love that does not merely affirm and celebrate the self, but love that gives to the other and receives from the other.[10] "You see a

---

10. There are significant Christian theologians who do not think that it is proper to speak of mutual love between the persons of the Trinity. A recent prominent exponent of this view is Karl Rahner, *The Trinity*, trans. Joseph Donceel (New York: Crossroad, 1998), 106.

Trinity if you see charity," wrote St. Augustine in his justly famous book on the Holy Trinity.[11]

The First Love

Because God is the Holy Trinity, God's eternal love is self-giving love rather than self-centered love. Consequently, God's love for humanity is a freely given love rather than a love motivated by the benefits that the object of love holds for the one who loves it. The one true God does not need anything from humans, but exists as self-complete and yet not self-enclosed plenitude of self-giving and other-receiving love. This circulating love, which is identical with the being of the One God, is the source of the world — the creaturely and therefore radically different other of God — and all its benefits.

If the eternal God *is* love in God's own self and in relation to creation, an important consequence follows: God's love is not a reactive love. And that takes us straight back to our text. "In this is love, not that we loved God but that he loved us" (1 John 4:10). A few verses later St. John writes that God's love is always "first" (v. 19), never second. St. Paul makes a similar point at the pinnacle of his epistle to the Romans: God never gives "in return" (Romans 11:35). So God's love is always the first love; it is never simply a response to the character or behavior of things that are "outside" God. It cannot be otherwise if love is the very being of the eternal God.

In his *Heidelberg Disputation* the great Protestant reformer Martin Luther famously, though a bit too sharply, contrasted God's love for creatures and human love: "The love of God does not find, but creates, that which is pleasing to it. The love of man comes into being through that which is pleasing to it."[12] For humans, mostly, an encounter with what is pleasing *elicits* love; we experience something lovable — eating a gourmet meal, viewing a beautiful work of art, holding a newborn baby — and love is born in us. With God it is different, Luther claimed. Objects do not elicit God's love by their qualities; God's love creates objects together with their

11. Augustine, *The Trinity*, trans. Edmund Hill (Brooklyn: New City, 1991), 8, 12.

12. See Martin Luther, *Luther's Works*, ed. Harold J. Grimm and Jaroslav Pelikan (Philadelphia: Fortress Press, 1957), vol. 31, sec. 28, p. 57.

qualities. And if God does not find what is pleasing in an object — if human beings have become un-godly — God does not abandon the object in disgust until it changes its character. Instead, God seeks to re-create it to become lovable again.

God loved us "first" — before we loved God. This theme is common in the Old Testament. God's love is not elicited by any special virtues of the people of Israel (Deuteronomy 7:7-8). Even more radically, according to the prophet Hosea, God's love remains first notwithstanding Israel's vices (11:1-11). The New Testament picks up and highlights the strand in the Old Testament that speaks of God's love notwithstanding human abandonment of God. In Romans, St. Paul writes of God's love for the "weak," the "ungodly," the "sinners," the "enemies" (5:6-10). Similarly, St. John underscores that out of love God sent Jesus Christ into the world not just "that we might live through him" (1 John 4:9) but, most pointedly, to be "the atoning sacrifice for our sins" (v. 10) and the sin of the whole world (2:2). God's love is "first" even toward sinners, the ungodly, the wrongdoers, and is not in any sense a response to anything they do — to their movement toward God or their emergent love of God.[13]

Infinite Love

For the most part, Muslims and Christians disagree about whether or not Christ died on the cross,[14] and if he did, whether he died as the atoning sacrifice for the sin of humanity. Here isn't the place to discuss this important issue. As our interest is in the meaning of the phrase "God is love," I

13. Some scholars argue that in 1 John the world is not the object of God's love (as in St. John's Gospel [3:16]) but only its showplace (Luise Schottroff, *Der Glaube und die feindliche Welt* [Neukirchen-Vluyn: Neukirchner Verlag, 1970], 287). But this argument does not take sufficiently into account the consequences of the fact that even if it were true that in 1 John God's love extends only to the community of faith, God still loves them *notwithstanding* their sin. This "notwithstanding-character" of God's love effectively would make particularism of loving some people but not others utterly arbitrary. Moreover, as Raymond Brown pointed out, "That the world has to be more than a showplace we see from 4:14 where 1 John speaks of Jesus as the 'Savior of the world'" (Raymond Brown, *The Epistles of John* [Garden City, N.Y.: Doubleday, 1982], 518).

14. But see Joseph Cumming, "Did Jesus Die on the Cross?" (paper presented at the Yale Center for Faith & Culture's Reconciliation Program, New Haven, Conn., May 2001), http://www.yale.edu/faith/rc/rc-rp.htm.

shall explore what Christ's atoning sacrifice implies about the character of God's love.[15]

First, God's love is *immeasurable*. "We know love by this, that he laid down his life for us" (1 John 3:16). Similarly, in St. John's Gospel, Jesus, addressing his disciples, says: "No one has greater love than this, to lay down one's life for one's friends" (John 15:13). The greatest human love is a window into the infinity of divine love.

Second, God's love is *utterly gratuitous* and therefore *completely unconditional*. God does not love only those who are worthy of God's love, but loves all people, without any distinction.[16] As Jesus Christ said according to St. Matthew's Gospel, God "makes his sun rise [both] on the evil and on the good" (5:45).

Third, God's love is *universal*. The One God is the God of all humanity; therefore the love that God is, is the love for all humanity, irrespective of any differences or divisions that exist between human beings. Absolutely no one is excluded and no deed is imaginable that would exclude anyone from God's love (though if there prove to be irredeemable wrongdoers — those who insist on transgressing against love — they will be excluded from "heaven" as God's world of love[17] not despite but because God's love is universal).

---

15. It is crucial both to connect and to distinguish (1) God's eternal love apart from God's relation to the world and (2) God's love as manifest in overcoming the sin of the world. If we disconnect them, we lose the unity of the divine being. If we equate them, we project conditions of finitude and sin into the being of God. There is only one love of God, and it takes on a certain character in encounter with human sin. Thus we can speak of two forms of the one divine love. The first form of God's love — love of the eternal God apart from the world — is self-giving and mutually glorifying love. The second form of God's love — love of that same eternal God toward creatures — is in part a self-sacrificing love, and it is the response of the God of love to human sin and enmity toward God. The first form of love is basic, and it leads to the second form of love under the conditions of human sin. Not to differentiate adequately between the two forms of the one divine love is one of the most fundamental problems in the work of the great Catholic theologian Hans Urs von Balthasar (see on this Linn Tonstad, "Trinity, Hierarchy, and Difference: Mapping the Christian Imaginary" [Ph.D. diss., Yale University, 2009], 65-135).

16. On God's love as unconditional and indiscriminate see Miroslav Volf, *Free of Charge: Giving and Forgiving in a Culture Stripped of Grace* (Grand Rapids: Zondervan, 2006).

17. This is, I take it, the main thrust of the somewhat mysterious saying about the "mortal sin" about which one should not pray and about God's not giving life to those who commit it (1 John 5:16).

Fourth, God's love is *indiscriminately forgiving* of every person and for every deed. God isn't just generous even to the unrighteous; God also forgives their unrighteousness so as to lead them through repentance back to the good they have abandoned. "If we confess our sins, he who is faithful and just will forgive us our sins and cleanse us from all unrighteousness" (1 John 1:9).

Finally, the *goal* of God's love is — *love*. It cannot be otherwise if God, as the source and goal of everything, is love. The term 1 John uses to express this goal is "communion" (1:3): communion of human beings with God — indeed, mutual indwelling of God and human beings (4:13-15) — and communion of human beings with one another (1:7).

Love and Judgment

That God's love is immeasurable, unconditional, universal, and forgiving is but the consequence of the simple fact that God *is* love. Is then the all-loving God indifferent to human sin, condoning of ungodliness and wrongdoing? No, God is not indifferent to ungodliness and wrongdoing. The whole epistle distinguishes sharply between light and darkness (1 John 2:8), love and hatred (2:9-10), truth and lie (2:21), justice and unrighteousness, good and evil (3:12), God and devil (3:10), Christ and antichrist (2:22-23), life and death (2:25). It does not come as a surprise, therefore, that just a few verses after our text St. John writes about God's *judgment* (4:17-18).

How is God's love related to God's judgment? The same divine love has different effects on people, depending on the basic orientation of their being and the moral character of their deeds. When we do what is right (basically, when we love), we experience God's love as delight and approval, as God's face "shining on us." When we do what is evil (basically, when we are indifferent or hate), we experience God's love as wrath and condemnation. Why wrath and condemnation? Not because God does not love us, but so that the loving God can return us to the good from which we have fallen.[18]

---

18. In the Christian tradition a distinction is often made between person and work: God loves the person, but not the work (if the work is sinful). Augustine puts the same idea, now applied to human love, this way: "Love not in the man his error, but the man: for the

Whether God is angry with us or delights in us, whether God approves of us or condemns us, God loves us with the same unchanging divine love rooted in, and indeed identical with, the very being of God. That is why those who "remain in love" and thereby remain "in God" have "confidence" in the day of judgment and need not fear (4:17-18).

Identifying God

What are the consequences of the claim that God is love for the knowledge of God? One consequence is obvious: From a Christian point of view, those who do deny that God is love do not know God properly. Martin Luther was deeply concerned with rightly identifying the character of God as love; indeed, one can say that, theologically and spiritually, the Protestant Reformation was greatly about the struggle over the proper understanding of God's character as love.[19]

Luther resisted vigorously — sometimes overzealously, I might add — two *false* forms of "knowing" God, both of which, he believed, entailed denial that God is love. First is the straightforward belief that God is ill-disposed toward human beings as sinners, that God hates them on account of their sin. That cannot be true, Luther insisted, because God is love. God cannot but love sinners and precisely because God loves them hate their sin. The second false opinion about God, which is just another version of the first, is that God is "favorably disposed toward me because of my efforts and works."[20] To come to God with one's noble deeds and good works expecting God's love in return is to commit three mistakes in one — mistakes about (1) human beings and their good deeds (by claiming as their possession what is in fact a gift from God); (2) God's character (by denying that God "is nothing but love"[21]); and (3) God's love (by contesting that God's love is such that it cannot be earned, that it comes utterly "without cost"[22]).

---

man God made, the error the man himself made. Love that which God made, love not that which the man himself made" (*Homilies*, homily 7, n. 11).

19. See, for instance, Simo Peura, "What God Gives Man Receives: Luther on Salvation," in *Union with Christ: The New Finnish Interpretation of Luther,* ed. Carl E. Braaten and Robert W. Jenson (Grand Rapids: Eerdmans, 1998), 76-95.

20. Luther, *Luther's Works*, vol. 30, p. 293.

21. Luther, *Luther's Works*, vol. 30, p. 293.

22. Luther, *Luther's Works*, vol. 30, p. 294.

Even though Luther was a fierce proponent of the idea that unconditional love describes the very being of God, he still did not think Jews and Muslims — not just fellow Catholic Christians — who, as he saw it, disagreed with him on this point, worshiped a false God. In his *Large Catechism* he insisted that Jews and Muslims do "believe in, and worship, only one true God," even if they do not "know what His mind towards them is,"[23] which is to say, even if they, according to his understanding of their faiths, do not believe that God's love toward them is utterly unconditional.[24] Those who deny that God is sheer love do not therefore worship a false God. Instead, they (partly) falsely describe the one true God. That was a grave enough problem for Luther — for not to believe and therefore not to trust that God is gracious to you is for you *not to have* a gracious God! But even he did not claim that those who (like himself) affirm the unconditionality of God's love and those who deny the unconditionality of God's love (Catholics, Jews, and Muslims) therefore do not believe in the same God! That he did not do so is all the more surprising, given that his views of both Muslims and Jews were famously and very disturbingly negative.

Knowing God — Loving Neighbor

The entire text of 1 John 4:7-12 assumes the importance of identifying the character of God rightly, but its main concern lies elsewhere — not in the way we think about God, but in the way we behave toward neighbors. "Everyone who loves is born of God and knows God" (4:7), which implies that everyone who does not love neighbor is not born of God. Why does it not suffice to love God? The reason is simple: God's love is not a love that remains contained within the Godhead but flows out toward creatures. Any human love that would lay claim to being "from God" and being like God's love must flow toward others, toward neighbors. A love simply returned to

---

23. Martin Luther, *Large Catechism* (Philadelphia: Muhlenberg, 1959), 63.

24. Notice that Luther did not believe that God's attitude of utterly unconditional love is limited to Christians. It extends to all people, even those who do not believe that God has such an attitude toward them (see Christoph Schwöbel, "The Same God? — The Perspective of Faith, the Identity of God, Tolerance and Dialogue" [paper presented at the God and Human Flourishing Consultation, Yale Center for Faith & Culture, New Haven, Conn., 2009], 16).

God is very much unlike divine love. Love passed on to the neighbor is like God's love. That is why everyone who is born of God loves, and everyone who loves is born of God. The point can be put tersely: no love of neighbor, no birth from God.

Similarly, no love of neighbor, no knowledge of God.[25] "Whoever does not love does not know God" (1 John 4:7). We can have accurate information about God, and we can also affirm as true all the accurate information about God we have, but still not know God. To know God it is not enough to give cognitive assent to truth about God; we must "do the truth" (1:6), we must act as God acts, be as God is (though, of course, always mindful of God's radical difference from creatures!). God is not known where neighbor is not loved. Knowledge of God is tied to affinity with God in who humans are and how they act.[26]

St. Augustine pushed the connection between love of neighbor and knowledge of God even a bit further. Commenting on verse 7 he wrote: "Whosoever therefore violates charity, let him say what he will with his tongue" — let him say all the right things about who Christ is and what the nature of God is — he still denies Christ and is therefore "an antichrist" and "acts against God."[27] Not to love neighbor is not just not to know God; it is actually to *deny* God. Clearly, Augustine believed, it is worse for concrete *deeds* toward neighbor to be misaligned with the character of God, than for *thoughts* about God to be misaligned with the character of God. If Augustine is correct in this assessment, the consequences for Christians' relation to non-Christians are astounding: non-believers or adherents of another religion, if they love, can be closer to God than Christians notwithstanding Christians' formally correct *beliefs* about God or even explicit, outward faith in Jesus Christ![28]

---

25. As Judith Lieu insists rightly in her fine commentary on 1 John, our text insists on "absolute nonnegotiability of love as the defining characteristic of those who would claim to know God" (Judith M. Lieu, *I, II, & III John. A Commentary* [Louisville: Westminster John Knox, 2008], 179).

26. This thought may be somewhat difficult. It may be made plausible if we reflect that one may not really know a person without in some sense participating in his or her projects. Max Scheler has plausibly advocated this idea. "The person of another can only be disclosed to me by my *joining in the performance* of his acts, either cognitively, by 'understanding' and vicarious 're-living', or morally, by 'following in his footsteps'" (*The Nature of Sympathy,* trans. Peter Heath [Hamden, Conn.: Archon, 1970], 167).

27. Augustine, *Homilies,* homily 7, n. 2, p. 1180, and n. 5, p. 1183.

28. Raymond Brown correctly claims that "the author's negative statement (4:8a), 'One

This elevation of deeds above beliefs and attitudes is the consequence of the claim that God is love. God loves, therefore those who know and love God must love their neighbors; God is love, therefore those who are born of God must "be" love — delighting and correcting love, supporting and resting love, and at all times benevolent, beneficent, and actively caring love.

Coming to Know God

But how can one come to know God properly? How can one come to act as God acts and be as God is? "Beloved, let us love one another, because love is from God" (1 John 4:7).[29] At one level, coming to act as God acts is a matter of obedience to a command. The statement I quoted is an exhortation — "let us" — but it has the force of a command (see 3:23). Love is from God, God is love; therefore we ought to love! The command, which concerns primarily actions, is appropriate, since indeed human beings ought to align their actions with those of their Creator, in whose image they are made. But the command is also insufficient. It fails to give what those who are to love need the most — sufficient motivation and power actually to obey and to love.

"Beloved, since God loved us so much, we also ought to love one another" (v. 11). At another and deeper level, coming to act as God acts is a matter of seeing who God is and how God has acted in loving humanity — immeasurably, unconditionally, universally, indiscriminately, forgivingly. God is a model of who human beings should be and how therefore they

who does not love has known nothing of God,' places the secessionists (against whom it is aimed) on the same level as 'the Jews' of John 16:3 who 'never knew the Father' and as the world which 'never knew [recognized] God' (1 John 3:1e)" (*The Epistles of John* [Garden City, N.Y.: Doubleday, 1982], 549). The statement in 4:8 is more general and applies more broadly than just to secessionists.

29. The command is directed to fellow believers and urges them to love one another. But this command is not simply a group-specific one. If God's love encompasses all, then all human beings are commanded to love, and they are commanded to love all human beings. This does not exclude the possibility that there can be group-specific and person-specific divine commands, a group's or individual's specific "callings" (see Robert M. Adams, "Vocation," *Faith and Philosophy* 4/4 [1987]: 448-63. See also Michael Wassenaar, "Four Types of Calling: The Ethics of Vocation in Kierkegaard, Brunner, Scheler and Barth" [Ph.D. diss., Yale University, 2009], 27-37).

should act. This takes us back to Luther's concern: If we ought to be as God is, it matters that we identify rightly who God is — in particular, who God is toward us. Hence the pervasive concern with the "right doctrine" in the epistle. Understanding properly who God is and how God loves us motivates us to love neighbors. At this second level, we come to know God in that we see, we are moved, and we seek to become like.

In the first and second ways of coming to know God — obedience to a command and imitation of an example — the relationship between God and us is an external one: we listen and obey, we observe and imitate. In the third way the relationship between God and us is more intimate — not one of spatial and temporal distance, but one of internal presence. It concerns both our being and our acting in their unity. "If we love one another, God lives in us," says our text (v. 12). A few verses later we read: "God is love, and those who abide in love abide in God, and God abides in them" (v. 16). Indwelled by God, we are conformed to God and act like God.

Having still in mind command and imitation as the first and second ways of doing the truth and being in the truth and so knowing God, we might be tempted to conclude that God will live in us *if* we show sufficient diligence in loving our neighbors. But that would be to turn things on their head. It would also make God's active love for us dependent on our love and therefore be to deny the gratuity of God's love and, in a sense, the very being of God.

Consider first that *all* love is "from God" (v. 7) — God is its ultimate source, not we ourselves or any creature. If we love, it is not because we have generated love ourselves, say, by deciding to imitate how God acts in Jesus Christ. If we love, it is only because God has somehow engendered love in us (say, by means of observing how God acted in Christ). Consider second that "God is love" (v. 8). When God gives love, God does not give something that God has, but something that God is. So the way God gives love is by giving God's own very self. God comes to "live in us," as our text says (v. 12). Love of neighbors is not the condition of God's presence in us; God's presence in us is the condition of love of neighbors. Living in us, God shapes the very character of our selves so that we can be and act in conformity with God. Love of neighbor is a *sign* of God's presence — a sign more sure than any other. Where genuine love is, God is there.

140

Manifestation of God

Ordinary love between ordinary human beings is a visible manifestation of the invisible God! God, whom no one can see, can in fact be seen — if we know how and where to look. St. Augustine writes eloquently about proper and improper ways to "see" God:

> But let no man imagine God to himself according to the lust of his eyes. For so he makes unto himself either a huge form, or a certain in-calculable magnitude which, like the light which he sees with the bodily eyes, he makes extend through all directions; field after field of space he gives it all the bigness he can; or, he represents to himself like as it were an old man of venerable form. None of these things do thou imagine. There is something thou mayest imagine, if thou wouldest see God; *God is love.* What sort of face hath love? what form hath it? what stature? what feet? what hands hath it? no man can say. And yet it hath feet, for these carry men to church: it hath hands; for these reach forth to the poor: it hath eyes; for thereby we consider the needy.[30]

When we encounter active love, when we give it and receive it, the invisible and unique God, who dwells in inapproachable light, becomes "visible" in the world — visible not to the physical eye, not even to the intellectual eye, but to the spiritual eye.

For Christians, all manifestations of the One God in the ordinariness of neighborly love are strictly speaking but echoes of God's self-manifestation in Jesus Christ. "God's love was revealed among us in this way: God sent his only Son into the world so that we might live through him" (1 John 4:9). The verse parallels a fuller one at the beginning of St. John's Gospel: "No one has ever seen God. It is God the only Son, who is close to the Father's heart, who has made him known" (1:18). As Jesus Christ fed the hungry, healed the sick, embraced the children, feasted with the outcasts; as he announced the nearness of God and preached repentance; as he was crucified as God's Lamb bearing the sin of the world, and as he rose again — in all these acts of love God's love was present, and in his life, the God who is love was fully made known.

---

30. Augustine, *Homilies,* homily 7, n. 10, p. 1186.

Conclusion: Six Theses

For Christians:

(1) God is love in God's very being apart from God's relation to creation;
(2) God's love of creatures is an expression of God's being and is therefore always "first" and utterly unconditional;
(3) We know that God is love and how God is through Jesus Christ, the unconditional love of God enacted in history;
(4) We ought to love our neighbors in a way that echoes in our own creaturely way God's unconditional and universal love for humanity;
(5) To know the God of love we must love neighbors, whoever these neighbors are;
(6) To love, the God who is love and who creates and redeems humanity out of love must engender our love and love through us.

In the Name of God Most High

Understanding the Meaning of Love: Eternal or Temporal? Self-Giving or Gift-Giving?

JOSEPH L. CUMMING

We read in the Holy Bible that "God is love, and those who abide in love abide in God, and God in them" (1 John 4:16).

اَللهُ مَحَبَّةٌ، وَمَنْ يَثْبُتْ فِي الْمَحَبَّةِ، يَثْبُتْ فِي اللهِ وَاللهُ فِيهِ. ¹

Because of this verse, and others like it, Christians believe that God's love is at the very center of their faith. Similarly, we read in the Holy Qur'ān that one of the Beautiful Names of God is *Al-Wadūd,* that is, "The Loving One." However, in the months since the open letter "A Common Word Between Us and You" was published, as well as the Yale Response, "Loving God and Neighbor Together," many Muslims and Christians have asked just exactly what we mean when we speak of the love of God, and whether we mean the same thing. In what follows below, this question will be addressed in relation to two more specific questions — one that has been raised by Muslims, and one that has been raised by Christians.

A question raised by some Muslims is whether love is an eternal, essential quality *(ṣifa)* in God, or whether it is a temporal "quality of act"

1. 1 John 4:16, Arabic Bustānī–Van Dyck translation.

In addition to the questions stated in the title of this paper, another question this paper might have addressed, as it has been raised by many observers, is whether God's love is conditional or unconditional. Because this question has been more than adequately addressed in Miroslav Volf's chapter titled "God Is Love," and indeed in the Yale Response itself, it would be superfluous to address it here.

(ṣifat al-fiʿl). Another way to put this question is whether God has from all eternity been "loving" in God's own self, or whether God is "loving" only in relation to the temporal created order. Many Western Christians are unaware that the distinction between God's "qualities of essence" and God's "qualities of act" is one made not only by Muslim theologians but also by both the Syriac- and Arabic-speaking Christian churches, who make the same distinction between God's qualities of essence and God's qualities of act.

For readers unfamiliar with this distinction, an explanation of these terms will demonstrate why the distinction is important. Qualities of essence are those qualities which have subsisted in God from eternity, without reference to temporal created things. For example, knowledge is a quality of essence, since God has known God's own self from all eternity, regardless of God's knowledge of the created universe that God brought into being in time. On the other hand, qualities of act are those qualities about which we can speak meaningfully only in relation to the temporal universe that God has created. For example, forgiveness is a temporal quality of act, since God forgives only in relation to sinful human beings, who need to be forgiven.[2]

So is God's love a quality of essence or a quality of act? That is, is God's love eternal and uncreated? Most Christians would answer this question with a strong "yes." Before addressing why Christians answer "yes," and what they mean by that "yes," let me address what I understand Muslims to mean by this question.[3]

The mainstream Sunnī theological tradition speaks of seven eternal, essential qualities in God. They are God's knowledge, God's power, God's life, God's word/speech, God's will, God's sight, and God's hearing. According to the Sunnī tradition, these seven qualities are not God's essence, nor are they anything other than God; rather they are uncreated eternal

---

2. This does not imply that God was "*un*forgiving" before creating humankind — only that the idea of forgiveness has meaning only in relation to temporal creatures who need to be forgiven.

3. At the Yale Common Word conference in July 2008, I asked the Muslim scholars present to correct any misunderstandings in what follows. They confirmed that what follows does accurately represent the Sunnī position, which led to an interesting discussion between Sunnī and Shīʿī scholars who were present. I have added here a paragraph on the Shīʿī position as expressed by Jaʿfarī Shīʿī scholars in this discussion. See footnote 14 below for more about this Sunnī-Shīʿī discussion at the conference.

"meanings"[4] subsisting in God's essence. This doctrine was articulated by Abū al-Ḥasan al-Ashʿarī, the famous Muslim theologian from the fourth century A.H./tenth century C.E. So if God's love is not one of these seven qualities, then it seemingly must be a Quality of act. That is, God loves in relation to created things, but perhaps one should not speak of love as a quality subsisting eternally in God. However, as will be seen in a moment, al-Ashʿarī can be interpreted as counting love as an eternal, uncreated quality of essence identical with God's will.

Most Shīʿī theologians would take a slightly different position on this point. They see these qualities of essence rather as being identical with God's essence or as being nothing more than different ways of speaking about God's essence. So whereas a Sunnī theologian might say that "God knows by His Knowledge, which eternally subsists in His Essence," the Shīʿī theologian might say, "God knows by His Knowledge, which *is* His eternal Essence."[5] In any case, in both the Sunnī system and the Shīʿī system, if God's love is a quality of essence, then it is eternal and uncreated, but if it is a quality of act, then it is meaningful only in relation to the temporal created order.

Most Christians hold that God's love is eternal and uncreated in God. They do so partly because of the verse quoted above, which says that "God is love," and also because of a tradition of theological reflection on other texts in the Holy Bible — for example Proverbs 8, which describes the relationship between God and God's wisdom before the creation of the universe, and in God's creation of the universe by God's wisdom.[6] This pas-

---

4. The Arabic word *maʿnā* (literally, "meaning") is a technical term in Islamic theology that, when used by Sunnī theologians, refers to an existent reality, or to the underlying reality of a thing — that is, the reality to which the word describing it points. See Daniel Gimaret, *La Doctrine d'al-Ashʿarī* (Paris: Cerf, 1990), 201ff. et passim; or see Richard M. Frank, "The Ashʿarite Ontology: I Primary Entities," *Arabic Sciences and Philosophy* 9 (Cambridge: Cambridge University Press, 1999), 163-231. See also my article "*Ṣifāt al-Dhāt* in al-Ashʿarī's Doctrine of God and Possible Christian Parallels," pages 5-11, available online at http://yale.edu/faith/downloads/rp/ashʿaripaper.pdf.

5. Cf. Moojan Momen, *An Introduction to Shiʿi Islam: The History and Doctrines of Twelver Shiʿism* (New Haven, Conn.: Yale University Press, 1985), 177. This paragraph focuses on the views of the majority of Twelver (Jaʿfarī) Shīʿa, not those of Ismāʿīlīs or Zaydīs.

6. Modern scholars of the Hebrew Bible interpret this passage in a variety of ways, but I am referencing here not so much the original *Sitz im Leben* of the text as the trajectory of its theological interpretation in the Christian tradition. I am interpreting the verb *qanā* in terms of the parallel verb *ḥolēl*.

sage of Scripture seems to describe the relationship between God and God's wisdom as a relationship of love before the creation of the universe.

Perhaps the most influential Christian thinker in the Western theological tradition is St. Augustine, the fourth-to-fifth century C.E. bishop of Berber ancestry from what is today Algeria. In his book *De Trinitate* ("On the Holy Trinity"), he speaks of the first hypostasis of the Trinity as God's *memoria*,[7] and the second hypostasis of the Trinity as God's understanding/knowledge or word *(intelligentia, verbum)*, and the third hypostasis of the Trinity as the bond of love *(vinculum caritatis, amor)* between God and God's understanding/knowledge/word. Thus in the Western Christian tradition love is understood as having eternally existed within God's essence.

In the Eastern Christian tradition of the Syriac- and Arabic-speaking churches it has been more common to speak of the third hypostasis of the Trinity (the Holy Spirit) as being God's life, noting passages in Scripture and in the creed that refer to God's Spirit as the "giver of life" (ζωοποιητός). Christian thinkers in this tradition often see God's love as being God's essence itself. Indeed, in the twentieth and twenty-first centuries C.E. this Eastern perspective on love as the very essence of God has influenced many Western thinkers as well.[8]

But regardless of whether Christians see God's love as being God's essence itself, or as being a hypostasis or quality subsisting in God's essence, nearly all would agree that God's love is eternal and uncreated. Nearly all would agree that God has loved within God's own self from before the creation of the universe.

As noted earlier, the Sunnī Ash'arite school of thought holds that God has seven eternal qualities of essence — knowledge, power, life, word/speech, will, sight, and hearing. At first glance one might suppose, then, that love is not an eternal quality in God but is a temporal quality of act. But al-Ash'arī's prominent disciple Ibn Fūrak offers us a different understanding of al-Ash'arī.

Ibn Fūrak (d. 406 A.H./1015 C.E.) was one of the leading Ash'arite theologians of his time, and only one generation stood between him and al-Ash'arī himself. In his book *Mujarrad Maqālāt al-Ash'arī* he sets forth

7. In this context Augustine uses the Latin word *memoria* with a meaning closer to the modern English concepts of "self," "consciousness," or "identity" than to the modern English word "memory."

8. Cf., for example, Jürgen Moltmann, *The Crucified God: The Cross of Christ as the Foundation and Criticism of Christian Theology* (London: SCM, 1974).

not his own ideas, but rather the ideas of al-Ashʿarī himself in al-Ashʿarī's own words. Since al-Ashʿarī wrote more than sixty books, and only five of them have survived until today, Ibn Fūrak must also be considered an important primary source on the thought of al-Ashʿarī.[9]

Ibn Fūrak tells us that al-Ashʿarī believed more than one word could be used to refer to the same quality of essence. Thus Ibn Fūrak writes:

وكان يقول إن معنى القادر والقويّ والقدرة والقوّة سواء...وكذلك كان
لا يفرّق بين العلم والدراية والفقه والفهم والفطنة والعقل والحسّ والمعرفة.

[Al-Ashʿarī] used to say that the meaning of Powerful [*qādir*] and Strong [*qawī*] and Power [*qudra*] and Strength [*quwwa*] is the same. . . . Likewise he did not distinguish among Knowledge [*ʿilm*] and Awareness [*dirāya*] and Understanding [*fiqh*] and Comprehension [*fahm*] and Sagacity [*fiṭna*] and Reason [*ʿaql*] and Sense [*ḥiss*] and Cognition [*maʿrifa*].[10]

Regarding God's love, Ibn Fūrak tells us the following about the teachings of al-Ashʿarī:

---

9. Daniel Gimaret argues:

> Je n'ai pas besoin de redire l'intérêt considérable de ce texte: chacun désormais pourra en juger par lui-même. La pensée d'Ašʿarī, certes, ne nous était pas complètement inconnue, du moins pour l'essentiel, grâce en particulier au K. al-Lumaʿ édité par McCarthy. C'était cependant bien peu de chose par rapport à la profusion d'information que nous apporte le Muǧarrad, et le mot de résurrection, en l'occurrence, n'est peut-être pas trop fort. Car, pour ceux qui pourraient encore en douter — tellement le personnage a été victime d'idées fausses — c'est bien l'authentique pensée d'Ašʿarī qui nous est ici restituée dans son intégralité: l'attestent non seulement l'autorité d'Ibn Fūrak, ainsi que les abondantes références aux oeuvres du maître (trente titres cités, dont certains plus de dix fois), mais aussi la parfaite conformité des thèses énoncées avec celles du K. al-Lumaʿ ou avec celles rapportés par Baġdādī, Ǧuwaynī, Abū l-Qāsim al-Anṣārī, etc.

(Gimaret, Introduction to Abū Bakr Muḥammad ibn al-Ḥasan ibn Fūrak, *Mujarrad Maqālāt al-Shaykh Abū al-Ḥasan al-Ashʿarī*, ed. Daniel Gimaret [Beirut: Dār al-Mashriq, 1987], 11-12.)

10. Ibn Fūrak (Gimaret ed.), 44.

فأما ما يوصف بأنه مُحِبّ راضٍ او ساخط مُعادٍ فذلك عنده يرجع الى الإرادة
وهو أنه كان يقول إن رِضا الله تعالى عن المؤمنين إرادتُه أن يُثيبهم ويمدحهم،
وسُخطه على الكافرين إرادته أن يعاقبهم ويذمّهم. وكذلك محبته وعداوته.

As for what is predicated by saying that [God] is Loving and Pleased, or Displeased or Hostile, for [al-Ashʿarī] that was a reference to [God's] Will. He used to say that God's pleasure (exalted is He) over believers is His Will to reward them and to praise them, and His displeasure over unbelievers is His Will to punish them and to censure them. The same is true of His Love and His Enmity.[11]

According to Ibn Fūrak's understanding of al-Ashʿarī, God's will is an eternal quality of God's essence; and God's love is simply another way of speaking of God's will. Thus, in this sense, God's love is an eternal quality of God's essence. Love is not merely a temporal quality of act. Interestingly, the Western, Augustinian Christian tradition also speaks of God's love as being God's will.[12]

I said that I would take up two questions in this paper — one that has been raised by Muslims, and one that has been raised by Christians. On the question of whether love is an eternal, essential quality in God, it seems that there is room for common ground. That is, Muslims and Christians alike can affirm that God's love is not merely a temporal quality of act, but is eternal and uncreated in God.

The second question, which has been raised by many Christians, is this: When we speak of love, do we mean that the one who loves must give of the giver's own self? Or do we mean only that the one who loves gives gifts external to the giver's self? For example, in a human family, if the father of the family gives his children food and clothing and shelter, but stays far away and does not spend time with his children, and thus does not give of his own self to them, can we say that he truly loves them?

The Christian answer to this question is rooted in the Christian understanding of God. That is, for Christians it is very important to affirm that God's love is such that God gives of God's own self.

The eighth-century C.E. theologian John of Damascus described the

---

11. Ibn Fūrak, 45.

12. E.g., Thomas Aquinas, *Summa Theologica* I, Q. 20, Art. 3. Cf. also Augustine, *De Trinitate*, XV, 38.

relationship among the hypostases of the divine Triunity with the Greek word *perichōrēsis* (περιχώρησις). The Christian tradition has understood this concept as implying that each hypostasis of the Triune God gives of itself to the others and opens itself to the others. That is, God loves in a self-giving way, within God's own self.

In the Christian view, when God created the human race, this same self-giving, self-opening love overflowed in God's love toward the human race. Thus, in the Christian view, God does not remain aloof from us, but rather God gives and opens God's very self to us. Christians agree with the verse in the Qur'ān in which God is described as saying:

$$وَنَحْنُ أَقْرَبُ إِلَيْهِ مِنْ حَبْلِ الْوَرِيدِ$$

We are closer to [humankind] than their jugular vein. (Sūrat Qāf [50]:16)

Thus, God does not only give us gifts that are external to God: in the Christian view, God gives to us of God's very self.

That is why it is impossible for Christians to think about the love of God toward humankind without thinking about God's eternal Word[13] assuming our human nature and being manifest to us in the person of Jesus Christ. Christians hold as precious the teaching of the New Testament concerning God's demonstration of love for us in coming among us as one of us. We read in the Gospel (John 1:1-14):

$$فِي الْبَدْءِ كَانَ الْكَلِمَةُ، وَالْكَلِمَةُ كَانَ عِنْدَ اللهِ، وَكَانَ الْكَلِمَةُ اللهَ. هَذَا كَانَ فِي الْبَدْءِ$$
$$عِنْدَ اللهِ. كُلُّ شَيْءٍ بِهِ كَانَ، وَبِغَيْرِهِ لَمْ يَكُنْ شَيْءٌ مِمَّا كَانَ. فِيهِ كَانَتِ الْحَيَاةُ،$$
$$وَالْحَيَاةُ كَانَتْ نُورَ النَّاسِ... وَالْكَلِمَةُ صَارَ جَسَدًا وَحَلَّ بَيْنَنَا، وَرَأَيْنَا مَجْدَهُ.$$

---

13. The Greek word *logos* (λόγος) has a broad range of meaning, which in the Christian philosophical and theological tradition encompasses "word" and "reason" and a number of other related meanings. It is beyond the scope of this paper to address the question of which of these meanings originally underlay the Johannine Prologue, but the Christian theological tradition has variously understood *logos* as meaning "word," "reason," "knowledge," and "understanding." See, for example, Augustine's use, noted above, of the Latin words *verbum* (word) and *intelligentia* (understanding or knowledge).

In the beginning was the Word, and the Word was with God and the Word was God. He was with God in the beginning. Through him all things were made and without him nothing was made that was made. In him was life and that life was the light of humankind. . . . The Word became flesh and dwelt among us, and we beheld his glory.[14]

Because human beings are tragically inclined toward sin against God, Christians also cannot think about God's love toward humankind without thinking about Jesus Christ's responding with self-giving, forgiving love when human beings rejected him on the cross. We read in the Holy Bible, in 1 John 3:16:

وَمِقْيَاسُ الْمَحَبَّةِ هُوَ الْعَمَلُ الَّذِي قَامَ بِهِ الْمَسِيحُ إِذْ بَذَلَ حَيَاتَهُ لِأَجْلِنَا. فَعَلَيْنَا نَحْنُ أَيْضاً أَنْ نَبْذُلَ حَيَاتَنَا لِأَجْلِ إِخْوَتِنَا.

This is how we know what love is: that Jesus Christ laid down his life for us, and so we should lay down our lives for our brothers and sisters.

Christians have traditionally[15] understood that by giving his life on the cross in forgiving love, Jesus Christ atoned for our sin and fulfilled the divine plan for our forgiveness.

Of course the Christian doctrine of God's Word being manifest in the person of Jesus Christ and the doctrine of the cross have been historic points of disagreement between Muslims and Christians. It would be beyond the scope of this paper to enter into that discussion here. In another article elsewhere I have analyzed the views of the major Qur'ān commentaries of the Sunnī Muslim tradition (al-Ṭabarī, al-Rāzī, al-Bayḍāwī, etc.)

---

14. At the Yale conference, Muslim theologians suggested that Sunnī theology could be seen as being in a sense parallel to the idea that "in the beginning was the Word . . . and the Word was *with* God," and Shī'ī theology could be seen as parallel to the idea that "in the beginning was the Word . . . and the Word *was* God." This suggestion prompted the amused observation that Christian theology on this subject was somewhere between these two great Islamic schools of thought in affirming that "in the beginning was the Word and the Word was with God and the Word was God."

15. Notably, but not only, in the Anselmian tradition. Cf. Anselm of Canterbury, *Cur Deus Homo*. See also Isaiah 53:5; Matthew 26:28; Mark 10:45; Romans 3:23-26; Romans 5:8-11; 1 Corinthians 15:3-4; and 1 John 4:9-11.

concerning the question of the death of Christ,[16] and I will not repeat that analysis here.

But even if Muslims may not agree with Christians about the historicity of the crucifixion of Jesus Christ, certainly Muslims and Christians alike (and also Jews) would affirm the idea that Christians should behave toward others with the same kind of self-giving, forgiving love that Christians believe Jesus demonstrated on the cross. If Christians would give of themselves in love to and for Muslims and Jews, forgiving any wrongs committed by others, then surely their doing so would be a good thing.

As a Western Christian it is difficult for me to speak to Muslims, Jews, and Eastern Christians about the idea that the cross calls Christians to give themselves in love for others, since for many the idea of the cross brings to mind the Crusades. Thus I believe that the Yale Response to the "Common Word" letter had to begin with an apology for the evil of the Crusades. Let me repeat here that I ask our Muslim, Jewish, and Eastern Christian neighbors to forgive us for that evil.

The Crusades were evil not only because the atrocities committed were wrong,[17] but especially because they were committed under the banner of the cross. The Bible tells us the following about love and the cross:

وَمِقْيَاسُ الْمَحَبَّةِ هُوَ الْعَمَلُ الَّذِي قَامَ بِهِ الْمَسِيحُ إِذْ بَذَلَ حَيَاتَهُ لأَجْلِنَا. فَعَلَيْنَا نَحْنُ أَيْضاً أَنْ نَبْذُلَ حَيَاتَنَا لأَجْلِ إِخْوَتِنَا.

This is how we know what love is: that Jesus Christ laid down his life for us, and so we should lay down our lives for our brothers and sisters. (1 John 3:16)

وَلَكِنَّ اللهَ بَيَّنَ مَحَبَّتَهُ لَنَا، لأَنَّهُ وَنَحْنُ بَعْدُ خُطَاةٌ مَاتَ الْمَسِيحُ لأَجْلِنَا.

But God demonstrates his love toward us in this: that while we were still sinners Christ died for us. (Romans 5:8)

---

16. Joseph Cumming, "Did Jesus Die on the Cross? The History of Reflection on the End of His Earthly Life in Sunnī Tafsīr Literature," in *Muslim and Christian Reflections on Peace*, ed. J. Dudley Woodberry, Osman Zümrüt, and Mustafa Köylü (Washington, D.C.: University Press of America, 2005), 32-50. This article is available online in English, Arabic, and Turkish at http://yale.edu/faith/rc/rc-rp.htm.

17. Comparable atrocities were committed by Tīmūr (Tamerlane), and worse were committed by Hitler, Stalin, and Pol Pot.

The Yale Response to the "Common Word" letter also quoted Jesus' prayer on the cross:

"Forgive them, for they know not what they do." (Luke 23:34)

اغْفِرْ لَهُمْ، لأَنَّهُمْ لاَ يَعْلَمُونَ مَاذَا يَفْعَلُونَ.

Thus the Christian understanding of the cross describes a love that gives itself for the other and forgives the other, and it calls Christians to imitate Christ in demonstrating this love toward others. The Crusades distorted the cross to mean the exact opposite of what it should mean. Instead of being a symbol that calls Christians to lay down their lives in forgiving love for others, it became a symbol that called Christians to kill others without forgiveness.

Even if not everyone will agree with the Christian doctrine, most likely everyone will agree that if we would forgive one another and give ourselves to one another and for one another in love, then the world would be a better place. In Islam and Judaism there also exist scriptural and theological resources for understanding God's love as self-giving and forgiving,[18] and therefore for calling us to give ourselves for one another in forgiving love.

Peace be with you, and the mercy of God.

---

18. Muslim and Jewish scholars at the Yale Common Word conference in July 2008 offered concrete examples of such resources.

Transforming Love

DAVID BURRELL, C.S.C.

Let us begin where we all begin, and where Jews, Christians, and Muslims concur: the free creation of the universe by the One God. As preposterous an assertion as that is, we become even more perplexed when we ask why the One would ever have undertaken such an initiative. Yet there can be but one answer to that question, which I found best articulated by my friend in Sarajevo, Rusmir Mahmutcehajic. Through his highly poetic reflections *On Love*, one may catch glimpses of that *love* which alone could "move" the One to create this world.[1] And we may obtain some inkling of that love as we find ourselves moved from calculation to *faith*. Now any grasp of divine realities will require commensurate alterations in ourselves; indeed, transformations that only a loving Creator can effect. Moreover, the same obtains for our own capacity to love: unless we acknowledge that it originates in a Creator's utterly gratuitous act animating our desire to respond to that generosity with a total gift in return, we will inevitably find we are deceiving ourselves in mouthing "I love you!" Rusmir's manner of interior recollection on the verses *(ayat)* of the Qur'ān allows them to become signs *(ayat)* of the divine presence and activity in a world whose actions and preoccupations are often so alien to God's intent.

That mode of appropriating qur'ānic verses *(dhikr)* will predispose those who practice it to grasp the unique relation of Creator to creatures:

---

1. Rusmir Mahmutcehajic, *On Love: In the Muslim Tradition*, trans. Celia Hawkesworth (Bronx, N.Y.: Fordham University Press, 2007).

for "all that a person has is nothing other than a gift they have received out of Fullness. But, as nothing can be fullness other than fullness itself, a person is essentially a poor man who through his essential emptiness bears witness to his own condition as debtor, for his possibility of stating 'there is no fullness other than Fullness' is at the same time his initial orientation towards the resolution of duality in his self."[2] Indeed, as Sara Grant — an English Religious of the Sacred Heart who spent her life in Pune, India — notes, Shankara's term of art "nonduality" offers a way of articulating the *sui generis* relation of creatures to Creator that is less misleading than ordinary statements, which will inevitably presume that Creator and creature are "two things" in the universe.[3] Rather is the love we receive from God more like the air we breathe, for our very existence originates in an utterly gratuitous love, so that our unimpeded response would be in kind. Yet not only is our response always impeded in one way or another, but even should we wish to do so, we will be unable to return *everything* to the One from whom we have received everything. We will need to hold something back, if only the very capacity by which we try to return it all! And overcoming that final obstacle can only be God's work, as Sufi writers aver in speaking of *fana'*.

Here is where the dynamic of love built into the Christian revelation of God in the person of Jesus can help us articulate the current of love that can effect such a return. For much as the Qur'ān came to be seen as the eternal Word of God, the Word of God who took flesh in Jesus is identified as the very One through whom the universe is made, a Word bearing fruit in love, which authentic understanding engenders. So as Aquinas puts it, knowledge of divine triunity is "'necessary' [that is, 'fitting'] for us to have the right idea of creation, to wit, that God did not produce things 'of necessity,' [for] when we say that in God there is a procession of love, we show that God produced creatures not out of need, nor for any other extrinsic reason, but on account of the love of God's own goodness"[4] — not even for the intrinsic reason of "God's own goodness," but out of God's love for that very goodness, where the reduplication gestures at an "interpersonal" life within the One that quite escapes philosophy. So "the right

2. Mahmutcehajic, *On Love*, 29.

3. Sara Grant, *Towards an Alternative Theology: Confessions of a Non-dualist Christian*, ed. Bradley Malkovsky (Notre Dame, Ind.: University of Notre Dame Press, 2002).

4. *Summa Theologiae* 1.32.1.3.

idea of creation" will elude reason operating unilluminated by revelation
— and here expressly Christian revelation — since reason itself could
never conclude to the divine Triunity to which we need to direct our thinking about intentional origination.

Yet by a similar reasoning, the precise sense in which God's creating
can be said to be free will escapes us as well. For if we were unable confidently to affirm it without having been informed of the divine Triunity,
which itself escapes our comprehension, then so will the freedom that
that Triunity announces and protects escape us. We have, of course,
moved well beyond logical necessity here, yet the generation of the Son
(Word) with the procession of the Holy Spirit (Love) in God, which in
Aquinas's thought best displays and secures the freedom of creation, cannot itself be a free act of God, but is presented as God's own revelation
displaying to creatures the inner life (or complete "nature") of the Creator. Once that life is revealed, then, it will be *necessary* that such a One
act freely, out of love, yet the manner whereby that loving free consent to
the divine goodness allows it to overflow into creation will utterly escape
us. Just how God is free in creating is not for us to know. So the Christian
revelation may offer a glimpse, but never a demonstration, of that initiating and sustaining love of God, in whose very current we are invited to
participate.

So the centrality of *love* in the Christian revelation — though too often lacking in the witness of Christians! — stems directly from the startling fact that the revelation of God is "in Christ," that is, in a person whose
theandric constitution so baffled the Christian community that it took
them four centuries to articulate the reality of Jesus in such a way as to
avoid affirming Jesus' reality as "alongside" that of God. What properly
impeded the Christian community for those centuries was, of course, the
shema: "Hear, O Israel, God our God is One" (Deuteronomy 6:4). Yet those
constraints run parallel to the central Muslim assertion of *tawhid*. And
while Jesus refers to himself as "Son" and God as "Father," the Gospel of
John begins with the startling assertion: "In the beginning was the Word,
and the Word was with God, and the Word was God" — all statements ap-
plicable, albeit in different ways, to the Qur'ān. So the telling similarity-
cum-difference of Islam and Christianity can be displayed in the parallel
formulae: Christians believe that Jesus is the Word of God made human,
while Muslims believe the Qur'ān to be the Word of God made *kitab* (or
"book," with all the qualifications Dan Madigan has noted in his cele-

brated study).[5] So the operative parallel is *not* between Bible and Qur'ān, or Jesus and Muhammad, but between Jesus and the Qur'ān. For *dhikr* (or meditative recitation) of the "beautiful names of God" culled from the Qur'ān functions for Muslims much the way reception of Holy Communion does for Christians. In each case, believers are given a way of appropriating for themselves the revelation linking the living God with God's creatures, so as to bring the persons involved to a palpable sense of the reality of a Creator's initiating love. As participating in the Eucharist links Christians "sacramentally" to the life, death, and resurrection of Jesus, precisely to empower them to live his lived message of loving God and God's creatures, so Muslims sharing personally in the revelation of the Qur'ān can come to assimilate the qualities of this "straight path" in such a way as to be empowered, little by little, to return everything to the One from whom we receive everything. The quality of love of God and others enjoined by the Qur'ān on believers is articulated in the ninety-nine "beautiful names of God," which are incorporated in Muslim practice as tangible reminders of the divine presence.[6]

5. Dan Madigan, *The Qur'ān's Self-image* (Princeton, N.J.: Princeton University Press, 2001).

6. See *Al-Ghazali on the Ninety-Nine Beautiful Names of God,* trans. David Burrell and Nazih Daher (Cambridge: Islamic Texts Society, 1992; Louisville, KY: Fons Vitae, 1998).

Loving Neighbor in Word and Deed:
What Jesus Meant

MARTIN ACCAD

"In Word" — The Ideal

One day, an expert in the Mosaic law asked Jesus about its most important commandment. Jesus replied: "Love the Lord your God with all your heart and with all your soul and with all your mind and with all your strength. The second is this: 'Love your neighbor as yourself.'" (Mark 12:28-31; Matthew 22:35-39; Luke 10:25-27)

Christians are thrilled that "A Common Word Between Us and You" emphasizes these two commandments as the most important teachings of both Christianity and Islam, for they are at the heart of Jesus' teaching. As the expert in the Law adds in Mark's account, and with Jesus' approval, for someone to follow these two commandments is "more important than all burnt offerings and sacrifices." In these two commandments is enshrined the foundation of our relationship with God *('ibādāt)* and relationship with people around us *(mu'āmalāt)*. Nevertheless, our attempt to get deeper into the second commandment naturally leads us together to ask, "Who is our neighbor?" And what did Jesus mean by his endorsement of the important command from the Pentateuch to "love your neighbor"?

To the Jews of Jesus' time, the category was quite clear. It referred primarily to "one of their own people" and could at best be extended to "the strangers living among [them]." Jews had learned this teaching from their own Scriptures, for God said (in Leviticus 19 in the Old Testament [*tawrāt*]):

Do not seek revenge or bear a grudge against one of your people, but love your neighbor as yourself. I am the LORD. (Leviticus 19:18)

The alien living with you must be treated as one of your native-born. Love him as yourself, for you were aliens in Egypt. I am the LORD your God. (Leviticus 19:34)

In Jesus' story, the expert goes on to ask the same question we are asking: "And who is my neighbor?" (Luke 10:29). In response, Jesus builds on what his audience understood from the text of the Old Testament and expands the definition far beyond their expectations in relating the parable of the good Samaritan (Luke 10:30-36):

Jesus said: "A man was going down from Jerusalem to Jericho, when he fell into the hands of robbers. They stripped him of his clothes, beat him and went away, leaving him half dead. A priest happened to be going down the same road, and when he saw the man, he passed by on the other side. So too, a Levite, when he came to the place and saw him, passed by on the other side. But a Samaritan, as he traveled, came where the man was; and when he saw him, he took pity on him. He went to him and bandaged his wounds, pouring on oil and wine. Then he put the man on his own donkey, took him to an inn and took care of him. The next day he took out two silver coins and gave them to the innkeeper. 'Look after him,' he said, 'and when I return, I will reimburse you for any extra expense you may have.'

"Which of these three do you think was a neighbor to the man who fell into the hands of robbers?" (from the New International Version)

Jesus' Definition of "Neighbor"

The "good neighbor" is now identified as the "Samaritan," Samaritans being conventionally considered archenemies of the Jews. The Samaritan in the story turns out to be a better neighbor to a helpless beaten Jew than his compatriots, a priest and a Levite, even though they belonged to the category of Jewish religious leaders responsible for the welfare of their people.

More importantly, however, instead of giving the legal expert a list of the types of people he might consider as "neighbors," Jesus is effectively saying, "It is not about whom you might consider to be your rightful social neighbor; it is rather about YOU! You are to *act* as a *good neighbor* toward everyone, including those classified by history and social convention as your enemies!"

Neighbors and Enemies

Jesus' definition of "neighbor" extends to one's enemies because considering everyone a neighbor precludes anyone's *becoming* an enemy! In the summary of his ethical teaching, known as the Sermon on the Mount (Matthew 5–7), Jesus affirms again the same principle: "Love your enemies and pray for those who persecute you" (Matthew 5:44). The question therefore arises, "How do I practice *love* toward persons whom history and social conventions have identified as my enemies?"

Jesus' most original and challenging command is no doubt his statement, "Love your enemies." Sadly, this supreme command of Jesus is betrayed over and over again. Michael Hart, in his *The 100: A Ranking of the Most Influential Persons in History,* places Jesus in the third position, after Muhammad and Isaac Newton:

> Now these ideas [about loving one's enemies] — which were not a part of the Judaism of Jesus' day, nor of most other religions — are surely among the most remarkable and original ethical ideas ever presented. If they were widely followed, I would have had no hesitation in placing Jesus first in this book. But the truth is that they are not widely followed. In fact, they are not even generally accepted. Most Christians consider the injunction to "Love your enemy" as — at most — an ideal which might be realized in some perfect world, but one which is not a reasonable guide to conduct in the actual world we live in. We do not normally practice it, do not expect others to practice it, and do not teach our children to practice it. *Jesus' most distinctive teaching, therefore, remains an intriguing but basically untried suggestion.*[1]

Some people, particularly Christians, may disagree with Michael Hart's assessment of the church's adherence to the teaching of their Master.

---

1. Michael Hart, *The 100: A Ranking of the Most Influential Persons in History* (New York: Citadel, 1978), 20-21; my emphasis.

Some Muslims also disagree with Hart's statement by claiming that Islam has advanced the same teaching, though in doing so they generally must refer to *hadīth* material rather than to the Qur'ān. Whatever one's opinion, it is clear that this command is absolutely central to Jesus' teaching and value system, whereas when it is found in the teaching of other masters, it is at most secondary.

"In Deed" — The Reality: Some Practical Applications

Now that we have examined the biblical text and considered the implications of Jesus' teaching on loving our neighbor, we should turn our attention to the implications of his teaching for us today, as communities of faith that hold his words in highest regard.

As a first step, let us look for parallels in both our history and the contemporary world — parallels to the situation Jesus was addressing in his own day. Just as at the time of Jesus Jews and Samaritans were conventional enemies, so also have Muslims and Christians often been conventional enemies throughout a burdened history. As a result of recent history, Israelis and Palestinians, and Muslims and Jews have become conventional enemies, too. And no doubt resulting from the multiple conflicts of the second half of the twentieth century leading up to September 11, 2001, Americans and Arabs have become conventional enemies. In fact, in the popularized view of the "clash of civilizations," as Christians and Muslims — as peoples living either in the East or in the West — we are all continuously invited to embrace the notion that we are conventional enemies.

The questions, then, are these: If a Christian is serious about seeking to implement the radical teaching of Jesus with regard to loving his or her neighbor (read "his or her conventional enemy"), what will that Christian do the next time he or she witnesses the slandering of Muslims and Islam? How are Jews and Christians (especially in the West) required to intervene as "good neighbors" in the case of the beaten and wounded Palestinian? What will Muslims do the next time they witness a Christian being persecuted in the Muslim world because of that Christian's faith in Christ, whether faith by birth or faith by conversion to Christianity?[2]

---

2. I am aware that this question is controversial and disturbing for many Muslims, who find it hard to accept the possibility that Christians could be persecuted in the Muslim

A Suggested Mandate for Our
Academic and Religious Institutions

So as not to remain in the realm of theory, let me conclude with some practical suggestions in the form of a mandate for our academic and religious institutions. Let us:

(1) improve the efficacy of intercultural dialogue, first by identifying and developing a realistic understanding of the distinct socio-cultural frameworks (worldviews) between East and West, and second by developing fruitful methodologies for addressing conflict and misunderstanding based on mutual worldview comprehension;

(2) set up initiatives of love and justice in the face of world poverty and injustice, tyrannical and dictatorial regimes, and the injustices experienced daily by the Palestinian people;

(3) for Christians in particular: reexamine classical mission methodologies and develop an ethic of mission that takes into account sociological realities of the Muslim world; for Muslims in particular: act against the persecution faced by the so-called "apostates" and against the resulting human rights abuses;

(4) implement the spirit of "A Common Word" at the grassroots level of our constituencies by developing mandates for our preachers and teachers and by continuously monitoring, evaluating, and adjusting interfaith strategies and peace initiatives;

(5) set up an interfaith monitoring platform by identifying the issues needing to be monitored on both sides, analyzing and researching issues arising in an ongoing fashion, and addressing jointly the issues through media statements and denunciations and through active initiatives.

---

world. I wish my statement not to be taken as a personal attack. I am referring primarily to those Muslims who choose to convert to Christianity and whose decision is seen as an affront and treason against Islam. I am keenly aware that there is much in this issue that is sociological in nature rather than purely religious; nevertheless, the corpus of Islamic jurisprudence is nearly unanimous regarding the harsh treatment that an "apostate" is to receive as a result of the *ridda*. Sadly, it is still an issue that leads to deep injustice and abuse of human rights, which is acceptable neither to Christianity nor to Islam.

Love and Speech:
With Remarks on Seduction and Sorcery

HARVEY COX

Love

The link between love and speech in the Bible is both clear and fundamental: God *is* love and God *is logos* ("speech/word"). Love and speech are not merely secondary attributes of God. Together they constitute the essence of the divine.

When God creates the heavens and the earth (a creation that is not complete, but continues), it is God's word that creates, and the creation is an act of love.

God *said,* "Let there be light," and there was light. (Genesis 1:3)

By the word of the LORD the heavens were made. (Psalm 33:6)

The same union of speech and love is true for the creation of human beings. Also, when God summons Abraham and promises that through him all the families of the earth will be blessed, it is an act of both speech and love. When God speaks to Moses from the burning bush, sending him to lead an enslaved people to freedom, it is an act of love. When God calls the prophets to tell forth his word of justice for the poor and the fatherless, it is love in action. When God sends his beloved Son to become one of us in our sin and suffering, he does it for love.

For God so loved the world, that he sent his only begotten son. (John 3:16)

162

The New Testament identifies Jesus Christ as the *logos* of God whose essence is *love*. Christians believe that Jesus Christ is both the love of God and the word of God in our midst. Thus incarnation, salvation, and redemption are all supreme acts of love.

Love means having respect for the freedom and integrity of the other. Love must be noncoercive or it is not love, and the response love evokes must also be uncoerced, or it is not love. Love that is not voluntary is not love. The Genesis stories make it clear that Adam and Eve were created with the capacity either to accept or to reject God's love, including the pattern God sets for the way they are to live. When God gives the Hebrew people the Ten Commandments on Mt. Sinai, they are free to accept or reject them. Indeed, Jewish and rabbinical thought for ages has always referred to Torah as a *gift*. This is something in which Christian theology, especially in those trends which try to set law against love, makes a serious mistake. In Psalm 119, the words "law" and "word" and "statute" are used interchangeably. And they all convey God's compassion and loving-kindness toward his often recalcitrant children. The identification of love with speech (word, *logos*) is not only a New Testament concept.

God's manner of speaking to the prophets, at least when prophecy came to full maturation, illustrates this well. Scholars of the Hebrew Scriptures rightly emphasize the importance of the following texts that underline this point:

> The lion has roared;
>> Who will not fear?
> The Lord GOD has spoken;
>> Who can but prophesy? (Amos 3:8)

Here it seems that there is almost an element of compulsion, but the full context of the citation indicates that the prophet — here Amos — although reluctant to prophesy, finally decides freely to do so. In fact, his reluctance largely stems from the fact that the message of God he is called to deliver to his people will seem like very bad news to them. The prophet Jeremiah struggles with this same dilemma. No one *wants* to be a bearer of bad news, but when the prophets accept their heavy responsibility, they do so freely. They are not mere instruments or channels, but free and responsible creatures who *choose* to become messengers of God. Just as importantly, God does not *force* them. Because God is love, God *calls* them.

This call-and-response pattern is illustrated in the call of the prophet Jeremiah. In this moving passage, Jeremiah confesses his deep ambivalence about prophethood, but his ultimate decision to prophesy:

> If I say, "I will not mention him,
>   Or speak anymore in his name,"
> There is in my heart as it were a burning fire
>   Shut up in my bones,
> And I am weary with holding it in,
>   And I cannot. (Jeremiah 20:9)

The key point in this passage is that the prophet at least considers the real possibility of remaining silent. Of course, the initiative is clearly God's, but *God communicates with human beings in such a way that, however strong the message or the call, they remain free to refuse it.* This is the way a genuine lover, as opposed to a seducer, communicates with the beloved. Thus God's mode of calling the prophets, inspired and guided by love, models the way human beings should communicate with each other.

In the life and message of Jesus, the "Living Word," Christians discern a radical universalizing of the commandment of God to love our neighbor. Now even the enemy is included in the scope of God's love and therefore of our responsibility to love. The whole enterprise of Christian ethics has been summed up as the question of how we are to live if the content of God's love/speech is love. A familiar question in Christian ethics is how love, which must be voluntary, can be commanded. The answer, of course, is that *the commandment to love is itself an act of love.* We are enabled to love because God first loved us.

In discussing the relationship between God's love for us and our love for each other, Karl Barth argues that although the latter can only follow, the two are not the same:

> The one cannot be replaced and made unnecessary by the other. But love to God — to the God who reconciles the world to himself in Jesus Christ — evokes love to the neighbor and brother. And love to the man who is made a neighbor and brother by Jesus Christ follows love to God.[1]

1. Karl Barth, *Church Dogmatics*, IV/1 (Edinburgh: T. & T. Clark, 1956), 106.

Another way to put this is that our love for our fellow creatures should *reflect* God's love for us. This means:

(1) God's indiscriminate goodness to all creation must lead us to do and to wish good for all without distinction;
(2) God's free forgiveness of sinners leads us to forgive those who have sinned against us;
(3) God's redeeming activity among all nations suggests that we are called upon to serve the forgotten and misused of all the earth.

In summary, this means that since God's love/speech for all is unqualified, we should love people — ascribing to them dignity and the freedom to respond or reject — regardless of whether they "qualify."

It is important at this point to remind ourselves that "speech" as communication can transcend "words" in the ordinary sense. In his *Language as Symbolic Action* Kenneth Burke points out that three familiar forms of religious communication — praise, invective, and lamentation — can all be expressed by infants before they can use words. Thus infantile cooing with delight can be related to praise, shrieking with rage to invective, and sobbing to lamentation.[2] Pentecostals and charismatic Christians know that the "prayer of the heart" does not need words. God's message sometimes comes through "the sound of silence."

Seduction and Sorcery

In a history-of-religions context, God's loving call-and-response mode can be contrasted to the familiar concept of "possession," in which the human being's freedom and integrity are not respected, but overwhelmed. It can also be contrasted to sorcery, in which speech can be used to bewilder listeners and silence genuine response. A brief word about seduction and sorcery will help clarify this point.

---

2. Kenneth Burke, *Language as Symbolic Action* (Berkeley: University of California Press, 1966).

Seduction

God's loving speech, which preserves the human capacity to accept or refuse it, evokes in human beings the desire and capacity to speak and love in
the same way — respecting the freedom and dignity of the other. One example of the opposite of this loving speech is seduction, which is a caricature and a reversal of speech-as-love. The classic expression of this inver-
sion in the Western literary canon is Goethe's *Faust*. In this story Faust is
an old, decrepit, and bored scholar who grieves over his lost youth and
yearns to restore it through a sexual liaison with a fresh and innocent
young woman. At the outset we can already see that this is not a case of
love, but a quest for power — the power Faust has lost through aging.

The victim of Faust's attentions is Gretchen, who trusts Faust because
she believes he can help her, a humble peasant, to become a fine lady. The
initial parallel with Pygmalion (and with *My Fair Lady*) is obvious, but the
endings differ dramatically. The *Faust* story ends tragically. Faust, after
making a contract with the devil, kills Gretchen's brother, and Gretchen
goes mad after killing her illegitimate child. The key idea already appears
in the first words Gretchen utters when she meets Faust. She says that she
is so impressed with his *talk* (his speech) that *she has no choice*, and that all
she can do is to say yes to whatever he tells her *(Beschämt nur stehe ich vor
ihm da / Und sag zu allem Sachen "ja")*.

Goethe's point is that whenever speech overwhelms and silences, it is
not the expression of love but of something else, in this case of Faust's desperation and greed for power. The Faust story is a kind of antiparable, a
grim portrayal of what happens when love and speech become unlinked,
when the speaker does not affirm the freedom and dignity of the one spoken to, but uses him or her for extrinsic purposes.

In the Christian story, on the other hand, another young maiden,
Mary of Nazareth, freely decides to say "yes" to God's annunciation to her
that she will become the mother of his prophet and messiah. As that story
unfolds, Jesus, who is described as God's Word, allows himself to be re-
buffed, refused, and even killed, thus preserving human freedom. But
through Jesus' resurrection God demonstrates that his loving word cannot
be abolished by death and that it continues to be present in human history.

Sorcery

Sorcery (using the word in its modern sense) also mocks and reverses God's loving speech. But God's love/speech not only inspires and evokes a matching form of speech from human beings; it also judges those patterns of human speech which contradict it. If we "love as God first loved us," we must also speak as God has spoken to us. This means that humans should communicate in ways that preserve and nourish the freedom and dignity of the people addressed, and in ways that encourage response, not fear, silence, confusion, or resentment. However, many current ways in which human beings communicate invert and subvert God's loving manner of communicating with us. They are the modern equivalent of sorcery.

(1) *Propaganda.* The essence of propaganda is to give its receivers no choice, to coerce them into believing something, whether or not it is true. It relies on bombast, intimidation, and especially on repetition (what Josef Goebels called "the big lie"). At its core, then, propaganda is the opposite of the response-evoking love/speech of God. It brooks no response. It is a sinful violation of the will of God.

(2) *Advertising.* In a consumer society shaped by a market economy, vast sums of money are expended on inducing people to buy things they do not need and do not really want. The economy has long since passed from "giving people what they want" to creating, shaping, and enlarging what people think they need. Here is another example of "loveless speech."

Advertising is propaganda in the commercial realm. It makes use of surveys, psychological testing, focus groups, and other modern techniques to discover what potential customers fear and what makes them anxious. Then the commodity is fused in the advertising with words and images that imply, or even promise, that it will eradicate the anxiety. Since for many people these anxieties are linked to loss of powers, sexual deprivation, and loneliness, it is not surprising that so much advertising is suffused with this kind of imagery ("Drink/eat/wear/drive this and it will change your life. You will no longer be lonely or unloved. Buy some today!"). It will not do this, of course, and the advertisers know it, but it does sell the product. Like political propaganda, this distortion of human speech flatly contradicts the love/speech of God.

(3) *Complexification.* From the earliest days of the human race, "experts" have tried to keep those who rely on them ignorant of how they operate. This "mystification" enhances their power. Magicians and sorcerers

have practiced it for centuries. Its newest expression is the unnecessary complexification woven by technical experts around their endeavors. Undoubtedly, technical information can be complex. But intentional complexification goes beyond the requirements of the project itself in order to guarantee the power of the experts over others. It "keeps people guessing." It is a modern equivalent of sorcery, and it violates the loving speech modeled by God, who demonstrates for us how to communicate in a way that enhances the dignity of the other. It is also a form of rejection of God's love/speech (and it is not unknown, alas, to the world of scholarship, including religious scholarship).

The literary critic Susan Sontag remarked that our age has become one in which we are drowned in a deluge of words. Words and word-symbols pound us from morning until night from every direction. They scream at us from radios, bulletin boards, TV screens, and the internet. Words have been twisted, distorted, and evacuated of meaning. At Starbuck's, "large" now means small. If you want a large, you must order "grande." No wonder, Sontag commented, that modern poets and writers such as Eliot and Joyce have sometimes resorted to inventing neologisms, or that certain types of antiverbal mysticism have reappeared. We are pushed toward Cistercian silence or charismatic glossolalia.

One wonders, however, whether what has gone so sour with language and speech is precisely their unlinking from love. Of Jesus it has been said, "His words were deeds, and his deeds were words." He *was* in every way the message he brought. God, as both the source of love and the source of language, remains also the source, the model, and the inspiration for a truly human way of speaking — one that is suffused with love.

PART IV

Frequently Asked Questions

Frequently Asked Questions That Muslims Have Been Asked about "A Common Word"

(by Christians, Muslims, Jews, and others — some via the internet)

GHAZI BIN MUHAMMAD AND AREF NAYED

What is this document really about?

Simply put, it is about the Two Golden Commandments — Love God, and Love Neighbor — and it is an invitation to join hands with Christians on such a basis, for the sake of God and for the sake of world peace and harmony.

Why was "A Common Word" launched at this particular time (October 13, 2007)?

The world is living in tension, if not turmoil, and the situation threatens to get even worse. We need peace and justice. The latest Gallup polls show that 60 percent of Christians worldwide harbor prejudice against Muslims, and 30 percent of Muslims harbor prejudice against Christians. Those percentages amount to about 2 billion people out of 4 billion Christians and Muslims (out of about 6.5 billion people on the planet) who dislike or misunderstand each other — a recipe for worldwide combustion. Something had to be done.

Is it not too late?

Better late than never; and it is never too late for hope. The various signatories, and other Muslims, have been vocal before, but individually or in small groups. What is new is the successful getting together to speak with one voice, a voice of mainstream Islam.

Is the group of signatures representative?

Yes, in that it includes people with different profiles: religious authorities, scholars, intellectuals, media experts, non-government organization (NGO) leaders, etc. — all people of knowledge ('Uamā'/Ulama) or society leaders (Ahl 'aqd wa-ḥāl). It also includes people from different schools of mainstream Islam: Sunnī (from Salafī to Ash'arī and Māturīdī to Ṣūfī, and from all four Madhhab, or schools of jurisprudence: Ḥanafī, Mālikī, Shāfi'ī, and Ḥanbalī), Shī'ī (Ja'farī, Ismā'īlī, and Zaydī), and Ibā'ī. It includes figures from Chad to Uzbekistan, from Indonesia to Mauritania, and from Canada to Sudan. To date (March 2009) the document has been endorsed by over three hundred Islamic leaders, thousands of ordinary Muslims, and five hundred or more Islamic organizations.

How representative can a mere 138 persons be?

Many of the individual signatories guide or influence millions of Muslims and hold positions of religious, social, and political responsibility. The accumulated influence of the signatories is immense and too significant to ignore.

Can you comment on the mixture of very prominent to junior signatories in the 138 figure?

Most of the signatories are very prominent. Many of the most important influential *Ulama* and preachers of the Islamic world have signed or supported "A Common Word." There is value in a mixture of ages, experiences, and backgrounds, for prominence and influence are always in a state of flux, and there is a need to include people that look likely to be very influential in the future. No one mold of person can singlehandedly engage all the varied issues we face today. Jointly, the group is effective and important.

Who is the author of this document?

H.R.H. Prince Ghazi bin Muhammad of Jordan is the author of the document, but in fact the document is mostly a careful selection of essential quotations from Christian and Muslim (and Jewish) scriptures or sacred texts. Moreover, the document was thoroughly checked and approved by a group of senior Ulama, including Grand Mufti Ali Gomaa of Egypt, Sheikh Abd Allah bin Bayyah of Mauritania, Sheikh Sa'id Ramadan al-Buti of Syria, Grand Mufti Mustafa Ceric of Bosnia, Habib Umar bin Hafith of Yemen, Ayatollah Damad, T. J. Winter, and Professor Seyyed Hossein Nasr.

What were the mechanics of the document's production?

Momentum for it started with the Amman Message (www.amman message.com) and its interfaith components. Then the idea was mentioned in summary at the end of the October 2006 "Open Letter to the Pope" from thirty-eight Muslim scholars (following the Pope's Regensburg address of September 2006). The momentum continued to grow over the following year through several gatherings and conferences, the last of which was one on "Love in the Qur'an" of the Royal Aal Al-Bayt Institute for Islamic Thought, held in Jordan in September 2006. The final draft emerged out of that conference, and the process of signing began. The experience of having worked out a document in union to respond to the Pope the previous year made this year's document easier to achieve. Shaykh Habib Ali Jiffri, Professor Aref Nayed, Professor Ibrahim Kalin, Shaykh Amr Khaled, Professor Ingrid Mattson, Sohayl Nakhooda, and a number of other religious scholars and leaders have built and maintained the consensus.

So, is this document really a consensus?

Yes, in the sense that it constitutes a normative Ijmāʿ by the Ummah's scholars. This consensus will get stronger and stronger as more people sign it and uphold it. One mechanism for doing so, through the Common Word website (www.acommonword.com), is already in place, and others are in the making.

Is this a Jordanian government document?

No, it is not. It is a joint document by the Ummah's scholars. Jordan is indeed a welcoming and respected nexus of peace and harmony, which makes it a good place of consensus building. The King of Jordan has been extremely supportive, and this initiative would not have been possible without his help. But the document is international in scope, written from religious leaders to religious leaders.

Is this a document of the Royal Aal al-Bayt Academy?

Yes, but only insofar as that Royal Aal Al-Bayt Academy includes one hundred leading international scholars, who offered a core base of signatories and supporters that could be expanded, and who helped in the networking needed for producing the document.

How will the gains made in consensus building and peacemaking be safe-guarded against erosion and dispersal?

A lot of traction has been achieved already in 2008 by way of spreading the consensus at the highest levels, with major conferences at Yale and Cambridge universities and discussions involving the Archbishop of Canterbury and the Pope himself. (The document was the basis for the first Catholic-Muslim Forum, November 4-6, 2008.) Already, master's theses in major universities have been written on "A Common Word," and discussions have been held at the local level in joint Christian-Muslim groups in a number of countries all over the world. In 2009 the Common Word initiative aims to move from "traction" to "trickledown," with a major independent institute being created to follow up its work, books and films being made about it, joint websites with approved Christian and Muslim reading lists being created as a basis for curricula, and a movement to bring it to political fruition, God willing.

Why are certain Eastern Patriarchs not addressed? Why are many Protestant churches not mentioned?

The Eastern Patriarchs who are not mentioned (e.g., the Melkite, Maronite, and Chaldaean Patriarchs) all recognize the primacy of the Pope and are in communion with the Catholic Church; they are therefore addressed through the person of the Pope. The mainline Protestant churches are mentioned, but since there are over 30,000 churches today, it was evidently easier to address everyone with the phrase "Leaders of Christian Churches everywhere." Thus everyone is indeed included.

Why is it that Jews are not addressed?

Jewish scriptures are invoked repeatedly and respectfully in the document. It is quite normal for documents to be bilateral without implying the exclusion of others. Moreover, "A Common Word" is a theological document, and the problems between Jews and Muslims are essentially political (and thus religious de facto and not theological de jure), with both religions having essentially the same understanding of the unity of the One God — as we see it, at least. Also, Jewish scholars and rabbis have participated in the Common Word conferences at Yale and Cambridge.

Why is "A Common Word" not addressed to people of other faiths, for example Hindus and Buddhists?

It makes sense to begin with the two largest, most intertwined, and yet most conflicting religions in the world and try to help there first. More documents will be forthcoming, God willing.

Are you deliberately excluding secularists and nonbelievers?

Muslims are concerned about all humanity and must respect and seek peace with every single human being, for all are made by God in the fairest image, but again it makes sense to start with these segments of the world's population, since they make up such a large percentage of it.

What if no one pays attention to this initiative? What if it is simply ignored?

By the grace of God, this has not been the case. But if it were the case, Muslims would still be obliged to continue trying to get through. It is a religious duty for all Muslims to wish the best for humanity, no matter what the response. For doing so is precisely a part of loving the neighbor.

What of the few skeptical responses?

Muslims should still strive to respond with more gentleness, compassion, and love. The Holy Qur'an and the Prophet Muhammad (peace be upon him) teach Muslims to ward off bad with good. We have kept a very interesting special log of the "naysayers" on the Common Word website (in the news section, at the end). They are a small minority, but there is still a lot of bitterness.

Should you not fix your own problems first and stop your infighting before you address others?

The basis of inner healing and reconciliation has already started with the Amman Message and the historical consensus on its "Three Points" (see www.ammanmessage.com). The two tasks are not mutually exclusive, and in fact must go together. Indeed, addressing others unites Muslim hearts in ways that can be healing to our own inner wounds. Only God's compassion can unite people. The more compassion Muslims practice toward others, the more compassion toward each other they will have.

Why do you think a document between religions is so important? Religions have always fought each other, but the world has still spun on its axis!

Religion is too important a factor in human history and life to ignore. It is the single greatest impulse in the lives of the majority of people in the world and over history. It has tremendous energies that can have positive or negative consequences. It is very important to unite positive religious energies for the good of humanity. *Religions must be used as part of the solutions, not misused so as to contribute to the problem* — and the problem includes violence, conflict, war, injustice, and hatred. Love and understanding are the solution — "love," we say, not mere lust, but rather compassionate love, with wisdom. The Twin Golden Commandments of Love — and the knowledge of them — are the basis of "A Common Word" — this *religious* love is *true* love.

Do you not think that you have overdone your stark, exaggerated warning about the future of the world?

No, not if you consider that we jointly constitute half of humanity and consider the amount of weaponry combined with huge misunderstandings and mutual stereotypes. Let us remember also the Bosnian Genocide of fifteen years ago (in which 300,000 Muslims were killed by Christians just for being Muslims), or the 9/11 attacks (and similar attacks in the U.K., Spain, Russia, India, and even in many Muslim countries), or the wars in Iraq and Afghanistan from 2001 to 2009, in which over 1.5 million people have died and are still dying. Even in the light of this incomplete list, I do not think it is possible to overstate the tragedy and ever-imminent danger of conflict and war.

Is your reference to the danger to world peace a disguised threat?

No, it is a compassionate plea for peace. Anyone who claims that it is a threat cannot have read the document properly and is attributing motives that are simply not there in reality.

What use is this effort if terrorists are not going to heed your words?

God willing, this initiative will influence young people and will create an atmosphere in which hatred is less likely to thrive. There is no quick fix to these problems, and a patient, wholesome discourse is very much needed as a foundation for a better future. While there will always be people who want to resort to violence for whatever grievances, imaginary or real, we think that 99.9 percent of Christians and Muslims (and Jews, of course, and all people in fact) would rather have peace, and want a way to achieve it.

Why is it that the document doesn't address real issues such as violence, religious freedom, women's issues, democracy, etc.?

"A Common Word" is a first step, but one that strives to lay a solid foundation for the construction of many worthy edifices. The document cannot be expected to do everything at once. Moreover, many of these issues were already addressed in the Amman Message (see www.amman message.com).

Is this document just another form of propaganda?

If one means by that question that "A Common Word" highlights the precedence Islam gives to compassion and gentleness in order to achieve peace, then yes. If one means by that question that "A Common Word" is spin merely for the sake of a hidden political agenda, then no. God sees our hearts. We want peace. We know from the generous and loving Christian responses that most Christians do, too.

N.B. Of all the people we approached about signing "A Common Word," only two Muslims declined (and did so for political reasons). One other Muslim (not a scholar) said the Christian scriptures were forged, so we should not quote them side by side with ours. Basically, not a single scholar objected to the content on scholarly grounds. A number of scholars wanted to add their own touches, which could not be done without restarting the process. Ninety-nine percent of the people we asked signed immediately and without hesitation. Later, some Muslims expressed the wish that they had been asked to be among the original signatories.

Praise be to God, the Lord, the King,
Who gives beyond all reckoning.

Answers to Frequently Asked
Questions Regarding the Yale Response to
"A Common Word Between Us and You"

ANDREW SAPERSTEIN, RICK LOVE, AND JOSEPH CUMMING

In the weeks immediately following the publication of Yale's response to "A Common Word Between Us and You," many questions arose from the broader Christian community and beyond. The issues addressed below represent some of the most significant and frequently asked of those questions. The answers given reflect dialogue occurring before, during, and after the July 2008 Yale conference, "Loving God and Neighbor in Word and Deed: Implications for Muslims and Christians."

Does the Qur'ān really emphasize love as strongly as the Bible does? Is the description of Islam in the "Common Word" letter accurate?

It is true that many Christians would not interpret Islam as it is described in "A Common Word." Many Christians would not see love as being the heart of the message of the Qur'ān. But even as we would be rightfully uncomfortable with Muslims' independently interpreting our faith without reference to what we as Christians say about it, we must similarly not draw our own independent conclusions about Islam without first affording Muslims the opportunity to interpret their own faith for us. As Christians, we rightfully take offense if Muslims insist that Christianity teaches polytheism, and we quite understandably view this common Muslim notion as a misinterpretation of our faith and of the Bible. In like manner, before we confidently assert the substance of Islam, it is appropriate for us to permit members of the Muslim community to interpret their own faith and sacred texts.

Beyond our doing so, however, if Muslim leaders of the world determine publicly to situate love at the center of their faith — as the touch-stone of true religion — and to initiate dialogue on that basis, then surely Christians should welcome that move. If the Muslim leaders of the world say to their fellow Muslims, "Your chief duty toward Christians is to love them," we should welcome that word with enthusiasm. If Muslim leaders say (as they do twice in their letter) that freedom of religion is "a crucial part of that love," we should be encouraged. As is reflected in further responses below, this welcoming stance clearly does not indicate that Muslims and Christians necessarily mean exactly the same thing when they speak of loving God and neighbor, but it does serve as an excellent starting point for concrete, substantive dialogue.

Haven't members of the Jewish community been included in this dialogue?

Yes, they have. The "Common Word" letter was drafted by Muslim leaders and addressed specifically to "leaders of Christian churches every-where" in order to address concrete issues and problems between Muslims and Christians. We therefore felt it appropriate to respond as Christians to that letter. But the Yale Response emphasizes in its opening paragraph that the call to love God and neighbor also "lies at the heart of the most ancient Abrahamic faith, Judaism." Both the Muslim leaders behind "A Common Word" and the Christians at Yale agreed from the outset that Jewish leaders and scholars should be invited to the meetings for dialogue we were planning. As a consequence, a number of prominent Jewish scholars and leaders participated in the July 2008 conference at Yale, and we are committed to ensuring significant Jewish participation in future events as well.

There are, nevertheless, times when Muslims and Christians, Muslims and Jews, and Jews and Christians will need to meet together without the presence of representatives from the third Abrahamic faith. Even as two siblings from a large family will on occasion find it necessary and appropriate to meet privately together to address matters unique to them, so too will pairs of siblings from the larger Abrahamic family of religions on occasion find it necessary to do the same. The World Congress of Imams and Rabbis for Peace, for instance, held every year in Seville, Spain, is a meeting designed to address issues specific to members of Muslim and Jewish communities. As Christians we do not feel excluded by that annual meeting; rather, we recognize that certain matters are of particular concern to our Muslim and Jewish Abrahamic siblings, and that Christian representation in Muslim-Jewish dialogue events may not always be necessary or even appropriate. It is fitting and proper for Muslims and Jews to discuss certain matters in private.

Similarly, the Common Word dialogue focuses on questions specific to Muslim-Christian relations. Even in the event that aspects of this unfolding dialogue may involve only Muslims and Christians, we are confident that our Jewish neighbors would welcome a world in which Muslims and Christians actively seek peaceful relations based on the love of God and neighbor — including their Jewish neighbors. Given the extent, however, to which Jewish concerns are intertwined with those of Christians and Muslims, and given the historic Muslim and Christian tendency inappropriately to exclude the Jewish community, we are deeply committed to seeking out Jewish leaders and scholars to play a central role in the ongoing Common Word dialogue.

What do you hope to gain from this dialogue?

As the Yale Response notes, peaceful relations between Muslims and Christians stand as a central challenge of our time. If current international developments are any indication, then world events will be deeply affected for the foreseeable future by the extent to which Christians and Muslims can learn to live together in peace. The Yale Response, as well as ongoing dialogue, takes seriously God's admonition to us through Paul: "If possible, so far as it depends on you, be at peace with all people" (Romans 12:18).

But for peaceful relations to become a reality, there first must exist a network of deep-trust relationships among Muslims and Christians around the world. At Yale's Reconciliation Program, we seek to establish and cultivate precisely such a network of relationships — the seeds of a growing community of Muslims and Christians who know one another personally, who understand each other's communities and convictions, and who are committed to warm and constructive interactions even in the face of significant tensions and differences. Such a community not only serves as the foundation upon which ongoing peacemaking ventures can be built, but also provides the critical private channels of communication for defusing crises — both religious and political — when they occur. And it is just such communities that stand to influence larger Muslim and Christian constituencies around the world for good. In the end, there is simply no substitute for Muslim and Christian leaders' logging the face-to-face hours necessary to cultivate relationships that go beyond superficial pleasantries. So far as it depends on us, we are committed to making such relationships a reality.

Thus, in response to the unambiguous scriptural mandate, and with a clear notion of the pragmatic benefits of peaceful Muslim-Christian relations before us, we embark on the hard road of building with Muslims the weight-bearing relationships that will make a difference in the world. "Blessed are the peacemakers," Jesus said, and if we as his disciples want to experience his blessing and create opportunities for our Muslim neighbors to do the same, then we must with joy and sobriety answer his call, and in so doing, further his purposes in the world. To the extent that we are successful, we will count it as great gain indeed.

Shouldn't the basis of our dialogue with Muslims center on the person and work of Christ rather than the command to love God and neighbor?

The "Common Word" letter and the Yale Response merely articulate the starting point for dialogue. The command to love God and neighbor provides a strong theological bridge that both parties can affirm. Ours is only a first step, but it is a big step.

We are persuaded that substantive dialogue is absolutely crucial — dialogue that allows all parties to hold to their convictions even as they seek reconciliation. Such substantive dialogue with our Muslim neighbors is absolutely crucial if we are to fulfill our calling as peacemakers. Substantive dialogue among religious leaders at this level can build relationships of trust that ultimately shape the course of international events in ways that mere political engagement cannot. And such dialogue has the potential to bring about change in the overall spiritual climate in which Muslims and Christians share their respective faiths with one another, opening doors for Christians to bear witness to the Gospel and for Muslims to bear witness to Islam. Ultimately Christians expect to bear witness respectfully, graciously, and cordially to our beliefs about Jesus Christ, and we expect that Muslims will bear witness to their own distinctive beliefs.

Does a commitment to the Common Word dialogue mean that the signatories are renouncing evangelism?

The Yale Response itself neither promotes nor renounces evangelism. It merely responds to an invitation to dialogue. The signatories of the Yale Response represent a broad spectrum of Christian belief, in the same way that the signatories to the "Common Word" letter represent a broad spectrum of Muslim belief. Among both the Muslim and Christian signatories to the letters are those who would oppose both Christian evangelism and

Islamic *da'wa* (literally, "inviting" or "calling"), as well as conversion from one religion to another. But the majority of signatories on both sides recognize that Islam and Christianity are both missionary faiths, which by their very nature bear witness to a message they believe is essential to all people.

The Yale Response seems to imply that Allah is the same God that Christians worship. Is this true?

Implicit in this question are at least two, more basic questions, namely: (1) Is it appropriate for Christians to refer to the God of the Bible as "Allah"? and (2) Do Muslims and Christians actually worship the same God?

Regarding the first question, we do not hesitate to refer to the God of the Bible as "Allah," as Arab Christians and Arabic-speaking Jews since long before the time of Muhammad have used the name "Allah" to refer to God. There is clearly nothing implicitly wrong or evil in the name "Allah" — it is simply the Arabic word for "God." Indeed, there is no other word for "God" in Arabic. Thus all Arabic Christian Bible translations of John 3:16 say, "For Allah so loved the world. . . ." In Acts 2:11, when Arab visitors to Jerusalem heard the apostles "declaring the mighty works of God" in their own tongue, Arabic, the name they must have heard coming from the apostles' lips could only have been the name "Allah," and this as a direct, miraculous work of the Holy Spirit on the day of Pentecost. Furthermore, the Arabic word "Allah" is the cognate of the Aramaic word "Alāhā," which the Syriac Peshitta Bible uses for "God." And that same Aramaic word for God (pronounced with a Canaanite-shifted accent) was used by Jesus on the cross when he cried out, "*Alohi, Alohi, lama sabachthani* [My God, my God, why have You forsaken me]?" This same word is also cognate with the Hebrew divine names "El," "Elohim," etc.

The second question is more complex, and is perhaps best addressed as follows: Both Muslims and Christians affirm that there exists only one God. In the *shahada*, the Muslim confession of faith, devout Muslims affirm multiple times daily, "There is no god but God, and Muhammad is the Messenger of God." While Christians do not similarly affirm the prophethood of Muhammad, they nonetheless share with Muslims the notion that there is only one God. In the *Shema*, the Jewish confession of faith (also embraced by the world's Christians), we are told, "Hear, O Israel! The LORD is our God, the LORD is one!" (Deuteronomy 6:4). The New

Testament later affirms that there is "one God and Father of all who is over all and through all and in all" (Ephesians 4:6). One essential distinctive of the three Abrahamic faiths is that all agree there is only one true God, and that this God alone is worthy of our worship. Muslims, Jews, and Christians alike, in fact, not only affirm the sole worthiness of the one true God, but also claim in practice to worship that one true God.

So if there exists only one true God, and if members of all three Abrahamic faiths claim to worship that one God, then perhaps the question "Do Muslims and Christians (and Jews) worship the same God?" is not the right question at all. A more appropriate question might be, "Do Muslims and Christians (and Jews) all worship God truly?" Perhaps the substance of our discussions with Muslims should focus more on how we might more truly know and worship the one true God, rather than on whether we are all in practice actually doing so.

Now clearly much of the substance of our worship relates to the attributes we ascribe to the one true God, and to the posture of heart we bring to our worship. Jesus approaches the matter of Samaritan and Jewish worship in these very terms: "an hour is coming, and now is, when the true worshipers will worship the Father in spirit and truth; for such people the Father seeks to be his worshipers. God is spirit, and those who worship him must worship in spirit and truth" (John 4:23-24). In this statement, Jesus focuses the question not so much on whether two groups of people are worshiping the same God, but on whether they are worshiping the one true God truly — "in spirit and truth." In Jesus' terms, one who worships truly will necessarily be worshiping the one true God, who desires that we all grow in the extent to which we worship truly — "in spirit and truth."

Jews, Muslims, and Christians all attribute many of the same qualities to the one true God. All three groups believe that the one true God is the creator of the heavens and the earth. They all believe that God is merciful and compassionate, that God rules the universe and guides the affairs of humankind, and that God will judge all people at the end of history. They all believe that God has sent prophets into the world to guide God's people and that God inspired some of those prophets to write holy books that they consider to be sacred scripture. There is clearly much they share regarding "truth" about God, and even the "spirit" in which they worship. But this is by no means the end of the story.

Christians maintain that they worship the one true God and also hold that Jesus Christ is the incarnate, full revelation of that one true God —

"the radiance of his glory and the exact representation of his nature" (Hebrews 1:3). Jews and Muslims, on the other hand, also maintain that they worship the one true God but generally do not hold that God has fully revealed himself in Jesus Christ. Christians affirm that God is One and believe the One God exists eternally as triune, while Jews and Muslims generally do not hold this view of the divine being. Muslims believe that the Prophet Muhammad received the final, authoritative revelation of the one true God in the Qur'ān, whereas Jews and Christians do not share this view. So while there is clearly a great deal that Jews, Muslims, and Christians do share, both in the statements they make about God and the manner and devotion with which they seek to worship God, there are nonetheless profound differences. For these and other reasons, the "Common Word" letter affirms that "Islam and Christianity are obviously different religions, and . . . there is no minimizing some of their formal differences." The Yale Response similarly refers to "undeniable differences" between the two faiths.

Even in this light, however, many Muslims would say that Christians and Muslims worship the same God. In the Qur'ān, Sūrat al-'Ankabūt (29:46) states that "Our God and your God is one." Some, but not all, Christians and Jews would say the same. And perhaps fewer Christians still would say that Christians and Jews are worshiping different gods, or that Jews worship an idol. It is significant that the New Testament refers in a number of places to people, both Jews and Gentiles, who "worship God," though in many cases these worshipers do not believe either in Christ or in the Trinity. In some cases this worship is described as "empty," and in other cases as accepted by God (cf. Acts 10:2; 13:50; 16:14; 17:4; 17:17; 18:7; Matthew 10:40; Luke 10:16).

What can be definitively said is that Muslims, Christians, and Jews all *aspire* to worship the one true God. To begin our interactions with Muslims and Jews by denying outright that they worship the one true God, and for Muslims and Jews to do similarly in regard to one another and to Christians, is to initiate an irresolvable cycle of claims and denials that shuts down meaningful discussion and yields little but acrimony. Rather, if we engage the matter by accepting one another's approaches to devotion as good-faith *attempts* to worship the one true God, even if some of us may consider one another's attempts to be ultimately misguided, then we can discuss the salient issues with dignity and respect. In the end, it is perhaps best to answer the question of whether Muslims and Christians worship the same God in terms more like "Well, I'm not sure. We both *desire* to worship the one true God and we both *claim* to be doing so. But our worship and our beliefs about God differ in significant ways, and this leaves us a lot to discuss. Let's start talking."

The "Common Word" letter asserts that love for God and neighbor is the common ground between Muslims and Christians. But are Muslim and Christian understandings of love really the same?

While we recognize and anticipate differences between various Muslim and Christian understandings of love, we are committed to granting one another the dignity of first listening respectfully to each other's characterizations of our religious traditions, and then engaging in earnest discussion of those characterizations. We are committed to being "quick to hear" and "slow to speak" (James 1:19), and committed to taking the time genuinely to understand one another's positions before assuming that we already fully understand them. It is certain that if we rely only on our existing notions, or on mere caricatures of one another's faith, then we will never be able to answer this question meaningfully. If we never sit down at the table to talk together face-to-face, it will be impossible to clarify the similarities and differences in our perspectives regarding love of God and neighbor.

It is for this reason that in the Yale Response we invite our Muslim correspondents to meet together and begin the earnest work of determining how God would have us fulfill the requirement that we love God and one another. In the July 2008 conference at Yale, as well as at other important recent gatherings, this is precisely the process that has begun. To help initiate this process, the Yale Response sets forth some of the core Christian convictions regarding the meaning of love — its unconditional character, its rootedness in God's own being as love, and its ultimate expression in Christ's self-giving forgiveness of his enemies on the cross.

The difficulties experienced in translating the Yale Response into Arabic exposed the complexity of some of the questions that need to be addressed. For example, is the name *al-Wadūd* (one of the ninety-nine names for God in the Islamic tradition) close in meaning to the statement in 1 John that God is *agapē*? Is *ikhlāṣ* toward God the same as *agape* toward God? Is God's love conditional or unconditional? Is it self-giving? Is our love for each other conditional or unconditional? The exchanges that have arisen out of the "Common Word" letter and the Yale Response stand as only the beginning of the discussions warranted by these crucial matters of love of God and neighbor. The initial exchange of letters and the ensuing conference and conversations are clearly only first steps in an ongoing and sustained dialogue.

Why did we ask for forgiveness for the Crusades and for "excesses of the 'war on terror'"? Don't Muslims have a lot more to apologize for than Christians do?

Some people have been troubled by the apology to the worldwide Muslim community that is found in the second paragraph of the Yale Response. The apology consists of the following statement: "Since Jesus Christ says, 'First take the log out of your own eye, and then you will see clearly to take the speck out of your neighbor's eye' (Matthew 7:5), we want to begin by acknowledging that in the past (e.g., in the Crusades) and in the present (e.g., in excesses of the 'war on terror') many Christians have been guilty of sinning against our Muslim neighbors." In the paragraphs that follow, we seek to address some of the questions that have arisen regarding this apology.

First, some have expressed concern that this apology dangerously equates the behavior of so-called "Christian civilization" or of specific Western governments with the behavior of the church. In the Yale Response, we were very careful to specify that it was "many Christians" who were guilty of sinning against their Muslim neighbors, both at the time of the Crusades and then later in the ongoing "war on terror." In choosing this language, we were not saying either that the entire church or that all Christians were guilty of these sins, nor were we declaring the church as a whole guilty of the sins of our own or any other governments, even if those sins were committed in the name of Christ or the church. We were simply acknowledging the uncontestable fact that some Christians have been guilty of sinning against their Muslim neighbors, both then and now.

Even given this clarification, however, others have objected to the fact that we, as modern followers of Jesus, should see fit to apologize for Christians who lived hundreds of years ago in far-off lands, or for Christians in our own age who have acted sinfully toward Muslims without any direct support from us. While it is true that we may not as individual Christians have personally committed these sins, we nonetheless are numbered with our Christian brothers and sisters who do bear direct responsibility for them. Jeremiah 14:20, Lamentations 5:7, and Daniel 9:3ff. are just a few among the many examples in Scripture of individually innocent believers repenting of the sins of their people and the sins of believers of past generations. Recognizing that we are one body, and that when one member sins, we all in some measure suffer its effects; and recognizing that the impact of one member's sin affects the reputation of the entire church, the signatories to the Yale Response, as members of the church, offer a good-faith gesture of acknowledgment and apology to the Muslim community; and before God and our Muslim neighbors, we seek God's mercy.

Others have asked whether apologizing for the Crusades was not redundant, since Pope John Paul II and other prominent Christian leaders have apologized for the Crusades in the past. Unfortunately, many if not most Muslims are unaware of these apologies. Just as many Christians, for example, are unaware of all of the Muslim leaders who have denounced the 9/11 attacks, so also many Muslims are unaware that Christians today do *not* believe that the Crusades faithfully represented the love of Jesus Christ.

Still others have expressed concern that many Muslims have also been similarly guilty of sinning against Christians, both during the Crusades and in other times, including our own. In offering an apology for wrongdoing by Christians, we are in no way minimizing wrongs done by Muslims against Christians. Rather, we are doing what Jesus says is the prerequisite for addressing wrongs done by our neighbors. As followers of Christ, we are called first to take the log out of our own eye (Matthew 7:3-5), and only then to address the faults and sins of others. In any conflict (whether in the family, the church, the community, or the world) we are responsible to deal with our own sins first, and Jesus says we must do so whether or not the other party also apologizes. While there have indeed been sins by each community against the other, and while we continue to sin against one another in serious ways, the debate about who wronged whom in the history of Christian-Muslim relations is endless. We are persuaded that until and unless one party is willing to acknowledge their own wrong first, there will be no healing of the relationship.

Nonetheless, Jesus also says that removing the logs from our own eyes will help us to see more clearly to help others with specks in theirs. Having offered a sincere apology to our Muslim neighbors, we will, in appropriate contexts, and with firmness and respect, speak frankly to them about the ways in which Muslims, both in the past and in the present, have sinned against Christians. Certainly both Christians and Muslims have perpetrated serious evil against one another. By offering a sincere apology to our Muslim friends, we do not support or condone their sins against us — we simply affirm that reconciliation must begin with humility and repentance.

Some Christians point out that some of the signatories of the "Common Word" letter have a record of slandering the Christian faith or promoting persecution of Christians in their countries. How can we engage in meaningful dialogue about freedom of religion with such people?

Various prominent Muslim leaders have indeed gone on record in very unconstructive ways regarding religious freedom, the Christian faith, and other matters, as also some Christian leaders have said unhelpful things about Islam and Muslims. It is frequently the case, however (as borne out in our own experience), that even people who have held to harsh positions will often look for legitimate, more moderate positions within their own scriptural tradition once they are engaged in warm, personal relations with someone from another faith. And face-to-face discussion of these crucial issues stands as one of the central ways to truly ascertain and influence the intentions of Muslim signatories and their colleagues. We have every reason to believe that the majority of Muslim signatories are sincere in their pursuit of peace, as private conversations with many of them have confirmed. It is our hope that Muslim leaders who have been harsh toward Christians in the past will be led to change their positions, in part as a result of having gone on record publicly in support of love of God and neighbor in "A Common Word." Similarly, we hope for Christian signatories (and nonsignatories) to grow in their understanding of what Jesus requires of us in regard to loving both our Muslim neighbors and our Muslim enemies.

Our response to "A Common Word" is only the first comment in a long conversation, not the only word we *can* say, or the final word we *want* to say. Thus, engaging with the Common Word initiative is an initial step toward addressing the suffering of fellow Christians in Muslim countries, just as we expect that Muslim leaders will address the sufferings their fellow Muslims experience in the West.

It is noteworthy that the "Common Word" letter twice mentions the importance of freedom of religion as "a crucial part of love." We applaud our Muslim colleagues for this explicit mention. Ultimately, we believe Muslims who live in the West should be free to express and share their faith respectfully. Christians who live in the Muslim world should be equally free to express and share their faith respectfully. No double standard should be allowed to exist. We are deeply committed to promoting the substance of the United Nations Universal Declaration of Human Rights, Article 18: "Everyone has the right to freedom of thought, conscience and religion; this right includes freedom to change his religion or belief, and freedom, either alone or in community with others and in public or private, to manifest his religion or belief in teaching, practice, worship and observance."

In the end, we see this exchange of letters and the resulting dialogue as the beginning of a conversation in which leaders from both communities will bear respectful witness to their deepest convictions, and in which issues arising from Christian evangelism, Islamic *da'wa,* and conversion in both directions can be discussed in an atmosphere of mutual respect and sensitivity.

Why did you use the Muslim-sounding name for God, "The All-Merciful One," in offering your apology?

Actually, this name was a Christian and Jewish name for God long before the birth of Muhammad. The rabbis of the Talmud (a central Jewish sacred text consisting of rabbinic discussions concerning Jewish law, history, ethical behavior, etc.) and of Midrash Rabbah (a collection of rabbinic commentaries on the Jewish scriptures) asserted that the divine Name (the Tetragrammaton) specifically denoted God's character as "The Merciful One." They based this assertion on Exodus 34:6, in which God proclaimed the divine Name as "YHWH, YHWH: God Merciful and Compassionate." This text is at the heart of Jewish *Selichot* prayers (traditional penitential prayers recited in anticipation of the Jewish high holidays), and it forms the basis for the Jewish doctrine of the Thirteen *Middot,* or divine attributes of mercy. New Testament texts such as James 5:11 and Ephesians 2:4 allude to Exodus 34:6 when they refer to God as "The Lord Merciful and Compassionate." Pre-Islamic Christian inscriptions from South Arabia show that *Rahmān* ("The Merciful One") was the name for God used by Yemeni Christians before the time of Muhammad in invocations such as "In the name of the Merciful One and His Messiah and the Holy Spirit." In Luke 6:36 Jesus tells us we should be merciful just as God our heavenly Father is merciful. In referring to God by this name, which is common to both the Qur'ān and the Bible, we are simply seeking to communicate respectfully our understanding of God to our Muslim correspondents by using a name for God that is meaningful to them.

PART V

Political Significance of "A Common Word"

Common Word, Dialogue,
and the Future of the World

SENATOR JOHN F. KERRY

The novelist Michael Chabon recently asked, "Is there anybody else who feels that it might be best if we just started the twenty-first century over again?"

As a man who narrowly lost the presidency of the United States in 2004, I try not to dwell on the "what ifs." However, speaking as a person of faith, it's hard to avoid a sense of regret over the ground we've lost in a few short years in our quest for interfaith tolerance and understanding.

We have barely broken the seal on the twenty-first century, but already it's been marked not just by burning buildings and occupying armies and riots and roiling images of bloodshed and humiliation, but also by an even more widespread and dangerous worry, by a question you hear whispered and spoken quietly: What if we can't live together? Maybe the gulfs that separate us are unbridgeable. Maybe we just need higher walls and fewer visas. Maybe coexistence is just too difficult.

While demagogues play cynically to the worst human instincts, most leaders of good conscience and people of genuine faith believe and talk otherwise. They believe we can, we must, and — God willing — we *will* find a way to live together.

In a world where today a Catholic, a Protestant, a Russian Orthodox Christian, a Confucian ex-Communist, a Hindu, a Muslim, and possibly

---

Keynote address given by Senator John Kerry at the Yale Common Word Conference, July 28, 2008.

even a Jewish finger sits on a nuclear button, it's a delusion to think we can retreat to our safe spaces. Not when Christians, Hindus, and Muslims number in the billions. Not when Islam is the second-largest faith in Europe and the third-largest in America. Not when people of all faiths are migrating and mingling like never before. Gallup says there are 1.3 billion Muslims worldwide. The Vatican recently announced that there are now more Muslims than Catholics. The poet Auden said it best: "We must love one another or die." It's a delusion to think we have any choice but to find a way to live together.

This is not a new issue, and it's not one Americans come to without experience. America has struggled with this for centuries. The quest for religious truth — and the challenge it poses to peaceful coexistence — is written into the fabric of our country and the history of the world, and it's actually written into my own family DNA.

John Winthrop, my great-grandfather eight times over — meaning ten generations ago — was the son of a lawyer born in England. His passionate faith and his disagreements with the Anglican Church inspired him to lead a ship full of religious dissidents across the Atlantic to America to seek freedom to worship. On the deck of the *Arabella,* he famously said: "For we must consider that we shall be as a city upon a hill. The eyes of all people are upon us."

It wasn't long before these religious dissidents — many of whom lived in the city of Salem, which takes its name from *salaam* or *shalom,* meaning "peace" — experienced their own religious strife. They accused women of witchcraft and burned them at the stake.

In this "city on a hill," Winthrop soon found himself in conflict with a rogue preacher named Samuel Gorton. When Gorton compared Winthrop to Pontius Pilate and his followers to idol-worshippers and vipers, Winthrop responded by putting him in shackles and having him arrested. When Gorton refused to stop preaching, Winthrop expelled him into the wilderness.

More doctrinal differences, this time over relations between church and state, would soon exile Roger Williams from Massachusetts. Accused of "wanting to banish God from government," Williams was threatened with deportation back to England. Instead, he left Boston for a place he named Providence, and started his own colony in Rhode Island.

Then, a theologian named Thomas Hooker broke with Massachusetts leadership because he believed that all authority, in state or religion, must rest on popular consent. It wasn't long before he left too, and founded Hartford, Connecticut, with his congregation.

Another pastor, John Davenport, called for his congregants to burn their rings, cloaks, wigs, and other vain personal items in a large bonfire — along with religious books he considered to be wicked. His strong beliefs took him first to Holland, then to Massachusetts, and then to found a colony in Connecticut — making him one of the first to forsake Cambridge, Massachusetts, for greener pastures right here in New Haven. Davenport College at Yale is named after him.

These disagreements — all among a group of Christians whose shared disagreements with the Anglican Church led them to the New World — remind me of a joke a Jewish friend of mine used to tell:

A Jewish man, miraculously rescued after years stranded alone on a desert island — welcomes some news crews. He shows them a bucket and says, "This is how I got my rainwater." He shows them his coconut tree, and walks them past a snake patch he learned to avoid. And then they arrive at a clearing, with two shining temples.

The man says, "These are my two synagogues." And the reporters ask, "If you were here all alone, why did you build two synagogues?" And the man points to one and says, "This one I go to every week." And he points to the other one, with a look of disgust. "That one . . . I would never set foot in!"

These are not new challenges. Every religion has a version of this joke because we all struggle with the divisiveness of religious differences — even small differences inside the same religion.

No faith enters this dialogue with clean hands. In Christianity we've had our own struggles, and America has dealt with its share of religious disputes and religious cruelty. And yet, though we're far from perfect, no place has ever welcomed so many different faiths to worship so freely. There are Buddhist temples in the farmlands of Minnesota, mosques in the cornfields of the Midwest, and Hindu temples in suburban Nashville, Tennessee. Ours is a country not only of white church steeples but also of synagogues, of minarets, of Muslim mosques, of the gold domes and shikara of Sikh temples, and of monasteries, Buddhist as well as Catholic. "E Pluribus Unum," "From Many, One" is our national creed.

From many faiths, one shared country. That achievement rests on our solution to the age-old question, Who defines the truth in public space? Our experiment has succeeded because we've allowed for different notions of truth in public life. To do otherwise is to invite permanent war.

My pride in America's successes is tempered by knowing that we are a long way from mutual understanding with the Muslim world today. One enormous problem in that effort is that we lack a forum to discuss these issues. Even among political leaders it happens far too rarely.

When people don't engage, they end up lacking answers to the most basic, fundamental questions: Why do you wear the *hijab?* Why do you go to Mecca? What is *jihad?* If you ask many Americans or Europeans, they don't know the answers because they aren't having the dialogue. We have major politicians who couldn't tell you the difference between Shi'a and Sunni — so it's no wonder that we attack a secular dictator in response to radical fundamentalist terrorists.

As a Catholic American politician, I know enough about Islam to know that I don't know very much — and when it comes to Islam, American politicians ought to do a lot more listening and maybe a little less talking. I believe we have a duty to understand each other in the name of living peacefully. We have a duty to engage with each other. The Abrahamic faiths — Christianity, Judaism, and Islam — have to find new meaning in the old notion of our shared descent. What really is our common inheritance? What does it mean to be brothers? Are we responsible for each other? Ultimately, our sense of kinship has to rest on something more basic than our common ancestry: it must rest on an acknowledgment of our shared humanity.

The good news I see is that, for all the challenges our differences present, all the major religions do have a sense of universal values — a moral truth based on the dignity of all human beings. Gandhi called the world's religions "beautiful flowers from the same garden." Every religion embraces a form of the Golden Rule, and the supreme importance of charity, compassion, and human improvement. When Jesus was asked, "Teacher, which is the greatest commandment in the Law," he replied first, "Love the Lord your God," and second, "Love your neighbor as yourself" (Matthew 22:37-39). "In everything, do to others what you would have them do to you, for this sums up the Law and the Prophets" (Matthew 7:12).

The Talmud says that in Roman times a nonbeliever approached the famous Rabbi Hillel and challenged him to teach the meaning of the Torah while standing on one leg. Holding up one foot, Hillel replied: "What is hateful to yourself, do not do to another. That is the whole of the Torah . . . the rest is commentary."

The Prophet Muhammad, who brought the Qur'ān to the people of seventh-century Arabia, said, "Not one of you truly believes until you wish for others what you wish for yourself."

Buddhist scriptures teach us to "treat not others in ways that you yourself would find hurtful." Native American spirituality proclaims that "all things are our relatives; what we do to everything, we do to ourselves."

Anyone who adheres to these basic principles must acknowledge that the moral challenges we all face today are immense, yes, but also shared. Billions of human beings live in poverty. People from Port-au-Prince to Cairo are struggling to feed their families. Children whose parents died of AIDS are raising their younger siblings in shantytowns in South Africa. A planet is being ravaged and radically altered by the pollution we've created. And people in every corner of the world are living lives of violence and desperation.

We should think of our shared struggle in terms of these unmet challenges. Sixty-five percent of the Middle East's population is under the age of twenty-five. There's a 15 percent unemployment rate, half of which is comprised of youths between ages 15 and 24 — and just to maintain this unacceptable status quo as the population grows, the region needs eighty million new jobs in the next fifteen years. Extremism and violent sectarianism often represent a human attempt to capitalize on the failures of governance and civil society. This applies to failed states such as Afghanistan, where in the 1990s the Taliban arose to fill a chaotic vacuum, but also to many other places where the state, the society, and the religious order don't do enough to remedy unfairness, lack of education, or social alienation. I don't just mean a place like Sadr City in Baghdad — this is true of Cairo or even the desolate immigrant suburbs around Paris. People exploit religion to drive a wedge and gain a foothold, and failed states, failed civil societies, and, frankly, corruption in governance empower them to do so.

In talking about our shared challenges, I don't seek to minimize the real differences between our religions. The specificity, the immediacy, the richness of each of our sacred texts, the greatness of our preferred theologians and thinkers — all are cheapened when dialogue tries to turn religion into some sort of undifferentiated feel-good mush. Nor can we hope to remove any influence of faith from our public life. If we're not shaped by our faith, we don't *have* faith.

It's important to remember what faith is. Faith, to the person who has it, is truth. But in the end, faith is a belief beyond the evidence — or as some people say, in the evidence yet to come. Who pronounces the truth? In the end, God does — not us.

It's a true article of faith — belief in what is not shown but simply believed — that separates our faiths: belief by Christians that Jesus is the Son of God; belief by Catholics in the Holy Trinity — a notion which Muslims and even some other Christians believe compromises the oneness of a monotheistic God; belief by Muslims that Jesus was a great prophet who didn't complete his mission, requiring Muhammad and the teachings of the Qur'ān; belief by Muslims and Jews that Jesus was an important teacher but that God could never become human. Each religion believes its basic tenets are supported by fact: that Muhammad received the Qur'ān; that the crucifixion was observed and recorded; that Moses led the Jews to the promised land. While each rests on basic facts, it still takes a leap of faith to weave these facts together into a religious narrative.

We don't need to agree on everything to get along — instead, we need to ask ourselves tough questions about coexistence. We need to search for how we might live together in some sort of peace and harmony that respects our differences while fashioning a common effort for human dignity. This theological discourse must include the pressing political and social questions — such as how to get along in a shrinking world. Somehow, we have to find a way to agree that faith may be worth dying for, but it cannot be worth killing for. We have to strive for a global ethic that allows each of our religious faiths to express themselves fully but also allows us to unite around common ethical ground.

My own faith, Roman Catholicism, has advanced a line of thinking that I believe can help structure this conversation. For many years Catholics have spoken of the common good, not just for Catholics, not just for a single people, not just for this or that nation, but for all the earth's people: an international common good.

In recent Catholic history, a crucial document of Vatican II labeled the common good "the sum of those conditions of social life which allow social groups and their individual members relatively thorough and ready access to their own fulfillment." These conditions include the right to fulfillment of material needs, a guarantee of fundamental freedoms, and the protection of relationships that are essential to participation in the life of society. These rights are bestowed on human beings by God and grounded in the nature and dignity of human persons. They are not created by society. Indeed, society has a duty to secure and protect them.

Can our great faith traditions come together and forge a consensus on what exactly the conditions of life are that will empower people to find their own fulfillment? Can we come together to seek these conditions that will lead to the flourishing of all humans? It seems to me that we cannot move forward as a planet if we do not come to some rough consensus on what these broad rights are. Beyond that we must find ways to secure these goods for everyone on our planet while simultaneously discussing, arguing, and sharing our particular understandings of God and God's call for how we are to live our lives.

There are many different ways that communities of faith and governments can contribute to nurturing this conversation. There are profound gaps in the mutual understanding not only between the major faiths, but also between nations populated by these faiths. Governments possess resources to sponsor educational exchanges, to make it easier for students to study abroad, to create venues for mutual intellectual collaboration and exploration.

We must also recognize that dialogue is not enough. We must also learn to match it with action and treat each other with respect. Napoleon, to give a negative illustration, arrived in Egypt declaring his love and respect for the Muslim religion, and even hinting that he himself was eager to become a Muslim. Then he pillaged the country. More recently, we've seen other leaders whose actions powerfully counteracted their words of respect for Islam. It's not enough to talk a good game — our actions must foster coexistence as well. And I happen to believe very deeply, as do many of my colleagues in government, that [for the American government] that will begin by putting the Middle East peace process in its comprehensiveness back on center stage and working as a legitimate, active, and creative agent for peace between all parties in order to right everybody's grievances.

All religions today include their moderate and extreme elements — those who value peaceful coexistence and those who don't. It's up to each of us to work within our faith communities and between them to influence people toward expressing their beliefs in a manner compatible with a peaceful world.

Gandhi said, "You must be the change you want to see in the world." We all want to see a great deal of change. Somewhere between religious war and religious harmony — the "love" that Auden wrote of — is tolerance, acceptance of others' freedom to believe. I am so impressed and so grateful to "A Common Word" for not merely longing for a better dialogue but also standing up and delivering one.

And so, as we embark on this interfaith dialogue, we face great challenges and thorny questions. Is there, as I have suggested, a duty to engage with other faiths? What should the goal be? Tolerance? Understanding? Love? Is there in fact a global ethic? And if so, what can religious leaders such as the many in this room do to strengthen it and flesh it out? How do we reconcile the demands of our particular faith with the need to live in a pluralistic world? How do we balance respect for religious truths with respect for those who don't share them? There are people of every faith who claim that their faith entitles them to actions that harm others. How and where do we as religious communities draw the lines of acceptable behavior?

These are just some of the questions with which we must grapple. Unfortunately I have no easy answers. But most importantly, we have come together to make an honest effort at understanding. When you do so, whatever your faith, I believe you are doing God's work.

My ancestor John Winthrop saw his colony in Massachusetts as a "city on a hill" — apart from the rest of humanity, an example to teach others how to live a true Christian life. That was then. Today we need a new kind of city on a hill. The new city on the hill cannot be walled off, and it cannot lock in shackles those who disagree, or send them into the wilderness. We still need to set an example for the world. We still need to teach humanity a lesson. Only now, the lesson is this: "We must love one another or die." We must learn how both to love our faiths and also to live them side by side. In the twenty-first century, that will be our city on the hill.

May God bless you all.

The Addressees and Signatories of
"A Common Word Between Us and You"

Addressees

His Holiness Pope Benedict XVI,

His All-Holiness Bartholomew I, Patriarch of Constantinople, New Rome,

His Beatitude Theodoros II, Pope and Patriarch of Alexandria and All Africa,

His Beatitude Ignatius IV, Patriarch of Antioch and All the East,

His Beatitude Theophilos III, Patriarch of the Holy City of Jerusalem,

His Beatitude Alexy II, Patriarch of Moscow and All Russia,

His Beatitude Pavle, Patriarch of Belgrade and Serbia,

His Beatitude Daniel, Patriarch of Romania,

His Beatitude Maxim, Patriarch of Bulgaria,

His Beatitude Ilia II, Archbishop of Mtskheta-Tbilisi, Catholicos-Patriarch of All Georgia,

His Beatitude Chrisostomos, Archbishop of Cyprus,

His Beatitude Christodoulos, Archbishop of Athens and All Greece,

His Beatitude Sawa, Metropolitan of Warsaw and All Poland,

His Beatitude Anastasios, Archbishop of Tirana, Duerres and All Albania,

His Beatitude Christoforos, Metropolitan of the Czech and Slovak Republics,

His Holiness Pope Shenouda III, Pope of Alexandria and Patriarch of All Africa on the Apostolic Throne of St. Mark,

His Beatitude Karekin II, Supreme Patriarch and Catholicos of All Armenians,

His Beatitude Ignatius Zakka I, Patriarch of Antioch and All the East, Supreme Head of the Universal Syrian Orthodox Church,

His Holiness Mar Thoma Didymos I, Catholicos of the East on the Apostolic Throne of St. Thomas and the Malankara Metropolitan,

His Holiness Abune Paulos, Fifth Patriarch and Catholicos of Ethiopia, Echege of the See of St. Tekle Haymanot, Archbishop of Axium,

His Beatitude Mar Dinkha IV, Patriarch of the Holy Apostolic Catholic Assyrian Church of the East,

The Most Rev. Rowan Williams, Archbishop of Canterbury,

Rev. Mark S. Hanson, Presiding Bishop of the Evangelical Lutheran Church in America, and President of the Lutheran World Federation,

Rev. George H. Freeman, General Secretary, World Methodist Council,

Rev. David Coffey, President of the Baptist World Alliance,

Rev. Setri Nyomi, General Secretary of the World Alliance of Reformed Churches,

Rev. Dr. Samuel Kobia, General Secretary, World Council of Churches,

And Leaders of Christian Churches, everywhere

Signatories (in Alphabetical Order)

His Royal Eminence Sultan Muhammadu Sa'ad Ababakar
The 20th Sultan of Sokoto; Leader of the Muslims of Nigeria

H.E. Shaykh Dr. Hussein Hasan Abakar
Imam of the Muslims, Chad; President, Higher Council for Islamic Affairs, Chad

H.E. Prof. Dr. Abdul-Salam Al-Abbadi
President of Aal Al-Bayt University; Former Minister of Religious Affairs, Jordan

Prof. Dr. Taha Abd Al-Rahman
President of the Wisdom Circle for Thinkers and Researchers, Morocco; Director of Al-Umma Al-Wasat Magazine, International Union of Muslim Scholars

Imam Feisal Abdul Rauf
Co-founder and Chairman of the Board of the Cordoba Initiative; Founder of the ASMA Society (American Society for Muslim Advancement); Imam of Masjid Al-Farah, New York, NY, USA

Sheikh Muhammad Nur Abdullah
Vice President of the Fiqh Council of North America, USA

Dr. Shaykh Abd Al-Quddus Abu Salah
President of the International League for Islamic Ethics; Editor of the Journal for Islamic Ethics, Riyadh, Saudi Arabia

H.E. Prof. Dr. Abd Al-Wahhab bin Ibrahim Abu Solaiman
Member of the Committee of Senior Ulama, Saudi Arabia

Dr. Lateef Oladimeji Adegbite
Acting Secretary and Legal Adviser, Nigerian Supreme Council for Islamic Affairs

H.E. Amb. Prof. Dr. Akbar Ahmed
Ibn Khaldun Chair of Islamic Studies, American University in Washington, DC, USA

H.E. Judge Prince Bola Ajibola
Former International High Court Judge; Former Minister of Justice of Nigeria; Former Attorney-General of Nigeria; Founder of the Crescent University and Founder of the Islamic Movement of Africa (IMA)

H.E. Prof. Dr. Kamil Al-Ajlouni
Head of National Centre for Diabetes; Founder of the Jordanian University of Science and Technology (JUST), Former Minister and Former Senator, Jordan

Shaykh Dr. Mohammed Salim Al-'Awa
Secretary General of the International Union of Muslim Scholars; Head of the Egyptian Association for Culture and Dialogue

Mr. Nihad Awad
National Executive Director and Co-founder of the Council on American-Islamic Relations (CAIR), USA

H.E. Prof. Dr. Al-Hadi Al-Bakkoush
Former Prime Minister of Tunisia, Author

H.E. Shaykh Al-Islam Dr. Allah-Shakur bin Hemmat Bashazada
Grand Mufti of Azerbaijan and Head of the Muslim Administration of the Caucasus

H.E. Dr. Issam El-Bashir
Secretary General of the International Moderation Centre, Kuwait; Former Minister of Religious Affairs, Sudan

H.E. Prof. Dr. *Allamah* Shaykh Abd Allah bin Mahfuz bin Bayyah
Professor, King Abdul Aziz University, Saudi Arabia; Former Minister of Justice, Former Minister of Education and Former Minister of Religious Affairs, Mauritania; Vice President of the International Union of Muslim Scholars; Founder and President, Global Center for Renewal and Guidance

Dr. Mohamed Bechari
President, Federal Society for Muslims in France; General Secretary of the European Islamic Conference (EIC), France; Member of the International Fiqh Academy

Prof. Dr. Ahmad Shawqi Benbin
Director of the Hasaniyya Library, Morocco

Prof. Dr. *Allamah* Shaykh Muhammad Saʿid Ramadan Al-Buti
Dean, Dept. of Religion, University of Damascus, Syria

Prof. Dr. Mustafa Çağrici
Mufti of Istanbul, Turkey

H.E. Shaykh Prof. Dr. Mustafa Cerić
Grand Mufti and Head of Ulema of Bosnia and Herzegovina

Professor Ibrahim Chabbuh
Director General of the Royal Aal al-Bayt Institute for Islamic Thought, Jordan; President of the Association for the Safeguarding of the City of Qayrawan, Tunisia

H.E. Prof. Dr. Mustafa Cherif
Muslim Intellectual; Former Minister of Higher Education and Former Ambassador, Algeria

Dr. Caner Dagli
Assistant Professor, Roanoke College, USA

Ayatollah Prof. Dr. *Seyyed* Mostafa Mohaghegh Damad
Dean of Department of Islamic Studies, The Academy of Sciences of Iran; Professor of Law and Islamic Philosophy, Tehran University; Fellow, The Iranian Academy of Sciences, Iran; Former Inspector General of Iran

Ayatollah *Seyyed* Abu Al-Qasim Al-Deebaji
Imam Zayn Al-Abideen Mosque, Kuwait

H.E. Prof. Dr. Shakir Al-Fahham
Head of the Arabic Language Academy, Damascus; Former Minister of Education, Syria

Shaykh *Seyyed* Hani Fahs
Member of Supreme Shia Committee, Lebanon; Founding Member of the Arab Committee for the Islamic-Christian Dialogue, and the Permanent Committee for the Lebanese Dialogue

H.E. Shaykh Salim Falahat
Director General of the Muslim Brotherhood, Jordan

Chief Abdul Wahab Iyanda Folawiyo
Member, Supreme Council for Islamic Affairs of Nigeria; Vice President, Jamaat Nasril Islam

H.E. Shaykh Ravil Gainutdin
Grand Mufti of Russia

Justice Ibrahim Kolapo Sulu Gambari
Justice of Nigerian Court of Appeal; National Vice Chairman, Nigerian Football Association (NFA)

Prof. Dr. Abd Al-Karim Gharaybeh
Historian and Senator, Jordan

H.E. Prof. Dr. Abdullah Yusuf Al-Ghoneim
Director of the Kuwaiti Centre for Research and Studies on Kuwait; Former Minister of Education, Kuwait

H.E. Prof. Dr. Bu Abd Allah bin al-Hajj Muhammad Al Ghulam Allah
Minister of Religious Affairs, Algeria

Prof. Dr. Alan Godlas
Co-Chair, Islamic Studies, University of Georgia, USA; Editor-in-chief,
Sufi News and Sufism World Report; *Director, Sufis Without Borders*

H.E. Shaykh Nezdad Grabus
Grand Mufti of Slovenia

H.E. Shaykh Dr. *Al-Habib* Ahmad bin Abd Al-Aziz Al-Haddad
Chief Mufti of Dubai, UAE

Shaykh *Al-Habib* Ali Mashhour bin Muhammad bin Salim bin Hafeeth
Imam of the Tarim Mosque and Head of Fatwa Council, Tarim, Yemen

Shaykh *Al-Habib* Umar bin Muhammad bin Salim bin Hafeeth
Dean, Dar Al-Mustafa, Tarim, Yemen

Professor Dr. Farouq Hamadah
Professor of the Sciences of Tradition, Mohammad V University,
Morocco

Prof. Dr. Hasan Hanafi
Muslim Intellectual, Department of Philosophy, Cairo University

Shaykh Hamza Yusuf Hanson
Founder and Director, Zaytuna Institute, California, USA

H.E. Shaykh Dr. Ahmad Badr Al-Din Hassoun
Grand Mufti of the Republic of Syria

H.E. Shaykh *Sayyed* Ali bin Abd Al-Rahman Al-Hashimi
Advisor to the President for Judiciary and Religious Affairs, UAE

Shaykh Kabir Helminski
Shaykh of the Mevlevi Tariqah; Co-Director of the Book Foundation,
USA

H.E. Shaykh Sa'id Hijjawi
Chief Scholar, The Royal Aal al-Bayt Institute for Islamic Thought;
Former Grand Mufti of Jordan

H.E. Prof. Dr. Shaykh Ahmad Hlayyel
Chief Islamic Justice of Jordan; Imam of the Hashemite Court; Former
Minister of Religious Affairs

H.E. Amb. Dr. Murad Hofmann
Author and Muslim Intellectual, Germany

H.E. Dr. Anwar Ibrahim
*Former Deputy Prime Minister of Malaysia; Honorary President of
AccountAbility*

H.E. Shaykh Dr. Izz Al-Din Ibrahim
Advisor for Cultural Affairs, Prime Ministry, UAE

H.E. Prof. Dr. Ekmeleddin Ihsanoglu
Secretary-General, Organization of the Islamic Conference (OIC)

H.E. Prof. Dr. Omar Jah
*Secretary of the Muslim Scholars Council, Gambia; Professor of Islamic
Civilization and Thought, University of Gambia*

H.E. Prof. Dr. Abbas Al-Jarari
Advisor to HM the King, Morocco

Shaykh *Al-Habib* Ali Zain Al-Abidin Al-Jifri
Founder and Director, Taba Institute, United Arab Emirates

H.E. Shaykh Prof. Dr. Ali Jum'a
Grand Mufti of the Republic of Egypt

Prof. Dr. Yahya Mahmud bin Junayd
*Secretary General, King Faisal Centre for Research and Islamic Studies,
Saudi Arabia*

Professor Dr. 'Abla Mohammed Kahlawi
*Dean of Islamic and Arabic Studies, Al-Azhar University (Women's
College), Egypt*

Dr. Ibrahim Kalin
*Director, SETA Foundation, Ankara, Turkey; Assistant Professor,
Georgetown University, USA*

H.E. Amb. Aref Kamal
Muslim Intellectual, Pakistan

Prof. Dr. Mohammad Hashim Kamali
*Dean and Professor, International Institute of Islamic Thought and
Civilization (ISTAC), International Islamic University, Malaysia*

Prof. Dr. Said Hibatullah Kamilev
Director, Moscow Institute of Islamic Civilisation, Russian Federation

Prof. Dr. *Hafiz* Yusuf Z. Kavakci
Resident Scholar, Islamic Association of North Texas, Founder and

Instructor of IANT Qur'anic Academy; Founding Dean of Suffa Islamic Seminary, Dallas, Texas, USA

Shaykh Dr. Nuh Ha Mim Keller
Shaykh in the Shadhili Order, USA

Shaykh Amr Khaled
Islamic Missionary, Preacher and Broadcaster, Egypt; Founder and Chairman, Right Start Foundation International

Prof. Dr. Abd Al-Karim Khalifah
President of the Jordanian Arabic Language Academy; Former President of Jordan University

H.E. Shaykh Ahmad Al-Khalili
Grand Mufti of the Sultanate of Oman

Seyyed Jawad Al-Khoei
Secretary-General, Al-Khoei International Foundation

Shaykh Dr. Ahmad Kubaisi
Founder of the 'Ulema Organization, Iraq

Mr. M. Ali Lakhani
Founder and Editor of Sacred Web: A Journal of Tradition and Modernity, *Canada*

Dr. Joseph Lumbard
Assistant Professor, Brandeis University, USA

H.E. Shaykh Mahmood A. Madani
Secretary General, Jamiat Ulama-i-Hind; Member of Parliament, India

H.E. Prof. Dr. Abdel-Kabeer Al-Alawi Al-Madghari
Director General of Bayt Mal Al-Quds Agency (Al-Quds Fund); Former Minister of Religious Affairs, Morocco

H.E. *Imam Sayyed* Al-Sadiq Al-Mahdi
Former Prime Minister of Sudan; Head of Ansar Movement, Sudan

H.E. Prof. Dr. Rusmir Mahmutcehajic
Professor, Sarajevo University; President of the International Forum Bosnia; Former Vice President of the Government of Bosnia and Herzegovina

Allamah Shaykh *Sayyed* Muhammad bin Muhammad Al-Mansour
High Authority (Marja') of Zeidi Muslims, Yemen

Prof. Dr. Bashshar Awwad Marouf
Former Rector of the Islamic University, Iraq

H.E. Prof. Dr. Ahmad Matloub
Former Minister of Culture; Acting President of the Iraqi Academy of Sciences, Iraq

Prof. Dr. Ingrid Mattson
Professor of Islamic Studies and Christian-Muslim Relations and Director, Islamic Chaplaincy Program, Hartford Seminary; President of the Islamic Society of North America (ISNA), USA

Dr. Yousef Meri
Special Scholar-in-Residence, Royal Aal al-Bayt Institute for Islamic Thought, Jordan

Dr. Jean-Louis Michon
Author; Muslim Scholar; Architect; Former UNESCO expert, Switzerland

Shaykh Abu Bakr Ahmad Al-Milibari
Secretary-General of the Ahl Al-Sunna Association, India

Pehin Dato Haj Suhaili bin Haj Mohiddin
Deputy Grand Mufti, Brunei

Ayatollah Sheikh Hussein Muayad
President and Founder, Knowledge Forum, Baghdad, Iraq

Prof. Dr. Izzedine Umar Musa
Professor of Islamic History, King Saʿud University, Saudi Arabia

Prof. Dr. Mohammad Farouk Al-Nabhan
Former Director of Dar Al-Hadith Al-Hasaniya, Morocco

Prof. Dr. Zaghloul El-Naggar
Professor, King Abd Al-Aziz University, Jeddah, Saudi Arabia; Head, Committee on Scientific Facts in the Glorious Qur'an, Supreme Council on Islamic Affairs, Egypt

Mr. Sohail Nakhooda
Editor-in-Chief, Islamica Magazine, *Jordan*

Prof. Dr. Hisham Nashabeh
Chairman of the Board of Higher Education; Dean of Education at Makassed Association, Lebanon

H.E. Professor Dr. *Seyyed* Hossein Nasr
University Professor of Islamic Studies, George Washington University, Washington, DC, USA

Prof. Dr. Aref Ali Nayed
Former Professor at the Pontifical Institute for Arabic and Islamic Studies (Rome); Former Professor at International Institute for Islamic Thought and Civilization (ISTAC, Malaysia); Senior Advisor to the Cambridge Interfaith Program at the Faculty of Divinity in Cambridge, UK

H.E. Shaykh Sevki Omarbasic
Grand Mufti of Croatia

Dato Dr. Abdul Hamid Othman
Advisor to H.E. the Prime Minister of Malaysia

Prof. Dr. Ali Ozek
Head of the Endowment for Islamic Scientific Studies, Istanbul, Turkey

Imam Yahya Sergio Yahe Pallavicini
Vice President of CO.RE.IS., Italy; Chairman of ISESCO Council for Education and Culture in the West; Advisor for Islamic Affairs of the Italian Minister of Interior

H.E. Shaykh Dr. Nuh Ali Salman Al-Qudah
Grand Mufti of the Hashemite Kingdom of Jordan

H.E. Shaykh Dr. Ikrima Said Sabri
Former Grand Mufti of Jerusalem and All of Palestine, Imam of the Blessed Al-Aqsa Mosque, and President of the Islamic Higher Council, Palestine

Ayatollah Al-Faqih *Seyyed* Hussein Ismail Al-Sadr
Baghdad, Iraq

Mr. Muhammad Al-Sammak
Secretary-General of the National Council for Islamic-Christian Dialogue; Secretary-General for the Islamic Spiritual Summit, Lebanon

Shaykh *Seyyed* Hasan Al-Saqqaf
Director of Dar Al-Imam Al-Nawawi, Jordan

Dr. Ayman Fuad Sayyid
Historian and Manuscript Expert, Former Secretary General of Dar al-Kutub Al-Misriyya, Cairo, Egypt

Prof. Dr. Suleiman Abdallah Schleifer
Professor Emeritus, The American University in Cairo

Dr. *Seyyed* Reza Shah-Kazemi
Author and Muslim Scholar, UK

Dr. Anas Al-Shaikh-Ali
*Chair, Association of Muslim Social Scientists, UK; Chair, Forum
Against Islamophobia and Racism, UK; Academic Advisor, IIIT, UK*

Imam Zaid Shakir
Lecturer and Scholar-in-Residence, Zaytuna Institute, CA, USA

H.E. Prof. Dr. Ali Abdullah Al-Shamlan
*Director General of the Kuwait Foundation for the Advancement of
Sciences (KFAS); Former Minister of Higher Education, Kuwait*

Eng. *Seyyed* Hasan Shariatmadari
Leader of the Iranian National Republican Party (INR)

H.E. Dr. Mohammad Abd Al-Ghaffar Al-Sharif
Secretary-General of the Ministry of Religious Affairs, Kuwait

Dr. Muhammad Alwani Al-Sharif
*Head of the European Academy of Islamic Culture and Sciences,
Brussels, Belgium*

Dr. Tayba Hassan Al-Sharif
*International Protection Officer, The United Nations High
Commissioner for Refugees, Darfur, Sudan*

Prof. Dr. Muhammad bin Sharifa
*Former Rector of Wajda University, Morocco; Fellow of the Royal
Moroccan Academy*

Prof. Dr. Muzammil H. Siddiqui, on behalf of the whole Fiqh Council of
North America
*Islamic Scholar and Theologian; Chairman of the Fiqh Council of North
America, USA*

Shaykh Ahmad bin Sa'ud Al-Siyabi
Secretary General of the Directorate of the Grand Mufti, Oman

Al-Haji Yusuf Maitama Sule
*Former Nigerian Permanent Representative to the United Nations;
Former Nigerian Minister of National Guidance*

Prof. Dr. Muhammad Abd Al-Rahim Sultan-al-Ulama
Deputy-Dean of Scientific Research Affairs, United Arab Emirates University, UAE

Shaykh Dr. Tariq Sweidan
Director-General of the Risalah Satellite Channel

Prof. Dr. H.R.H. Prince Ghazi bin Muhammad bin Talal
Personal Envoy and Special Advisor of H.M. King Abdullah II; Chairman of the Board of the Royal Aal al-Bayt Institute for Islamic Thought, Jordan

Prof. Dr. Ammar Al-Talibi
Former Member of Parliament, Professor of Philosophy, University of Algeria

H.E. Shaykh Ahmad Muhammad Muti'i Tamim
The Head of the Religious Administration of Ukrainian Muslims, and Mufti of Ukraine

H.E. Shaykh Izz Al-Din Al-Tamimi
Senator; Former Chief Islamic Justice, Minister of Religious Affairs and Grand Mufti of Jordan

H.E. Shaykh Dr. Tayseer Rajab Al-Tamimi
Chief Islamic Justice of Palestine; Head of The Palestinian Center for Religion and Civilization Dialogue

Ayatollah Shaykh Muhammad Ali Taskhiri
Secretary General of the World Assembly for Proximity of Islamic Schools of Thought (WAPIST), Iran

H.E. Prof. Dr. Shaykh Ahmad Muhammad Al-Tayeb
President of Al-Azhar University; Former Grand Mufti of Egypt

Prof. Dr. Muddathir Abdel-Rahim Al-Tayib
Professor of Political Science and Islamic Studies, International Institute of Islamic Thought and Civilization (ISTAC), Malaysia

H.E. Amb. Prof. Dr. Abdel-Hadi Al-Tazi
Fellow of the Royal Moroccan Academy

H.E. Shaykh Naim Trnava
Grand Mufti of Kosovo

H.E. Dr. Abd Al-Aziz bin 'Uthman Al-Tweijiri
Director-General of the Islamic Educational, Scientific and Cultural Organization (ISESCO)

H.E. Prof. Dr. Nasaruddin Umar
Rector of the Institute for Advanced Qur'anic Studies; Secretary General of the Nahdhatul Ulama Consultative Council; Lecturer at the State Islamic University Syarif Hidayatullah, Jakarta, Indonesia

Shaykh Muhammad Hasan 'Usayran
Jafari Mufti of Sidon and Al-Zahrani, Lebanon

Allamah Justice Mufti Muhammad Taqi Usmani
Vice President, Darul Uloom Karachi, Pakistan

Prof. Dr. Akhtarul Wasey
Director, Zakir Husain Institute of Islamic Studies, Jamia Milla Islamiya University, India

Shaykh Dr. Abdal Hakim Murad Winter
Shaykh Zayed Lecturer in Islamic Studies, Divinity School, University of Cambridge; Director of the Muslim Academic Trust, UK

Prof. Dr. Mohammed El-Mokhtar Ould Bah
President, Chinguitt Modern University, Mauritania

H.E. Shaykh Muhammad Sodiq Mohammad Yusuf
Former Grand Mufti of the Muslim Spiritual Administration of Central Asia, Uzbekistan; Translator and Commentator of the Holy Qur'an

Prof. Dr. Shaykh Wahba Mustafa Al-Zuhayli
Dean, Department of Islamic Jurisprudence, University of Damascus, Syria

H.E. Shaykh Mu'ammar Zukoulic
Mufti of Sanjak, Bosnia

APPENDIX 2:
The Signatories of the Yale Response, "Loving God and Neighbor Together"

The Yale Response was first issued by the following four scholars:

Harold W. Attridge
> *Dean and Lillian Claus Professor of New Testament, Yale Divinity School*

Joseph Cumming
> *Director of the Reconciliation Program, Yale Center for Faith and Culture*

Emilie M. Townes
> *Andrew Mellon Professor of African American Religion and Theology and President-elect of the American Academy of Religion*

Miroslav Volf
> *Founder and Director of the Yale Center for Faith and Culture, Henry B. Wright Professor of Theology, Yale University*

The statement was subsequently endorsed by many other Christian theologians and leaders. A selection of prominent signatories follows:

Capt. Bradford E. Ableson
> *Chaplain Corps, US Navy and Senior Episcopal Chaplain in the US Navy*

Dr. Martin Accad
> *Academic Dean, Arab Baptist Theological Seminary (Lebanon); Director, Institute of Middle East Studies (Lebanon); Associate Professor of Islamic Studies, Fuller School of Intercultural Studies*

Scott C. Alexander
> *Associate Professor of Islam and Director, Catholic-Muslim Studies, Catholic Theological Union*

Roger Allen
> *Professor of Arabic and Comparative Literature and Chair, Department of Near Eastern Languages and Civilizations, University of Pennsylvania; member of Middle East Study Group of the Episcopal Diocese of Pennsylvania*

Jean Amore, CSJ
> *for the Leadership Team of the Sisters of St. Joseph, Brentwood, NY*

Leith Anderson
> *President, National Association of Evangelicals*

Rev. Daniel S. Appleyard
> *Rector, Christ Episcopal Church, Dearborn, MI*

William Aramony
> *Consultant*

Dr. Don Argue
> *Chancellor, Northwest University; Former President, National Association of Evangelicals; Commissioner, United States Commission on International Religious Freedom*

Yvette A. Assem
> *Student, Interdenominational Theological Center, Atlanta, Georgia*

David Augsburger
> *Professor of Pastoral Care and Counseling, Fuller Theological Seminary*

Gerald R. Baer, M.D.
> *Minister of Christian Education, Landisville, PA*

Dwight P. Baker
> *Associate Director, Overseas Ministries Study Center*

Dr. Ray Bakke
> *Convening Chair, Evangelicals for Middle East Understanding: An International Coalition, Tempe, AZ*

His Lordship Bishop Camillo Ballin, MCCI
> *Vicar Apostolic of Kuwait*

Leonard Bartlotti
> *Associate Professor of Intercultural Studies, Biola University*

Charles L. Bartow
Carl and Helen Egner Professor of Speech Communication in Ministry, Princeton Theological Seminary

Dr. Mogamat-Ali Behardien
Minister, African Reformed Church, Paarl, South Africa

Rt. Rev. Barry Beisner
Bishop, Episcopal Diocese of Northern California

Federico Bertuzzi
President, PM Internacional, Latin America

James A. Beverley
Professor of Christian Thought and Ethics, Tyndale Seminary, Toronto, Canada

J. D. Bindenagel
former US Ambassador and Vice President, DePaul University, Chicago, IL

Rev. Dr. Thomas W. Blair
The Second Presbyterian Church of Baltimore

Walter R. Bodine
Pastor, International Church at Yale, and Research Affiliate, Near Eastern Languages, Yale University

Rev. Timothy A. Boggs
St. Alban's Episcopal Church, Washington, DC

Regina A. Boisclair
Cardinal Newman Chair of Theology, Alaska Pacific University, Anchorage, AK

David Bok
Independent Bible Teacher, Hartford Seminary, Hartford, CT

Rev. Jim Bonewald
Pastor, Knox Presbyterian Church, Cedar Rapids, IA

Jonathan J. Bonk
Executive Director, Overseas Ministries Study Center and Editor, International Bulletin of Missionary Research

Rev. Michael S. Bos
Director, Al Amana Centre, Sultanate of Oman

Steven Bouma-Prediger
Professor of Religion, Hope College, Holland, MI

Gerhard Böwering
Professor of Religious Studies, Yale University

Mary C. Boys
Skinner and McAlpin Professor of Practical Theology, Union Theological Seminary, New York, NY

Dan Brannen
International Students, Inc.

Revs. Scott and Katarina Breslin
Protestant House Church Network, Istanbul, Turkey

Rev. Dr. Stuart Briscoe
Minister at Large, Elmbrook Church, Brookfield, WI; Founder, Telling the Truth, Inc.

Joseph Britton
Dean, Berkeley Divinity School at Yale

Rev. Douglas Brown
Pastor, Valley View United Methodist Church Overland Park, KS

Huib Bruinink
Developer of Marketing, PT. Puteri Mawar Sari, Central Java, Indonesia

John M. Buchanan
Editor/Publisher, The Christian Century

James J. Buckley
Dean, College of Arts and Sciences, Loyola College in Maryland

Eugene W. Bunkowske, Ph.D.
Fiechtner Chair Professor of Christian Outreach, Oswald Huffman School of Christian Outreach, Concordia University, St. Paul, Minnesota

John R. Burkholder
Professor Emeritus, Religion and Peace Studies, Goshen College, Goshen, IN

David Burkum
Pastor, Valley Christian Church, Lakeville, MN

Rt. Rev. Joe Goodwin Burnett
Bishop, Episcopal Diocese of Nebraska

Allen Busenitz
International Student Ministry, West Lafayette, IN

Very Rev. Samuel G. Candler
Dean, Cathedral of St. Philip (Anglican), Atlanta, GA

Juan Carlos Cárdenas
Academic Director, Instituto Iberoamericano de Estudios Transculturales, Granada, Spain

Joseph Castleberry
President, Northwest University

Rev. Colin Chapman
Former Lecturer in Islamic Studies, Near East School of Theology, Beirut, Lebanon, and author of Whose Promised Land?

Ellen T. Charry
Associate Professor of Systematic Theology, Princeton Theological Seminary

David Yonggi Cho
Founder and Senior Pastor of Yoido Full Gospel Church, Seoul, Korea

Hyung Kyun Chung
Associate Professor of Ecumenical Studies, Union Theological Seminary, New York, NY

Rev. Richard Cizik
Vice President of Governmental Affairs, National Association of Evangelicals

Rev. Dr. Emmanuel Clapsis
Professor of Systematic Theology, Holy Cross Greek Orthodox School of Theology, Brookline, MA

William Clarkson IV
President, The Westminster Schools, Atlanta, GA

Emily Click
Lecturer on Ministry and Assistant Dean for Ministry Studies and Field Education, Harvard Divinity School

Corneliu Constantineanu
Dean and Associate Professor of New Testament, Evangelical Theological Seminary, Osijek, Croatia

Robert E. Cooley
President Emeritus, Gordon-Conwell Theological Seminary, South Hamilton, MA

Rev. Shawn Coons
St. Philip Presbyterian, Houston, TX

Harvey Cox
Hollis Professor of Divinity, Harvard Divinity School

Daniel A. Cunningham
Executive Pastor, Temple Bible Church, Temple, TX

Bryant L. Cureton
President, Elmhurst College, Elmhurst, IL

Fr. John D'Alton
President, Melbourne Institute for Orthodox Christian Studies, Melbourne, Australia

Fr. Joseph P. Daoust, S.J.
President, Jesuit School of Theology at Berkeley, CA

Rev. David R. Davis
Special Projects Coordinator, The Evangelical Alliance Mission, Wheaton, IL

John Deacon
Leader, Branch Out Ministries, The Olive Branch Community Church, Markham, Ontario, Canada

Rev. Joseph C. Delahunt
Senior Pastor, Silliman Memorial Baptist Church, Bridgeport, CT

André Delbecq
Thomas J. and Kathleen L. McCarthy University Professor, Center for Spirituality of Organizational Leadership, and former Dean of the Leavey School of Business at the University of Santa Clara

Dr. John Dendiu
Assistant Professor of Religion, Bethel College (Indiana)

David A. Depew
President, Seed of Abraham Association, broadcasting radio Bible studies in the Middle East

Keith DeRose
Allison Foundation Professor of Philosophy, Yale University

Curtiss Paul DeYoung
Professor of Reconciliation Studies, Bethel University

Andrew Dimmock
Director, Doulos Community, Nouakchott, Mauritania

Chip Dobbs-Allsopp
Associate Professor of Old Testament, Princeton Theological Seminary

Linda Tempesta Ducrot
President, Chez Ducrot, Inc., Plymouth, MA

Andrés Alonso Duncan
CEO, Latinoamerica Global, A.C.

Kent A. Eaton
Professor of Pastoral Ministry and Associate Dean, Bethel Seminary San Diego, CA

Diana L. Eck
Professor of Comparative Religion and Indian Studies in Arts and Sciences and member of the Faculty of Divinity, Harvard University

Mike Edens
Professor of Theology and Islamic Studies, Associate Dean of Graduate Studies, New Orleans Baptist Theological Seminary, New Orleans, LA

Mark U. Edwards, Jr.
Senior Advisor to the Dean, Harvard Divinity School

James Ehrman
Director, Global Ministries Office, Evangelical Congregational Church

Bertil Ekstrom
Executive Director, Mission Commission, World Evangelical Alliance

Nancie Erhard
Assistant Professor of Comparative Religious Ethics, Saint Mary's University, Halifax, Nova Scotia

John Esposito
University Professor and Founding Director of the Prince Alwaleed Bin Talal Center for Muslim-Christian Understanding, Georgetown University

Chester E. Falby
Priest Associate, St. Catherine's Episcopal Church, Manzanita, OR

Thomas P. Finger
Mennonite Central Committee, Evanston, IL

Rev. Dr. David C. Fisher
Senior Minister, Plymouth Church, Brooklyn, NY

David Ford
Regius Professor of Divinity, Cambridge University

Marlene Malahoo Forte
2007 Yale World Fellow, Fuller Theological Seminary, Pasadena, CA

Rev. Susan L. Gabbard
St. John's United Church of Christ, Mifflinburg, PA

Millard Garrett
Vice President, Eastern Mennonite Missions, Salunga, PA

Siobhan Garrigan
Assistant Professor of Liturgical Studies and Assistant Dean for Marquand Chapel, Yale Divinity School

Timothy George
Dean, Beeson Divinity School, Samford University

William Goettler
Assistant Dean for Assessment and Ministerial Studies, Yale Divinity School

Michael J. Goggin
Chairperson, North American Interfaith Network (NAIN)

Robert S. Goizueta
Professor of Theology, Boston College

Bruce Gordon
Professor of History, University of St. Andrews

William A. Graham
Albertson Professor of Middle Eastern Studies in Arts and Sciences and O'Brian Professor of Divinity and Dean in the Divinity School, Harvard University

Wesley Granberg-Michaelson
General Secretary, Reformed Church in America

Rev. Bruce Green
Bridge Building Facilitator, FCM Foundation, Centerville Presbyterian Church, Fremont, CA

Joel B. Green
Professor of New Testament Interpretation, Fuller Theological Seminary

Lynn Green
International Chairman, Youth with a Mission

Frank Griffel
Associate Professor of Islamic Studies, Yale University

Rev. Giorgio Grlj
Pastor, Rijeka Baptist Church, Baptist Union of Croatia

Rev. Kent Claussen Gubrud
Christus Victor Lutheran Church, Apple Valley, MN

Rt. Rev. Edwin F. Gulick, Jr.
Bishop, Episcopal Diocese of Kentucky

Judith Gundry
Adjunct Associate Professor of New Testament, Yale Divinity School

David P. Gushee
Distinguished Professor of Christian Ethics, McAfee School of Theology at Mercer University and President, Evangelicals for Human Rights

Kim B. Gustafson
President, Common Ground Consultants, Inc.

Elie Haddad
Provost, Arab Baptist Theological Seminary, Lebanon

Heidi Hadsell
President, Hartford Seminary, Hartford, CT

Dr. Anette Hagan
Elder, Mayfield Salisbury Parish Church, Edinburgh, Scotland

Martin Hailer
Professor of Theology, Leuphana University, Lüneburg, Germany

Rev. L. Ann Hallisey
Hallisey Consulting and Counseling, Interim Vicar, Good Shepherd Episcopal Church, Berkeley, CA

Gloria K. Hannas
Member, Peacemaking Mission Team of the Presbytery of Chicago, PCUSA, La Grange, IL

Paul D. Hanson
> *Florence Corliss Lamont Professor of Divinity, Harvard Divinity School*

Pastor Peter Hanson
> *Director of Studies, Department of Theology and Training, Lutheran Church of Senegal*

David Heim
> *Executive Editor,* The Christian Century

Richard Henderson
> *Director of Studies, Westbrook Hay, United Kingdom*

Mary E. Hess
> *Associate Professor of Educational Leadership, Luther Seminary*

Richard Heyduck
> *Pastor, First United Methodist Church, Pittsburg, TX*

Rev. Dr. David M. Hindman
> *United Methodist campus minister, The Wesley Foundation at The College of William and Mary, Williamsburg, VA*

Rev. Norman A. Hjelm
> *Director, Commission on Faith and Order (retired), National Council of the Churches of Christ in the USA*

Carl R. Holladay
> *Charles Howard Candler Professor of New Testament, Candler School of Theology, Emory University*

Jan Holton
> *Assistant Professor of Pastoral Care, Yale Divinity School*

Marian E. Hostetler
> *former worker, Mennonite Mission Network and Eastern Mennonite Mission, Elkhart, IN*

Joseph Hough
> *President and William E. Dodge Professor of Social Ethics, Union Theological Seminary in New York*

Bill Hybels
> *Founder and Senior Pastor, Willow Creek Community Church, South Barrington, IL*

Dale T. Irvin
President and Professor of World Christianity, New York Theological Seminary, New York, NY

Dr. Nabeel T. Jabbour
Consultant, Professor, Colorado Springs, CO

Todd Jenkins
Pastor, First Presbyterian Church, Fayetteville, TN

David L. Johnston
Lecturer, Religious Studies Department, University of Pennsylvania

Robert K. Johnston
Professor of Theology and Culture, Fuller Theological Seminary

Rt. Rev. Shannon Sherwood Johnston
Bishop Coadjutor, Episcopal Diocese of Virginia

Rt. Rev. David Colin Jones
Bishop Suffragan, Episcopal Diocese of Virginia

Gary D. Jones
Rector, St. Stephen's Episcopal Church, Richmond, VA

Tony Jones
National Coordinator, Emergent Village

Stefan Jung
Economist, Germany

Rev. Dr. Riad A. Kassis
Theologian, Author, and Consultant

Sister Helen Kearney
Sisters of Saint Joseph, Brentwood, NY

Sister Janet Kinney, CSJ
Sisters of St. Joseph, Brentwood, NY

Doris G. Kinney
Associate Editor (ret.), Time Inc., New York, NY

Steve Knight
National Coordinating Group Member, Emergent Village, Charlotte, NC

Paul Knitter
Paul Tillich Professor of Theology, World Religions and Culture, Union Theological Seminary in New York

Dr. Manfred W. Kohl
Vice President of Overseas Council International, USA

Rev. John A. Koski
Assemblies of God, Dearborn, MI

Very Rev. Dr. James A. Kowalski
Dean, The Cathedral Church of Saint John the Divine, New York, NY

James R. Krabill
Senior Executive for Global Ministries, Mennonite Mission Network, Elkhart, IN

Hank Kraus
Founder and Director, PeaceMark

Sharon Kugler
University Chaplain, Yale University

Catherine Kurtz
Landisville Mennonite Church, Landisville, PA

Peter Kuzmic
Eva B. and Paul E. Toms Distinguished Professor of World Missions and European Studies, Gordon-Conwell Theological Seminary, and Rektor, Evandjeoski Teoloski Fakultet, Osijek, Croatia

Jonathan L. Kvanvig
Distinguised Professor of Philosophy, Baylor University

David Lamarre-Vincent
Executive Director, New Hampshire Council of Churches

John A. Lapp
Executive Secretary Emeritus, Mennonite Central Committee, Akron, PA

Dr. Warren Larson
Director of the Zwemer Center for Muslim Studies, Columbia International University, Columbia, SC

Traugott Lawler
Professor of English emeritus, Yale University

Dr. Maurice Lee
post-doctoral fellow, Harvard University

Rt. Rev. Peter J. Lee
Bishop, Episcopal Diocese of Virginia

Kristen Leslie
Associate Professor of Pastoral Care, Yale Divinity School

Linda LeSourd Lader
President, Renaissance Institute, Charleston, SC

Rev. R. Charles Lewis, Jr.
Parish Associate, First Presbyterian-Vintage Faith Church, Santa Cruz, CA

Julyan Lidstone, OM
Glasgow, Scotland

Erik Lincoln
Author of Peace Generation tolerance curriculum for Muslim Students, Indonesia

John Lindner
Director of External Relations, Yale Divinity School

Greg Livingstone
Founder of Frontiers and historian of Muslim-Christian encounter

Albert C. Lobe
Interim Executive Director, Mennonite Central Committee, Akron, PA

Rick Love
International Director, Frontiers; Adjunct Associate Professor of Islamic Studies, Fuller Theological Seminary; author of Peacemaking

Donald Luidens
Professor of Sociology, Hope College, Holland, MI

Owen Lynch
Associate Pastor, Trent Vineyard, Nottingham, UK

Douglas Magnuson
Associate Professor of Intercultural Programs and Director of Muslim Studies, Bethel University

Peter Maiden
International Coordinator, OM

Jozef Majewski
Doctor of Theology, Professor of Media Studies at the University of Gdansk, Poland

Danut Manastireanu
>   *Director for Faith and Development, Middle East and East Europe Region, World Vision International, Iasi, Romania*

Rev. Steven D. Martin
>   *President, Vital Visions Incorporated, and Pastor, United Methodist Church, Oak Ridge, TN*

Rev. Dr. John T. Mathew
>   *Minister, St. Mark's United Church of Canada, and Department of Religious Studies, Huntington/Laurentian Universities, Sudbury, ON Canada*

Harold E. Masback III
>   *Senior Minister, The Congregational Church of New Canaan*

Rt. Rev. Gerald N. McAllister
>   *Retired Bishop, Episcopal Diocese of Oklahoma*

The Rev. Donald M. McCoid
>   *Executive for Ecumenical and Inter-Religious Relations, Evangelical Lutheran Church in America*

C. Douglas McConnell, Ph.D.
>   *Dean, School of Intercultural Studies, Fuller Seminary*

Sister Mary McConnell, CSJ
>   *Sisters of St. Joseph, Brentwood, NY*

Don McCurry
>   *President, Ministries to Muslims*

Jeanne McGorry, CSJ
>   *Sisters of St. Joseph, Brentwood, NY*

Elsie McKee
>   *Archibald Alexander Professor of Reformation Studies and the History of Worship, Princeton Theological Seminary*

Scot McKnight
>   *Karl A. Olsson Professor in Religious Studies, North Park University, Chicago, IL*

Brian D. McLaren
>   *Author, Speaker, Activist*

C. Edward McVaney
>   *Retired Chairman, CEO, and President, J. D. Edwards and Company*

Kathleen E. McVey
J. Ross Stevenson Professor of Early and Eastern Church History, Princeton Theological Seminary

Carl Medearis
President, International Initiatives, Denver, CO

Greg Meland
Director of Formation, Supervised Ministry and Placement, Bethel Seminary, Minnesota

Judith Mendelsohn Rood, Ph.D.
Associate Professor of History and Middle Eastern Studies, Department of History, Government, and Social Science School of Arts and Sciences, Biola University

Mennonite Central Committee, Akron, PA

Harold E. Metzler
Member, Church of the Brethren and heritor of the Amish/Mennonite tradition

Alan E. Miller
Lead Pastor, Conestoga Church of the Brethren, Leola, PA

David B. Miller
Pastor, University Mennonite Church, State College, PA

Rev. Dr. Sid L. Mohn
President, Heartland Alliance for Human Needs and Human Rights, Chicago, IL

Brother Benilde Montgomery, O.S.F.
Franciscan Brother of Brooklyn

Steve Moore
President and CEO, The Mission Exchange

Douglas Morgan
Director, Adventist Peace Fellowship

Richard Mouw
President and Professor of Christian Philosophy, Fuller Theological Seminary

Salim J. Munayer
Academic Dean, Bethlehem Bible College, Jerusalem

Rich Nathan
Senior Pastor, Vineyard Church of Columbus

David Neff
Editor in Chief and Vice-President, Christianity Today Media Group

Alexander Negrov
President, Saint Petersburg Christian University, St. Petersburg, Russia

Arnold Neufeldt-Fast
Associate Dean, Tyndale Seminary, Toronto

Craig Noll
Assistant Editor, International Bulletin of Missionary Research, *Overseas Ministries Study Center*

Rev. Roy Oksnevad
Institute of Strategic Evangelism at Wheaton College

Dennis Olsen
Charles T. Haley Professor of Old Testament Theology, Princeton Theological Seminary

Richard R. Osmer
Thomas Synnot Professor of Christian Education, Princeton Theological Seminary

Rev. Canon Mark Oxbrow
International Mission Director, Church Mission Society, UK

Rt. Rev. George E. Packard
Bishop Suffragan for Chaplaincies of the Episcopal Church

George Parsenios
Assistant Professor of New Testament, Princeton Theological Seminary

Greg H. Parsons
General Director, US Center for World Mission (USCWM), Pasadena, CA

Stephanie A. Paulsell
Houghton Professor of the Practice of Ministry Studies, Harvard Divinity School

James R. Payton, Jr.
Professor of History, Redeemer University College, Ancaster, Ontario, Canada, and President, Christians Associated for Relationships with Eastern Europe

Emily A. Peacock
Circuit Judge, 13th Judicial Circuit of Florida, Tampa, FL

Doug Pennoyer
Dean, School of Intercultural Studies, Biola University

Howard Pepper, M.A., M.Div.
President, Nurture Press, San Diego, CA

Douglas Petersen
Margaret S. Smith Professor of Intercultural Studies, Vanguard University of Southern California

Rev. Edward Prevost
Rector, Christ Church, Winnetka, IL

Bruce G. Privratsky
Elder, Holston Conference, United Methodist Church

Sally M. Promey
Professor of Religion and Visual Culture, Professor of American Studies, Professor of Religious Studies and Deputy Director, Institute of Sacred Music, Yale University

Rev. Erl G. Purnell
Rector, Old Saint Andrew's Episcopal Church, Bloomfield, CT

Rev. John C. Ramey
President, Aslan Child Rescue Ministries, and President, The Olive Branch Institute

Robert M. Randolph
Chaplain to the Massachusetts Institute of Technology, Cambridge, MA

Thomas P. Rausch, S.J.
T. Marie Chilton Professor of Catholic Theology, Loyola Marymount University, Los Angeles, CA

James D. Redington, S.J.
Associate Professor in the Dwan Family Chair of Interreligious Dialogue, Jesuit School of Theology at Berkeley/Graduate Theological Union, CA

David A. Reed
Professor Emeritus of Pastoral Theology and Research, Wycliffe College, University of Toronto, Canada

Neil Rees
International Director, World Horizons

Rev. Warren Reeve
  Lead Pastor, Bandung International Church, Bandung, West Java, Indonesia, and Founder and Facilitator of the Missional International Church Network

Rodney Allen Reeves
  Former Moderator of the Christian Church (Disciples of Christ) in Oregon, and board member, Greater Portland Institute for Christian-Muslim Understanding, and member, Interfaith Council of Greater Portland

Dr. Evelyne A. Reisacher
  Assistant Professor of Islamic Studies and International Relations, Fuller Theological Seminary, Pasadena, CA

Cornel G. Rempel
  Retired pastor, chaplain and supervisor of clinical pastoral education, Winnipeg, Manitoba, Canada

Steve Robbins
  Pastor and Director, Vineyard Leadership Institute

Cecil M. Robeck, Jr.
  Professor of Church History and Ecumenics, Fuller Theological Seminary, and the Director of the David du Plessis Center for Christian Spirituality

Leonard Rodgers
  Executive Director, Evangelicals for Middle East Understanding: An International Coalition, Tempe, AZ

Dudley C. Rose
  Lecturer on Ministry and Associate Dean for Ministry Study, Harvard Divinity School

Rev. Herschel Rosser
  Associate Pastor, Vineyard Church of Sugar Land, Stafford, TX, and Texas Area Church Planting Coordinator, Vineyard, USA

Glenna N. Roukes
  Elder, First Presbyterian Church, Santa Cruz, CA, and Secretary, Mission Team

Philip Ruge-Jones
  Associate Professor of Theology, Texas Lutheran University, Seguin, TX

William L. Sachs
Director, Center for Reconciliation and Mission, St. Stephen's Episcopal Church, Richmond, VA

Robert A. Sain
Pastor, Messiah Lutheran Church, ELCA, Hildebran, NC

Lamin Sanneh
D. Willis James Professor of Missions and World Christianity, Yale University

Andrew D. Saperstein
Associate Director of the Reconciliation Program at the Yale Center for Faith and Culture

Tyler Savage
Missionary with Church Resource Ministries, Germany and South Africa

Meritt Lohr Sawyer
International Program Director, Langham Partnership International

Warren C. Sawyer
President and CEO, The Caleb Foundation, Swampscott, MA

Rev. Dr. Christian Scharen
Director, Faith as a Way of Life Program, Yale Center for Faith and Culture

Rev. Dr. Robert Schuller
Founder, Crystal Cathedral and Hour of Power

Elisabeth Schüssler Fiorenza
Krister Stendahl Professor of Divinity, Harvard Divinity School

Francis Schüssler Fiorenza
Stillman Professor of Roman Catholic Studies, Harvard Divinity School

William Schweiker
Edward L. Ryerson Distinguished Service Professor of Theological Ethics, University of Chicago

Waldron Scott
President emeritus, Holistic Ministries International, Paterson, NJ

Andrew J. Sebanc
Senior Pastor, Green Timbers Covenant Church, Surrey, British Columbia, Canada

Rev. Donald Senior, C.P.
President, Catholic Theological Union, Chicago, IL

C. L. Seow
Henry Snyder Gehman Professor of Old Testament Language and Literature, Princeton Theological Seminary

Rev. Dr. Perry Shaw
Chair, Faculty of Ministerial Studies, Arab Baptist Theological Seminary, Beirut, Lebanon

Michael T. Shelley
Director, Center of Christian-Muslim Engagement for Peace and Justice, Lutheran School of Theology at Chicago

David W. and K. Grace Shenk
Global Consultants, Eastern Mennonite Missions, Salunga, PA

Wilbert R. Shenk
Senior Professor of Mission History and Contemporary Culture, Fuller Theological Seminary

John N. Sheveland
Assistant Professor of Comparative Theology, Gonzaga University, Spokane, WA

Marguerite Shuster
Harold John Ockenga Professor of Preaching and Theology, Fuller Theological Seminary

Frederick J. Sigworth
Professor, Department of Cellular and Molecular Physiology, Yale University

Mark Siljander
Member of the US Congress (retired) and former US Ambassador to the UN (alternate delegate)

Walt Simmerman
Pastor, First United Methodist Church, Galax, VA

The Community Council of the Sisters of the Precious Blood, Dayton,
OH:
Sister Florence Seifert, CPPS, President
Sister Jeanette Buehler, CPPS, Vice-President
Sister Madonna Ratermann, CPPS, Councilor
Sister Edna Hess, CPPS, Councilor
Sister Marita Beumer, CPPS, Councilor

C. Donald Smedley
Associate Director, The Rivendell Institute, New Haven, CT

John D. Spalding
Founder and Editor, SOMAreview.com

Rev. Andrew Spurr
Vicar of Evesham with Norton and Lenchwick Diocese of Worcester

John G. Stackhouse, Jr.
*Sangwoo Youtong Chee Professor of Theology and Culture, Regent
College, Vancouver, Canada*

Glen H. Stassen
*Lewis B. Smedes Professor of Chrisian Ethics, Fuller Theological
Seminary*

Sally Steenland
*Senior Policy Advisor, Faith and Progressive Policy Initiative, Center for
American Progress, Washington, DC*

Wilbur P. Stone
*Program Director and Lead Faculty, Global and Contextual Studies,
Bethel University/Seminary*

Rev. Dr. John Stott
Rector Emeritus, All Souls Church, Langham Place, London, UK

Frederick J. Streets
*The Carl and Dorothy Bennett Professor in Pastoral Counseling, The
Wurzweiler School of Social Work, Yeshiva University; Adjunct Associate
Professor of Pastoral Theology, Yale Divinity School; Former Yale
University Chaplain*

Diana Swancutt
Associate Professor of New Testament, Yale Divinity School

Merlin Swartz
Professor of Islamic Studies, Boston University

Donald K. Swearer
Director, Center for the Study of World Religions, Harvard Divinity School

Dr. Glen A. Taylor
Cooperative Studies Teaching Fellow, Tajikistan State National University, Dushanbe, Tjikistan

William Taylor
Global Ambassador, World Evangelical Alliance

Harvey Thiessen
Executive Director, OM Canada

Rev. John Thomas
General Minister and President, United Church of Christ

Stephen Thomas
European Team Leader, Salt and Light Ministries Senior Pastor, Oxford, UK

Dr. J. Milburn Thompson
Chair and Professor of Theology, Bellarmine University, Louisville, KY

Iain Torrance
President, Princeton Theological Seminary

Michael W. Treneer
International President, The Navigators, Colorado Springs, CO

Geoff Tunnicliffe
International Director, World Evangelical Alliance

Fr. Benjamin J. Urmston, S.J.
Director Emeritus Peace and Justice Programs, Xavier University, Cincinnati, OH

Birgit Van Hout
Executive Director, MCCJ, Florida

George Verwer
Founder and former International Director, OM

Harold Vogelaar
Director Emeritus, A Center of Christian-Muslim Engagement for Peace and Justice, Lutheran School of Theology at Chicago

Fr. H. Eberhard von Waldow
Professor Emeritus, Pittsburgh Theological Seminary

Rev. Berten A. Waggoner
National Director, Association of Vineyard Churches

Robin Wainwright
President, Middle East Fellowship, Pasadena, CA, and Chairman of the Executive Committee, Oxford Centre for Mission Studies

Dr. Dale F. Walker
Affiliate Professor, Asbury Theological Seminary, Wilmore, KY

Jim Wallis
President, Sojourners

Charlotte R. Ward
Associate Professor of Physics, Emerita, Auburn University, and Life Deacon, Auburn First Baptist Church

Charles H. Warnock III
Senior Pastor, Chatham Baptist Church, Chatham, VA

Rick Warren
Founder and Senior Pastor, Saddleback Church and The Purpose Driven Life, Lake Forest, CA

Very Rev. Debra Warwick-Sabino
Rector, Grace Episcopal Church, Fairfield, CA

Mark R. Wenger
Director of Pastoral Studies, Lancaster Eastern Mennonite Seminary P.O., Lancaster, PA

Dr. Bob Wenz
Renewing Total Worship Ministries, Colorado Springs, CO

Rev. Laura Westby
Pastor, First Congregational Church of Danbury, CT

Rev. Michael D. Wilker
Executive Director, Lutheran Volunteer Corps, Washington, DC

Robert R. Wilson
Hoober Professor of Religious Studies, Associate Dean for Academic Affairs, Yale Divinity School

Leslie Withers
Coordinator, Interfaith Pilgrimage Project, Friendship Force International, Atlanta, GA

Dr. John Wolfersberger
Retired Executive, Christian Church (Disciples of Christ), Southern California

Nicholas Wolterstorff
Senior Fellow, Institute for Advanced Studies in Culture, University of Virginia

J. Dudley Woodberry
Professor of Islamic Studies and Dean Emeritus of the Fuller School of International Studies

Rev. Dr. Christopher J. H. Wright
International Director, Langham Partnership International, London, UK

John Wright
Senior Pastor, Trent Vineyard, Nottingham, England

Godfrey Yogarajah
General Secretary, Evangelical Fellowship of Asia

Rev. Andrea Zaki Stephanous
Vice President of the Protestant Church in Egypt, Director of Dar El Thaquafa Communications House-CEOSS

Rev. John D. Zeigler
First Presbyterian Church, PCUSA, Canton, TX

Contributors

Martin Accad was born in Lebanon of Lebanese and Swiss parents, and lived there through the civil war (1975-1990). He undertook seminary studies in Beirut and then completed a Master's degree (M.Phil.) and a Ph.D. (D.Phil.) at the University of Oxford in the U.K. before returning to Lebanon in 2001. Currently his time is divided between Lebanon (Arab Baptist Theological Seminary) and Pasadena, California (Fuller Theological Seminary), where he teaches in the fields of Islam and Christian-Muslim relations. He has published numerous articles and is currently working on a book on conflict and Christian-Muslim relations. As director of ABTS's Institute of Middle East Studies in Lebanon, he purposes to "bring about positive transformation in thinking and practice between Christians and Muslims in the Middle East and the West."

Born in 1934 to the Owu royal family, **Judge Bola Ajibola** obtained a degree in law from the University of London in 1962, and was called to the Bar as Honourable Barrister-at-Law of Lincoln's Inn that same year. Among his awards are: Knight of the Order of the British Empire (KBE) — from Queen Elizabeth II (1989); World Jurist Award (1987); Fellow of the Nigerian Institute of Advanced Legal Studies; Honorary Fellow of the Society for Advanced Legal Studies; and Commander of the Federal Republic of Nigeria (CFR). He founded African Concern in 1994, the Islamic Mission for Africa (IMA) in 1996, and Crescent University in Abeokuta, Nigeria, in 2005.

Habib Ali Al-Jifri was born in Jeddah, Saudi Arabia, and traces his ancestry to Yemen's Hadramaut Valley, an area historically associated with traditional Islamic spirituality and masters who trace their ancestry back to the Prophet Muhammad (Peace Be Upon Him). Having received his training from some of the leading masters of our time, he went on to found the Abu-Dhabi based Tabah foundation, in which he presently serves as General Director. He lectures internationally as both a scholar and religious leader. He is also a lecturer and Deputy Dean at the Tarim-based Dar al Mustafa for Islamic Studies.

David Burrell has been working since 1982 in comparative issues in philosophical theology in Judaism, Christianity, and Islam, as evidenced in *Knowing the Unknowable God: Ibn-Sina, Maimonides, Aquinas* (1986), *Freedom and Creation in Three Traditions* (1993), and two translations of al-Ghazali: *Al-Ghazali on the Ninety-Nine Beautiful Names of God* (1993) and *Al-Ghazali on Faith in Divine Unity and Trust in Divine Providence* (2001). A corresponding member of the Dominican Institute for Oriental Studies in Cairo, as well as the Tantur Ecumenical Institute in Jerusalem, he is currently Professor of Ethics and Development at Uganda Martyrs University.

Harvey Cox is Hollis Professor of Divinity at Harvard, where he has been teaching since 1965, both at Harvard Divinity School and in the Faculty of Arts and Sciences. An American Baptist minister, he was the Protestant chaplain at Temple University and the director of religious activities at Oberlin College, an ecumenical fraternal worker in Berlin, and a professor at Andover Newton Theological School. His research and teaching interests focus on the interaction of religion, culture, and politics. He has been a visiting professor at Brandeis University, Seminario Bautista de Mexico, the Naropa Institute, and the University of Michigan. One of his many books, *Secular City* (1965), became an international bestseller and was selected by the University of Marburg as one of the most influential twentieth-century books of Protestant theology.

Joseph Cumming is Director of the Reconciliation Program at the Yale Center for Faith and Culture. Born and raised in New York City, Joseph has lived most of his adult life in the Islamic Republic of Mauritania, where he continues to oversee major humanitarian work. He has served as Director of Doulos Community, a Christian humanitarian organization whose largest program provided food and health education to 30,000 Mauritanian children and mothers. He teaches courses in Islamic Studies at Fuller Theological Seminary and is completing his Ph.D. in Islamic Studies and Christian Theology at Yale University. Fluent in several languages and an ordained Christian minister (Assemblies of God), Joseph has in recent years been involved in Muslim-Christian dialogue, including at al-Azhar University in Cairo and the Doha Conference on Interfaith Dialogue.

H.R.H. Prince Ghazi bin Muhammad bin Talal of Jordan received a B.A. *Summa Cum Laude* from Princeton University in 1988, and a Ph.D. from Cambridge University in the U.K. in 1993. He was Cultural Secretary and Advisor for Tribal Affairs to the late H.M. King Hussein and is presently Personal Envoy and Special Advisor to H.M. King Abdullah II. He is also the Chairman of the Royal Aal al-Bayt Institute for Islamic Thought, and the founder of Al-Belqa Applied University (1996), W.I.S.E. University (2007), The Baptism Site National Park (1997), and the "*Great Tafsir* Project" (2001). He was the head of the *Amman Message* Committee and the author of the historical "A Common Word" Open Letter of 2007.

John Kerry, born 1943, is a United States Senator from Massachusetts and chairman of the Senate Foreign Relations Committee. He received his B.A. in political science from Yale University in 1966, and his Juris Doctor (J.D.) from Boston College in 1976. After serving as a soldier in the Vietnam War, he became the spokesman for Vietnam Veterans Against the War. He was elected Lieutenant Governor of Massachusetts in 1982, and a United States Senator in 1984 where he was recently reelected for a fifth term. He has provided significant leadership in areas related to the Iran-Contra scandal, global AIDS, East Asian and Pacific Affairs, North Korea, American policy in Iraq and Afghanistan, the war on terrorism, and the Middle East peace process.

Rick Love has been involved in Christian-Muslim relations for the last thirty years. He has a D.Min. in Urban Studies from Westminster Theological Seminary and a Ph.D. in Intercultural Studies from Fuller Theological Seminary. He lived in Indonesia from 1984 to 1992. He specializes in coaching faith-based organizations in cross-cultural communication and Christian-Muslim relationships. In the spring and summer of 2008 he served as a Postdoctoral Fellow at the Yale Center for Faith and Culture's Reconciliation Program. He is presently a consultant for Christian-Muslim Relations in the Association of Vineyard Churches, USA.

Seyyed Hossein Nasr, currently University Professor of Islamic Studies at George Washington University, Washington, D.C., has authored over fifty books and five hundred articles which have been translated into several major Islamic, European, and Asian languages. Professor Nasr regularly speaks at academic conferences and seminars, university and public lectures, and also radio and television programs. He was a professor at Tehran University from 1958 until the Iranian revolution in 1979, and then taught at Temple University in Philadelphia from 1979 to 1984 before coming to George Washington University. He has been active in dialogue with other religions and especially Christianity for over a half century.

Dr. Aref Ali Nayed is Founder and Director of Kalam Research & Media, Dubai. He is Senior Advisor to the Cambridge Inter-Faith Programme, and Fellow of the Royal Aal Al-Bayt Institute in Jordan. He was Professor at the Pontifical Institute for Arabic and Islamic Studies (Rome) and the International Institute for Islamic Thought and Civilization (Malaysia). He received his B.Sc. in engineering, M.A. in the philosophy of science, and a Ph.D. in hermeneutics from the University of Guelph (Canada). He has been involved in various inter-faith initiatives since 1987, including the recent "A Common Word" process, and has authored several scholarly works.

Andrew Saperstein serves as the Associate Director of the Reconciliation Program at the Yale Center for Faith and Culture. He holds degrees in linguistics from the University of Chicago (B.A.) and Ohio State University (M.A. and Ph.D.), and worked for several years as a Fulbright scholar in Peshawar and Quetta, Pakistan. From 1998 to 2006, he helped oversee an educational development program in Samarqand, Uzbekistan, and taught sociolinguistics at the Samarqand State Institute of Foreign Languages. He has served as a consultant to several non-government agencies working in Pakistan and Afghanistan and has traveled extensively in both countries. He serves as a lay leader in the Association of Vineyard churches and is deeply involved in local church development and leadership.

Reza Shah-Kazemi was born in the U.K. of mixed Persian-Pakistani parents. He studied international politics to M.A. level, before turning to the field of comparative religion, completing his doctoral thesis, a study of Shankara, Ibn Arabi, and Meister Eckhart, at Kent University in 1994. He has published widely in Islamic studies, Sufism, and Shi'ism. His latest publication was *My Mercy Encompasses All: The Koran's Teachings on Compassion, Peace and Love.* He is currently a Research Associate at the Institute of Ismaili Studies, London.

Miroslav Volf serves as Director of the Yale Center for Faith & Culture and Henry B. Wright Professor of Theology at Yale Divinity School. He received a B.A. from the Evangelical-Theological Faculty in Osijek, Croatia, an M.A. from Fuller Theological Seminary, and a Dr. theol. and Dr. theol. habil. from the University of Tübingen, Germany. The author of numerous books and articles, his book *Exclusion and Embrace: A Theological Exploration of Identity, Otherness and Reconciliation* (which received the 2002 Grawemeyer Award) offers the idea of embrace as a theological response to the problem of conflict between peoples.

Melissa Yarrington is Research Fellow for Muslim-Christian Relations at the Yale Center for Faith & Culture's Reconciliation Program.